Praise for
Coming of Age . . . All Over Again

"Charming, funny, filled with great resources, and written by two great gals."
    —Sharon Stone

"An amazingly comprehensive guide for facing the challenges of midlife and beyond. If *Coming of Age* doesn't address it, it's just not an issue."
    —Libby Gill, author of *Traveling Hopefully*

"A wise, funny, and exhaustive how-to guide for the midlife moment when you're just beginning to need a new perspective."
    —Lynda Obst, producer of *Sleepless in Seattle* and
        How to Lose a Guy in 10 Days

"The midlife journey for women gets a little easier with Buffy and Kate along as traveling companions. An essential tool for women dealing with midlife issues."
    —Pat Gaudette, coauthor of *How to Survive Your Husband's*
        Midlife Crisis

"Not to fear, friends are here. Kate and Buffy will feel like *your* best friends as they lead you through a warm, funny, and spot-on guide to getting the most out of the second chapter of your life. Their writing is so personal and vibrant, you'll feel like they're in your kitchen having coffee with you."
    —Joanna Johnson, writer and creator of the TV series
        Hope & Faith

"My midlife crisis began when I read this book and realized all the things I needed to start doing. . . . This is a must-read for all grown-up women!"
    —Laurie David, activist

Coming of Age ...
All Over Again

The Ultimate Midlife Handbook

Kate Klimo and Buffy Shutt

SPRINGBOARD PRESS

NEW YORK BOSTON

Springboard Press
Hachette Book Group USA
1271 Avenue of the Americas
New York, NY 10020
Visit our Web site at www.HachetteBookGroupUSA.com

Springboard Press is an imprint of Warner Books, Inc. The Springboard name and logo are trademarks of Hachette Book Group USA.

155.66
KLIM

First Edition: January 2007

This book contains opinions and ideas of its authors. It is intended to provide helpful and informative advice on the subjects addressed. It is sold with the understanding that the authors and the publisher are not engaged in rendering medical, psychiatric, health, or any other kind of personal professional services in the book. The reader should consult his or her medical, health, or other competent professional before adopting any of the suggestions in this book or drawing inferences from it. While every effort has been made to ensure its accuracy, the authors and the publisher specifically disclaim all responsibility for any liability, loss, or risk, personal or otherwise, which may be incurred as a consequence, directly or indirectly, of the use of this book.

Library of Congress Cataloging-in-Publication Data
Kate Klimo and Buffy Shutt. — 1st ed.
    p.   cm.
  ISBN-10: 0-8212-5839-7
  ISBN-13: 978-0-8212-5839-2
  1. Middle-aged persons — Life skills guides.   2. Middle-aged persons — Conduct of life.
3. Middle-aged persons — Health and hygiene.   4. Middle-age.   I. Shutt, Buffy.   II. Title.
HQ1059.4.K58   2007
646.70084'4 — dc22   2006009785

Q-FF

Design by Meryl Sussman Levavi

PRINTED IN THE UNITED STATES OF AMERICA

FEB 0 9 2007

To our Super Seniors — Middie, Big Topper, and Sandy
And with love to all our friends at the tea party,
with a special welcome back to Justine

Contents

Coming of Age ...
All Over Again

Introduction

Our Own Private Iowa

Three years ago, a couple of things happened that made the two of us sit up and take notice.

A week after her fiftieth birthday, Buffy received her AARP membership card in the mail, and her first thought was, "Excuse me, but there must be some mistake!" She wasn't ready to join the grizzled ranks of the retired. And then, two months later on Thanksgiving night, both of her parents slipped and fell coming out of their house. Luckily, neither was hurt badly, but it was the tipping point for Buffy and her siblings. It was time for the folks to move from their big house into a more senior-friendly apartment. But they didn't even want to talk about it. They were adamant that, in their mideighties, they could live by themselves in a two-story house with a spiral staircase made of marble. They weren't ready to scale down. They weren't even ready to consider the next steps. They had no plan.

It was then Buffy realized that the AARP membership card—however unexpected and even unwelcome—was a sort of early signal telling her that if she couldn't affect her parents' choices, at least she could have some control over her own. Buffy realized that now was the time to start planning the second half of her life.

And whenever something really important comes along, Buffy calls her best friend, Kate. She told Kate, "We need to figure out this getting old thing now."

Kate started laughing. Only the day before, her eighty-four-year-old mother had deposited a brand-new pair of $10,000 hearing aids into a bowl of foaming Polident.

"Count me in," Kate said.

WHO ARE WE, ANYWAY?

We're two women in our fifties, best friends since our first day of college more than thirty years ago. Kate, a children's book publisher with three young adult sons and a husband who teaches college, lives in upstate New York. Buffy, a movie and television producer with a background in marketing, two young adult children, and a husband who writes for movies and television, lives in the Los Angeles area. In spite of the continent that lies between us, we have kept in touch over the years with visits, e-mails, and phone calls. Although we live on opposite coasts, we like to think that our friendship has thrived in an imaginary, heart-warmed place that lies somewhere in between. We call it Our Own Private Iowa. ("Idaho" was already taken.)

Over the years, we've kept ourselves busy in that Iowa, talking constantly and staying in touch with what happens in each other's life. And let's just say that we've been visiting Our Own Private Iowa a lot more frequently in recent years, as we've found ourselves dealing with a whole new set of midlife issues and trying to figure them out together.

SO THAT MAKES US EXPERTS?

Other than in our chosen fields, we don't consider ourselves experts. But on the subject of living the second half of our lives, who needs experts? We figure we've made it through the first half having learned enough about ourselves and the world to make the second half of our lives the better half. And after doing the research and study that led to the writing of this book, we think of ourselves as being something much more useful, something we all need to be as we start to think about living the second half of our lives: prepared. Being properly prepared will make *you* the first and best expert on how to live the second half of your life with style, wit, and a dash of imagination.

READY, SET, RESEARCH!

One week after that fateful "AARP card incident," Kate happened to come out to the West Coast on business. Deciding to take full advantage of this unexpected time together, our first stop was a bookstore. While we have come to love and rely on the Internet, we both crave the intimacy of words on a printed page. We were in search of a book that would help us plan the second half of our lives. Wanting the full-tilt bookstore experience — coffee, easy chairs, and an awesome selection — off we went to the fabulous, one-hundred-and-ten-year-old Vroman's Bookstore in Pasadena.

There was, as you must know, no dearth of books in the self-help section, many directed toward people — well, let's put it this way — one heck of a lot older than we think of ourselves. We found lots of books about fighting old age, negative thinking, wrinkles, cholesterol, cancer, and fat, fat, fat. We found books on coping with menopause, impotence, toxic mothers, boomerang children, and stress, stress, stress. We found books empowering the inner child, the outer adult, the creative spirit, and the entrepreneur in you. We found books about where to retire, when to retire, and how to retire with enough money that you don't have to subsist on cat food.

Good ideas abounded in all of these books, but they just weren't *the* book we were looking for: a single, handy volume, a handbook if you will, that would tell relatively young people — people in their midforties to midsixties — how to pull it all together and start gearing up for the second half of their lives. Because there wasn't such a book, we decided to give ourselves some time to explore, experiment, and share with each other concrete ways in which we could start to prepare and plan for the next phase. Before we knew it, something uncannily like the book we had gone looking for that day in Vroman's began to take shape.

We talked once a week on the phone and exchanged innumerable e-mails — a sampling of which you'll see throughout the text — as we divided up assignments, reported on our progress, interviewed people, swapped notes, books, CDs, and Web sites, and generally tried to keep ourselves on task when we lagged and to bolster each other when we got discouraged. As the project grew and expanded in scope, our excitement began to mount. We felt like two kids on a secret journey—facing forward fear-lessly, embracing the future, and determined never to look back.

COMING OF AGE . . . ALL OVER AGAIN

We began to feel a bit like we did our senior year of high school: poised be-tween two of life's grand phases. In fact, we felt as if we were coming of age, in a new and wonderful way, all over again. As Buffy watched her daughter, Daisy, complete her senior year in high school, it occurred to her that, like Daisy, she and Kate stood on the threshold of a larger world. As adults, we stand between family, career, and—all right, if we have to say it we will but just this once—retirement. From here on in, we will mostly refrain from using the *R* word, not just because it conjures up images of blue-haired ladies and doddering codgers parked on porches relentlessly rocking their way into oblivion, but also because—in case you haven't already noticed—retirement, as our parents and their parents knew it, is being radically re-defined. Not only are we living longer, healthier lives, but we're also working longer, and not always because we must, but just as often because it's what we choose to do.

Not so very long ago, people greeted the onset of their older years by shifting down, phasing out, fading away. That is not what we're talking about here. On the contrary, we are talking about gearing up, reinventing, and reengaging. In the sixties, baby boomers brought about a cultural revolution, the ripples of which extended to every corner of our lives: from the poli-tics we practiced to the clothes we wore to the food we ate to the rock and roll we loved. Now, in the early years of the new millennium, we stand per-fectly poised to bring about a second revolution, one that will transform the very concept of what it is to venture beyond age fifty and do so in style.

ASK YOURSELF SOME QUESTIONS

Beyond the obvious and irrefutable fact of your age, perhaps you are won-dering whether there are any prerequisites for reading this book. It might help if you are a woman. We both view the world from a very female point of view and, therefore, are more comfortable addressing ourselves to other women. But when we really think about it, the major prerequisite is that you be ready and willing to open yourself up to a world of questions. Questions such as:

- Am I happy?
- What is my work-to-play ratio?
- How do I feel about my body?
- Do I feel healthy? Fit?
- What are my passions, hidden or otherwise?
- Do I make enough time for my friends?
- How do I rate as a mate? A parent? A child? A sibling?
- What is the last book I read?
- Am I in touch with my innermost self?
- How much money is enough?
- Am I a good citizen?
- How do I want to spend the days and nights of the second half of my life?

As these questions crop up—along with lots of others—it's very important to remember that you don't have to answer them right away. In fact, you may just want to let them hang in your mind for a while. Don't try to force or contrive your answers. Go about the business of your day-to-day life, then let the answers work themselves out for you gradually and naturally. The answers will come.

LIFE IS JUST A LAYER CAKE

We love this metaphor. We could eat it up with a fork. Life is a veritable multilayered extravaganza. This book is divided into chapters meant to prepare, coach, and encourage you to gear up for the important business of designing the second half of your life. The chapters cover the whole cake, the essential layers of your life. Each chapter includes discussions, shared experiences, exercises, and specific ideas to help you plan joyfully.

Within each chapter, you'll find seven tools, "seven candles" if you will, that you can use to help sort out the second half of your life. These candles represent seven bright lights, practical approaches we came upon as we wrote this book. You'll get the hang of using them as we go along, but here's a quick first look:

1. *Create time.* What did Alfred Lord Tennyson call time? "A maniac scattering dust." But it doesn't have to be like that. We'll show you ways to slow down and make the time you need to live your life mindfully.

2. *Reflect.* Once you've found more time in your life, you'll have the space to see and understand things more clearly. We'll share some techniques, including breathing (yes, there is a right way to do it) and meditation (it's not as scary as it sounds), to help you slow down and look deep inside yourself for calm, clarity, and focus.

3. *Practice patience.* Resist judging yourself and others. It doesn't help. We'll share some strategies to help you curb impatience and set realistic goals, then meet or even exceed them.

4. *Research.* We aren't experts on a lot of the issues covered here, but we have done copious amounts of research so we can bring you the best available resources. We synthesize information for you and offer additional resources—books, Web sites, newsletters, tapes, and CDs—if you want even more information.

5. *Find role models.* Now that you're older and wiser, you can choose your own role models rather than having them thrust upon you. We'll offer suggestions to help you find them and share some of our own.

6. *Write it down.* Writing things down gives them power. We'll show you how to record your thoughts and plans for the future. If you write it down when you're in your forties, fifties, and sixties, you can make it happen in your seventies and eighties.

7. *Get together.* We boomers hatched together in numbers so staggering that the world is still reeling. But somewhere along the way, we pulled back into ourselves and hunkered down in our family bunkers, watching the world on our TVs and now our computer screens. We'll teach you how

to reconnect with old friends and make some new ones so you won't go through this whole "coming of age" process alone.

As you may have already guessed, this is not your granny's self-help manual. It's not even your mommy's. This one's for you, so hold the Geritol, and ix-nay on the blue hair. It is a book that we trust you will be drawn to again and again, as a source of both information and inspiration. It is a book that you work through as much as you read.

For these reasons, we recommend that you nibble at it steadily, rather than devouring it from cover to cover. Take it one chapter at a time, and make the time to do each chapter right. Ask yourself the important questions, do the exercises, and conduct any research you feel you need before you move on to the next. You might want to give yourself a week or even a month to do each chapter. Or maybe you'll want to spend a season with each part. Do whatever it takes, but do not let yourself feel overwhelmed. Set reasonable goals and practice patience. Congratulate yourself for even the smallest achievement. And never, ever get down on yourself for not doing enough. Whatever you can handle is enough. Whatever you do is great.

We heartily encourage you to get together with a friend or two to work through this book. We got together to create it and know that we got, oh, at least twice as much out of it as we would have had we done it alone, so we think it's a great idea for you to do the book with a friend, a mate, or a small group. Do the exercises together. Share your experiences. Offer love and support and cheer each other along. Swap resources. Learn. Grow. Plan. Strive to make these the best years of your life.

Myself

Enough about you. What about *me*?

Remember those days of yore, before you had a mate or kids or a career or a job? Remember how you had lots of time to sit around and think about who you were and what you were going to be when you grew up? You had a whole lifetime to contemplate and dream about. So you got together with your friends, your parents, your teachers, and your guidance counselor, and you made plans. You were coming of age, and it was a sweet, exciting time in your life.

And then what happened? Life happened. Life came along, grabbed you by the collar, and dragged you off to spend the next thirty years planning for others, thinking of others, doing for others, and pretty much letting life make its plans for *you*.

Now it's time to grab back your life, smooth out your collar, and take stock of your mind and your body. That's what the first four chapters are about—you! We'll start by asking you to get in touch with your long-lost inner self so you can figure out exactly who you are, where you are, and precisely what you want out of the second half of your life. Then we'll talk about getting you on a weekly regimen of exercise and planning for a lifelong health maintenance program. Because your body isn't much good to you if your mind takes early retirement, we'll discuss some strategies to keep your mind engaged and engaging.

Why spend all this time focusing on yourself? Because if you don't have a solid relationship with yourself, it's impossible to have one with your family, friends, coworkers, community, and the world at large. So find a good notebook, take a deep breath, and let's go knocking on the door of your Inner Guidance Counselor.

Who Am I Again?

Reconnecting with the real you

Dear Buffy: What do I have to do to get some peace and quiet around here? If the phone rings, I swear, it zaps me like a cattle prod. If somebody walks in on me while I'm meditating, I feel like I'm undergoing a hostile invasion. Noah came in the other day to ask for some lunch money. I levitated three feet, spun around, and spewed green slime in his face. Poor kid. Not exactly the path to enlightenment, is it? Love, Kate

Dear Kate: You have a lock on your bedroom door, right? And your kids can read, right? So a Do Not Disturb sign is all you need. How's that for enlightenment? Love, Buffy

Dear Buffy: Hey, buddy, thanks for the light. Love, Kate

THE LONG-LOST YOU

This chapter is about getting in touch with your inner self, the rich gooey bottom layer of your cake. Remember that self? It's down there somewhere. It's the self that you neglected or suppressed over the decades while you commuted to work, put in overtime, paid the bills, helped the kids with those last-minute science projects, and seethed at your mate for failing to shift the wet laundry into the dryer. The you who has been trapped inside and not allowed out to play. The you who has been drowned out by the din and lost in the shuffle of family and work for the past twenty or thirty years. The you who knows what you want and what you need to be happy and healthy. That's the person we're going to tap into to help make the rest of your life the best of your life.

Kate Checks Out of Jerry Springer's Green Room

So I had reached a point in my life where I was beginning to feel like a regular on the *Jerry Springer Show*. My kids all seemed to be in crisis at once. My husband and I were barely on speaking terms. My job was stressful and life outside it nearly nonexistent. I was sleep deprived, recreationally challenged, and nearly crippled from a hideous session with a sadistic trainer. My family was not helping with the housework. And my mother — once the head of the cavalry that had always come charging to my rescue — had moved into my dining room following a stroke and didn't know who I was, much less that I could have used a little support. I know it sounds like I'm laying it on a little thick, but Buffy has the e-mails and the phone bills to prove that it's all true.

Friends and coworkers wagged their heads in sympathy and amazement as I reeled off, in masochistically macho fashion, my long list of woes. My suggestion box was overflowing with their well-meaning ideas, helpful hints, and surefire prescriptions:

Family therapy is always an option.
How about couples therapy?
Go away for a weekend.
Pamper yourself.
There's a Chinese herbalist off Flatbush Avenue you absolutely must see, but I hear there's a three-month wait.
I know a really good chiropractor.
Fire your trainer.
You know, you really should consider going to a therapist.
Ever thought of taking up a nice relaxing hobby?
I'm sure there's a book out there that can help you.
Get your kids to pick up their own socks.
There's this really great marriage counselor in Brooklyn.

Far from comforting me, these suggestions only irritated me. I was incapable of taking any advice, no matter how well meaning or promising. And for every idea and suggestion offered, I had a ready rebuttal:

My kids would no more undertake family therapy than join a macrobiotic commune.

Therapy is so self-indulgent.

Don't have time.

Don't have money.

Herbs schmerbs.

Aren't chiropractors quacks?

My trainer is making me strong.

I don't think you heard me the first time: therapy is self-indulgent.

A hobby? You must be mistaking me for your Uncle Herbie.

They haven't written a self-help book that can help me.

It's easier to pick up their dirty socks than to nag them into doing it.

Marriage counseling is for sissies and whiners.

   "I'm fine," I told myself. "I'm fine," I told my husband and family. "I'm
fine," I told my friends. "I'm really really fine! I can handle it. I really can. I'm
tough stuff! Haven't I always handled it? Aren't I Wonder Woman?"

   Looking back, of course, it's easy to see what the problem was. I was
completely overwhelmed by events, out of touch with myself, and, perhaps more important, out of sympathy with my own plight. My poor over-
loaded self was crying out for help and I just kept saying, "We're fine.
Move along, folks. There's no problem here." And I probably would have
gone on indefinitely in this fashion had my mother not been felled by that
stroke. Losing my cavalry was, I suppose you could say, the final insult. I
had no choice but to take a big deep breath and say uncle.

   Did I cure all my woes at once? Not by a long shot. As a matter
of fact, during the course of researching and writing this book, I addressed one thing at a time, gradually. Have I eliminated all my woes?
Don't be silly. Life is all about woes, but the quality of our lives depends
on how we ride them out. And the important thing is that I have established the habit of checking in with myself on a regular basis to make
sure I am giving myself the love and support I need. And guess what? Because of that, I'm getting more love and support from everyone around
me. The reason? I have begun to develop a much clearer self-concept.

And I'm happy to say that I've finally checked out of Jerry Springer's green room.

DEVELOPING A HEALTHY SELF-CONCEPT

Exactly who you are is inextricably bound up with your self-concept, how you see yourself. What makes you happy and what makes you unhappy? What inspires you and what drives you right up the wall? Your self-concept is a knowledge of your strengths and your weaknesses. Once you have a clear self-concept, you will be better able to steer yourself toward situations that will yield positive benefits in the second half of your life and avoid situations that will bring you unhappiness.

Having a strong self-concept involves self-appreciation, self-acceptance, self-enjoyment, self-confidence, self-sufficiency, and self-comfort. Take some time to review each of these six happy outcomes, and rate yourself on a scale of 1 to 10, with 1 meaning *needs improvement* and 10 meaning *darned near perfect*. Try to be as honest and specific as possible, and to see yourself within the context of your daily life. We'll talk you through it, point by point, and Kate will take the test with you.

Self-Appreciation

Self-appreciation means understanding and savoring what makes you unique, lovable, and interesting.

Relax. This one doesn't require a rating. Instead, list at least five traits that you appreciate in yourself that make you unique. Let's call this your "personality thumbprint." List the whorls and swirls and curlicues of your personality.

Here is Kate's Personality Thumbprint to give you the idea:

1. I have a great deal of energy and can energize the people around me.
2. I see what there is to love in most people.
3. I like to make things with my hands: gardens, meals, embroidery, dinner parties.

4. I am happier when I am working; free time makes me anxious.
5. I have a wicked, irrepressible sense of humor.

Self-Acceptance

Self-acceptance is about making peace with who you are, warts and all. After all, you've lived with yourself for half a century and it's about time you called a truce with yourself.

How do you rate your self-acceptance? Can you list your warts? Perhaps one of your warts is that you tend to be stubborn. Perhaps you have a quick temper or are easily disappointed.

These are Kate's warts: she is a sloppy multitasker, she refuses to accept help, and she indulges in ongoing self-deprecation. She gives herself a 5.

What about you? Have you made peace with your warts? Even better, have you learned to harness them in a positive way? Negative traits, if properly channeled, can be used for positive ends. Stubbornness, for example, can help you persevere when tasks are difficult. Anger may motivate you to stand up for yourself.

Self-Enjoyment

Self-enjoyment involves being able to savor the pleasure of your own company. When you can enjoy being alone, you come to appreciate yourself in a new and satisfying way.

How do you rate your self-enjoyment? Can you spend the day by yourself and derive pleasure from it? Can you eat out alone? Go to the movies or take a class or browse in a bookstore alone, or if you do, are you all the while obsessed by your aloneness?

Kate has learned to enjoy her solitude while commuting on the train and reading and meditating at home. But she prefers company. Perhaps too much. She wouldn't dream of eating out or going to a movie or a museum by herself. On weekends without company, she tends to get depressed. Too much entertaining exhausts her. What's a gal to do? She gets a 7.

Self-Confidence

Self-confidence is about having faith in your own strength and wisdom. Nearly everything you need to know to live a wise, happy, and fulfilled life lies somewhere within you. Not out there someplace, but in there someplace, inside you. All you need to do is access it. Let that knowledge bubble up into your life like an inexhaustible, sustaining underground spring.

How do you rate your self-confidence? In a pinch, do you look inside yourself for the answers, or do you copy off your neighbor's paper? Or maybe you go running to the nearest authority figure? Sounding boards are great, but you've lived half a lifetime and have vast stores of your own experience to call on.

Kate comes across as smart, funny, and knowledgeable, and for the most part, that's who she really is. But she uses humor and her quick wit to cover fairly deep, dark pockets of self-doubt. She gives herself an 8.

Self-Sufficiency

Self-sufficiency means that you're able to support yourself emotionally, possibly even financially, without looking for someone else to hold you up, buck you up, or sustain you.

How do you rate your self-sufficiency? Do you feel helpless without others? Would you be lost without your mate or your friends? It's OK to travel with a clique, but if they all transferred to another school tomorrow, would you still be able to hold your head up in the hallways and the cafeteria?

Kate has been the major wage earner in her family for the past twenty-six years, so, financially speaking, she feels pretty self-sufficient. Emotionally and socially, she is perhaps too self-sufficient and could benefit from a little more interaction and socializing. She gets an 8.

Self-Comfort

Self-comfort is the absence of self-consciousness — easier said than done, particularly because many of us have been battling painful self-consciousness since adolescence or even earlier. Self-consciousness is about shame. It's about letting others determine how you feel about yourself. It's about living your life for others instead of for yourself. Isn't it time to get comfortable with yourself so you can live your own life?

How do you rate your degree of self-comfort? Do you blush beet red when you are asked to speak at a conference or on a dais? Are you ashamed of yourself, the way you look, and the way your mind works? Or, all things considered, do you feel pretty comfortable in your own skin?

Kate can stand up in front of large groups of sales representatives and convince them in a matter of minutes that the book she is pitching will charm children, wow critics, and curry awards. But pretty comfy in her own skin? She's been self-conscious about her large breasts since they popped out of her chest at age twelve, spent a pretty penny getting reduction surgery, and *still* feels self-conscious. She gets a 7.

OK, so now you know your starting point—your self-concept, how you see yourself today. In the rest of the book, we'll work hard to help you figure out who, what, and where you want to be in the future. It may very well be that you'll find your self-concept evolving along the way. Remember the seven candles? Now's the time for them to shine, and we'll start by applying them to the most challenging and most important part of your life: you.

CREATE TIME

Time's the thing, isn't it? You're too busy to take time out for yourself. The demands of your busy life eat up time and rob you of solitude, of the peace and quiet you need to get in touch with your Inner Guidance Counselor. Now that you've spent half a lifetime putting everyone else first, don't you finally deserve to give yourself more of that most precious resource?

We'll share some ways to carve out time for yourself in your hectic life. But first, ask yourself a few important questions. (You might want to write down the answers in a journal or notebook to really give yourself a chance to think them through.)

- What role does time play in your life?
- How do you feel about time?
- If you were to assign time a human identity, what form would it take?

For example, would time be a strutting general who demands that you march forward? Would it be a malicious imp, pestering you to do, do, do or die? Or would it be, like Kate's, Mistress of Pain, a leather-clad dominatrix snarling and cracking a whip? Exactly how is time personified for you? For many of us, time is not particularly kind. Start with your current perception of time, then see if you can gradually transform it into something positive — from a beast into an ally or from a devil into an angel who is looking out for you.

Take Time to Breathe

One important way to create time for yourself is to breathe mindfully. "Take time to breathe" sounds funny, doesn't it? As though we are all holding our breath. Well, in a way, most of us are. Breathing is unquestionably the single most important controllable function that our bodies perform. We do it automatically, yet most of us fail to breathe in a full, healthy, mindful way.

Have you ever stood over a crib and watched a newborn baby breathe? She does it deeply and naturally, using her lungs, diaphragm, and stomach. On inhalation, her lungs fill with air and her diaphragm goes down. On exhalation, her diaphragm rises, expanding her rib cage and pressing her stomach outward. As we grow, we gradually lose the knack of breathing deeply and fully. We begin to breathe in a tight, shallow fashion, restricted to our upper chest and throat. Why does this happen? Poor posture, tight clothing, self-consciousness about having our stomachs pooch out, and stress are some of the reasons. So we have to retrain ourselves to breathe properly — like sweet, calm, happy babies whose parents love them very much.

You can't force deeper breathing. Forcing it just produces tension. But you can start to be more aware of it. Start by listening to your breathing, observing its patterns and rhythms. How does your state of mind affect the level and rate of your respiration? You can't expect to change your breathing patterns overnight. It will take time, but it is worth the effort; you are worth the effort.

Deep, controlled breathing can be a powerful force. Athletes and actors know its power. Opera singers certainly do as well. You may have experienced its power if you used Lamaze or yoga breathing techniques during natural childbirth. The power afforded us by breathing more deeply is always available. Harness it now for your long-term health.

The Daily Breather

This exercise will get you in touch with your breathing patterns. Each time you perform this exercise, you will have succeeded in making time for yourself.

Wear loose, comfortable clothing. Make sure you won't be interrupted, and close your bedroom door. You might want to post a DO NOT DISTURB sign on your door to discourage interruptions. Lie down on the floor. If your neck and head bother you, roll up a medium-sized towel and tuck it behind your neck. If your lower back starts talking to you, bend your knees slightly and place a pillow behind them.

1. Lie very still and breathe normally. Notice which part of your body is moving. Place your hand on that part of your body. Is your hand on your upper chest? This is the area to which most of us restrict our breathing.
2. Now gradually start breathing more deeply. Inhale through your nose, and exhale through your mouth. Try to pull down the breath more deeply into your lungs, into that less used, lower two-thirds.
3. Think of your lungs as two balloons. Fill them up as you inhale, and as you exhale let the air empty out and the balloons deflate.
4. As you inhale, feel your stomach expand like a third balloon. Blow

Breathing: The Master Key to Self Healing by Andrew Weil, MD (Sounds True). "If I had to limit my advice to healthier living to just one tip," says Weil, "it would be simply to learn how to breathe correctly." The CD includes eight useful breathing exercises.

In Praise of Slowness by Carl Honore (Insight). Honore calls this itch to get on to the next item on the agenda the cult of speed. We can cure this by breathing deeply, slowing down, and learning to savor the moment.

Without Reservations by Alice Steinbach (Random House). Steinbach took nearly a year's leave of absence from her job as a reporter for a Baltimore newspaper to travel alone, live in the moment, and rediscover the lost Alice — the Alice who wasn't defined by her deadlines, house, kids, or even her cat.

up the balloon nice and big and round. Don't worry. It won't pop. And no one's around to think your stomach is fat. Now exhale.

5. Again, inhale. Draw the air down into your diaphragm. As you slowly exhale, feel the vertebrae in your lower back press into the floor. Repeat.

It might help to visualize your breath as having a color, say blue. Imagine your lungs and stomach filling up with refreshing blue vapor as you inhale, the blue vapor gradually draining out as you exhale.

During the day, whenever you can manage it, whenever you're feeling a bit lint-headed, foggy, or stressed, take a Breather. You don't have to retreat to your bedroom to do it. When you're sitting at your desk waiting for your computer to boot up, sitting in your car waiting for the light to change, or simply walking down the street, inhale for a count of four or five, hold your breath for the same count, then exhale for twice that count. Do this several times. It doesn't matter how long you do this exercise. It isn't about time, it's about time-out. We call these "out-and-about breathers."

Begin to be mindful of the thoughts that go through your head during and after a Breather. Bring this quality of mindfulness to your inner life. Before long, you will find that your thoughts are coming into sharper focus. Your energy level will be higher, and you will feel more relaxed and confident as you welcome the day's joys and challenges.

REFLECT

Throughout this book, we will ask you to spend time reflecting on yourself, your actions, and your future. We believe that it is only through quiet contemplation that you will be able to gear up, take control, and design the rest of your life.

Pausing to reflect is something most of us do without even knowing it. It's sometimes called "wool gathering" or "staring into space." A more structured way to gather wool is to meditate. If deep breathing offers a squeegee for your mental windshield, then meditation removes the windshield altogether and lets you see your thoughts, your challenges, and your dreams with perfect clarity. Once you are breathing more mindfully, meditation is the natural next step.

We know what some of you are thinking: "That's New Age stuff, and it's not for me." Try to keep an open mind. If twenty years ago someone had told Kate, a busy, no-nonsense New Yorker, that in her fifties she would be meditating twice a week, she would have told him to get outta town and join an ashram. But Kate discovered that the only way she can clear some space in her busy, noisy life, the only way she can truly be alone with her thoughts, is by meditating.

During one of your wool-gathering expeditions, ask yourself what four things in this world make you really happy. Why is it important to identify these things? Because, on some level, you can and should design the second half of your life around them. Hold those four items in your mind as you make your way through this book. Work them into the theme of your design. They can be your warp and your woof. They can also change, and that's OK. Don't worry if you only came up with two, or you couldn't narrow your list down from twenty. Just starting to focus on what makes you happy is the crucial part of this exercise. Do be aware, however, if one of your items contradicts or cancels out another. Try to resolve such contradictions as you progress.

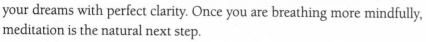

Creative Visualization by Shakti Gawain (New World Library Audio); available as a book and on CD. Gawain is probably the foremost popularizer of meditation and visualization. She leads you through the stages of relaxation into meditation, offers affirmations, and helps you create an inner sanctuary, where you can explore your thoughts and ideas in peace and safety.

Dear Buffy: OK, so did you get a chance to do the "Four Things That Make You Really Happy" meditation? Love, Kate

Dear Kate: Yep. I came up with: money, money, money, money. Kidding! Let's see. It was Peter, my kids, writing, and touching. Love, Buffy

Dear Buffy: Here's what popped into my head: family, riding, writing, you. Love, Kate

Dear Kate: That's so sweet! Now I feel guilty. Love, Buffy

Dear Buffy: You'd better. Love, Kate

The Beginner's Guide to Meditation: How to Start Enjoying the Benefits of Meditation Immediately by Shinzen Young (Sounds True). On this CD, a Buddhist monk offers a cogent and fascinating lecture on the internal science of meditation and gives exercises to get you to settle in, breathe mindfully, relax your body, and radiate love for yourself and others.

Eat, Pray, Love: One Woman's Search for Everything Across Italy, India and Indonesia by Elizabeth Gilbert (Viking). Coming off a painful divorce, the author embarks on a journey of self-discovery, spending four months in each of three wildly dissimilar parts of the world. She spends the second leg of her sojourn at an Indian ashram, exploring some mind-blowing meditation techniques.

Kate, the Reluctant Swami

OK, so I am not exactly swami material. I can't do the lotus position. I can't even sit cross-legged. This is not a function of age. Even in kindergarten, during circle time, when I sat on the floor with my legs crossed, my feet would fall asleep and my knees would get the screaming meemies.

So instead, I lie down on my bedroom floor. Before I lie down, I make sure I have hung the sign Buffy sent me on the bedroom doorknob. It says Go Away in very polite needlepoint letters, and so far has successfully warded off intruders, despite eliciting an occasional snide remark from my kids. I put a pillow behind my knees, and I roll a towel under my neck. That way I'm comfortable, but my spine is still straight. (In order for meditation to be successful, energy needs to flow up and down a straight spine.) I close my eyes and begin to breathe deeply and mindfully. I imagine that I am a feather, dropping gently from high atop a steep bluff. Slowly, slowly, with each breath, I drift ever downward to the soft, mossy ground below, becoming more tranquil and more relaxed with each breath.

I guess you'd say I'm a practical meditator. I always have an agenda, a problem I want to solve or ponder. I find that if the answer doesn't come to me during the meditation, it usually does within the next several hours. It just appears. Like magic. I feel a little bit like an ancient Greek consulting an oracle. But, hey, it's a technique that works for me, and I'm glad I opened my previously closed mind to it.

PRACTICE PATIENCE

As you begin to ponder the second half of your life, you must recognize the important role patience will play in creating your future. There is a lot to do. It cannot be done overnight. You are committing to a journey of discovery, and patience needs to be your helpmate.

So many of us have type A personalities: when we want something, we want it *now*. Patience doesn't always come easily. And the heightened pace of modern life, rather than satisfying us, seems only to fuel our impatience, transforming us into type A plus personalities. That's a grade that none of us should want. We live in a world with five hundred television channels, 24/7 news, voice mail, instant messaging, e-mail, faxes, cell phones, and a Starbucks on practically every corner. All of these modern conveniences, many of which have made us smarter and more efficient, have also put us on overload and given rise to a whole host of habits we like to call "edge behavior." Edge Behavior includes everything from multitasking to hyperventilating to overdosing on caffeine. We need to find ways to modify this behavior, to sand down our edge. Here is an exercise to help you do just that.

Sanding Down the Edge

Start by making a list of your habitual Edge Behaviors. Your Edge Behaviors might include any or all of the following. (These happen to be Buffy's Edge Behaviors.) See how many of them you can lay claim to. How many others can you come up with?

- Drinking three or more cups of coffee per day
- Driving over the speed limit, running yellow lights
- Multitasking
- Eating standing up, eating food quickly
- Feeling impatient with inanimate objects, such as computers, cars, cell phones, and land lines, and activities, such as waiting for services and being put on hold
- Intolerance of strangers
- Jumping to conclusions, flying off the handle
- Picking cuticles
- Hyperventilating

Now spend some time thinking about what's on your list. What does it tell you about yourself? How do you feel when you succumb to the edge? Breathless, overstimulated, rushed, hostile? How about so impatient you could bite a steel girder in half? Do you know what you need? Do you know what we all need? A personal prescription for practicing patience.

There are lots of great music CDs that might help you be your own guide, among them: *The Most Relaxing Classical Album in the World . . . Ever* (Virgin) and *Mozart for Meditation* (Philips).

Also, we've found a few Web sites with some great free information about meditation.

www.learningmeditation .com
This online guide to meditation explains how to make your daily life more serene and calm. Includes free meditations that you can listen to online.

www.meditationcenter .com
The World Wide Online Meditation Center provides a glossary, FAQs, and straight-forward instructions so you can quickly and easily learn meditation techniques that will benefit your daily life.

Full Catastrophe Living: Using the Wisdom of Your Body and Mind to Face Stress, Pain, and Illness by John Kabat-Zinn, PhD (Delta). Don't let the subtitle stress you out or put you off. In this book there's plenty of good advice about sanding down the edge, living in the moment, and being a mindful individual rather than a mindless blob of pure panic. (Sound like anyone you know?)

CrazyBusy: Over-stretched, Overbooked, and About to Snap! Strategies for Coping with a World Gone ADD by Dr. Edward M. Hallowell (Ballantine). The author, an expert on ADD, explains the phenomenon of brain overload brought about by our cell-phone chirping, BlackBerry-thumbing global society and offers step-by-step advice on how to untangle the tangled web of our sped-up lives.

To give you an idea of how to come up with your own prescription, here's Buffy's (based on her Edge Behaviors):

- Replace at least one cup of coffee with decaf, herbal tea, or water.
- Drive within the speed limit; slow down at yellow lights.
- Do one thing at a time. (Well, at least some of the time; make an earnest effort.)
- Sit down and eat slowly; enjoy each mouthful of each meal.
- Give strangers the benefit of the doubt.
- Practice deep breathing while waiting in line—for the light to change, for the computer to boot up, for my husband to show up—and before making tough decisions.
- Use cuticle oil or, if desperate, rub Chapstick on my cuticles.
- Place my tongue behind my upper teeth, then relax my jaw, lips, and tongue.

As you design your own prescription for patience, try to make the remedies as specific as you can. Refrain from using words like *don't, stop, quit, never,* and *have to.* Take care to couch your prescription in positive terms.

Write down your prescription on three index cards. Post one where you will see it every morning, post one in the car, and keep one in your purse, backpack, or wallet. Read it often to remind yourself exactly how you will practice patience today. You can revise these cards at any time, and we encourage you to do so. As you get to know yourself better, you may realize that you have conquered some forms of impatience but find other pockets of impatience that you had overlooked, hidden, or plumb ignored.

RESEARCH

Research means looking closely for new ways of listening to both yourself and others. There are many paths, many ways to open your mind to new ideas and different perspectives, but all of them require that you listen *actively.* An important part of self-discovery is asking questions and actually hearing and considering the answers, listening deeply, and being open to new beliefs and different viewpoints. Consider using the following suggestions to increase your ability to listen actively.

Listen to Your Dreams

Sigmund Freud called the interpretation of dreams "the royal road" to the unknown life within us. Dreams give us important clues to our deeper selves and provide us with fresh perspectives on our thoughts and actions. Keeping a dream log is one of the best ways to access the content of your dreams. Dream interpretation is mainly intuitive and endlessly fascinating.

Here are some questions to ask yourself when recalling a dream: What happened in the dream? Where did it take place? Who were the principal players? What was said? How did you feel during the dream? What images do you recall?

Listen to Your Therapist

Therapy can be an extremely useful guide to self-discovery, especially when you have something specific you want to manage, accomplish, or solve, like how to design the second half of your life.

It's also important to consider seeing a therapist if your Edge Behaviors or other problems are taking over your life.

Listen to Your Spiritual Adviser

A church, temple, or mosque is an ideal place to sit in silent contemplation, meditation, and prayer. Seek the counsel of your priest, rabbi, reverend, or minister. Share your ideas with your higher power in prayer.

Listen to a Teacher

Learning and belief systems abound in today's world. Teachers and experts offer advice in books and magazines, on TV, the radio, and the Internet. But teachers are often more available than experts. A wise teacher,

The Bedside Guide to Dreams by Stase Michaels (Ballantine). Dreams are fascinating, but in our experience books about dreams are either a bit too scholarly (like Freud and Carl Jung) or too gee-whiz, like something a bunch of high-school girls might pore over at a slumber party. In this great one-book resource, the author offers a sensible five-step approach to "dream recovery" and categorizes dreams into twenty-seven specific types.

The Committee of Sleep: How Artists, Scientists, and Athletes Use Dreams for Creative Problem Solving by Deirdre Barrett, PhD (Crown). John Steinbeck said: "A problem difficult at night is resolved in the morning after the committee of sleep has worked on it." In her excellent book, Barrett, a faculty member at Harvard Medical School, gives examples, exercises, and techniques for dream recall and reaping.

www.belief.net
This nondenominational, multifaith online community offers resources to help meet specific religious and spiritual needs.

www.dreambank.net
Think you have weird dreams? You're not alone. Check out this searchable collection of dream reports and dream journals.

www.dreamresearch.net This site from the University of California, Santa Cruz, cannot interpret your dreams but nonetheless provides a lot of interesting data.

www.soundstrue.com This audio, video, and music publishing company calls itself an "interfaith university that embraces the world's spiritual traditions and the arts and humanities." It's good one-stop shopping for CDs, kits, videos, and even games that explain alternative ways of thinking and living.

www.retreatsonline.com This site might provide a decent springboard for finding a retreat. It provides links to retreat centers in the United States and abroad.

www.yogajournal.com This is the trusted online source for yoga poses, teachers, travel, and ideas.

instructor, friend, boss, or coworker can be wonderfully helpful when you air ideas for the second half of your life.

Listen to Yourself

Go on a retreat and take time to listen to yourself. There are many different kinds of retreats: health, yoga, nature, travel, meditation, business, couples', women's. Some, like yoga or meditation retreats, offer you an opportunity to practice extended periods of silence. Being silent for a day, a few days, or even longer can be a powerful and compelling opportunity to spend time with your own thoughts and to commune with and pay heed to your Inner Guidance Counselor.

FIND ROLE MODELS

When you seek out people whom you admire, you are identifying role models. We often use role models unconsciously as points of comparison for ourselves. Now we want to use role models consciously. Seek out people you know and don't know and observe how they are living the second half of their lives. They can serve as guides to the life you are just beginning to contemplate living. Role models are valuable. Cultivate and treasure them.

Kate has come to know a woman who is a good role model for self-knowledge. At age seventy, Jane lives an active life. She gives art lessons, does ceramics, belongs to a book group, keeps a journal, sings in her church choir, and stays in constant touch with her four children and her six grandchildren. She and her husband have friends over for dinner at least once a week. But despite all that activity, she lives her life with an ear keenly attuned to her inner self.

Jane considers almost everything she does, even cleaning the house, to be a form of active meditation. For her, teaching, cooking, reading, and singing are all forms of meditation in motion. Jane makes sure that every day—no matter how mundane the tasks that fill it—resounds with a celebration of her spirit and the spirits of those she touches. Jane lives life authentically, and her every action and gesture vibrates positively with energy and love.

WRITE IT DOWN

Writing down your thoughts, ideas, and plans will help you make them happen. In each chapter of this book, we will ask you to write down your dreams so you can use those important and transforming thoughts to design the second half of your life. Writing down your thoughts gives them power. *Commit* yourself to paper.

If you don't already keep a journal, you might want to start now. Find a notebook that pleases you, preferably one that lies flat when opened and has lines. Keep it and a pen near your bed, and write in it nightly when you're a little bit sleepy, your guard is down, and the day's events are still fresh in your mind. Or write when you are on the subway or bus, during your lunch break, or right before you start watching your favorite TV program. Create a special time to write down your thoughts. Don't worry about your penmanship, grammar, or literary style. If you find that you are boring yourself silly with mundane details, like what you ate, where you went, and what you did, try to include how you felt, what you learned, and what you are grateful for. Think of yourself as the hero of your own personal adventure.

Consider carrying this notebook—or a smaller, more portable journal—with you throughout the day, and use it to capture your daydreams, passing thoughts, plans, and lists of things that are important to you. Whether bedside or in your bag or hip pocket, a journal can link your mind with your inner self through your writing hand. Your ideas, recollections, ambitions, concerns, and dreams are vital to understanding who you are now and who you hope to be in the future. Take time to record as much of this as you can.

Talk about alone! *Sailing Alone Around the World* by Joshua Slocum, Captain (Shambhala). Slocum's account of his late nineteenth century voyage, the first solo sail around the world.

Making Journals by Hand by Jason Thompson (Quarry Books). Kate has always had trouble committing to keeping a journal. She buys scads of them and winds up losing them, using them at work, writing her shopping lists in them, or tossing them. This book inspired her to make her own journal from scratch.

Life's Companion: Journal Writing As a Spiritual Quest by Christine Baldwin (Bantam). This book deals with practical questions, like whether to use lined or blank paper, colored or white paper, marker or pen, regular entries or spontaneous ones.

The Zen of Seeing: Seeing/Drawing As Meditation by Frederick Franck (Vintage). In this book, hand-lettered and illustrated by the author, we learn that a journal doesn't have to be just words. Especially if you are inclined to doodle or draw (but even if you're not), this book shows you how to see in new ways and to capture the life around you in sketch form.

www.livejournal.com This is a large online journaling community.

Dear Buffy: When we thought my mother was going to die, I got in bed one night — it was my old bedroom in the house I grew up in — and read all of her journals. Every single one of them, from cover to cover. I learned so much about her. For the past ten years, it seemed like all she did was worry about money. I knew she had been concerned about paying the bills. That's why I helped her out when I could. But I never realized she was downright scared. I also never knew how shaky her self-confidence was. She had always come across as so self-assured, so strong. I met a different woman in those pages. Then, when it turned out that she wasn't going to die, not yet at least, I felt guilty at first for having invaded her privacy. Then I was glad I did, because it helped me understand her better. Now I see the whole woman. Love, Kate

Dear Kate: That's a good way to look at a journal. It's the one place where you can be yourself, minus the public persona. Your true self. It's also a way to freeze time, I think. Where else do you have the time and space to dwell on a single event or emotion? It's so easy to let life blaze past us without giving it a second thought. I've kept a journal since college but not as religiously as I would like. I also have too many notebooks and feel a little scattered. Love, Buffy

Dear Buffy: I'm shocked. You? Scattered? That's not the Virgo I know and love. Love, Kate

GET TOGETHER

Getting together with a friend or two to work through this book, just as we did in Our Own Private Iowa, is a great idea. Each of us will chart our own paths through the second half of life, but that doesn't mean we can't compare the routes we'll take or share the discoveries we make along the way with a friend or even a small circle of friends.

If a meditation class is being offered nearby and you feel funny or shy about going, invite a friend to go along, and explore the process together. Does the idea of going on a retreat freeze your feet? Invite a friend and thaw those feet: go together. Vet and swap CDs and DVDs, and share any positive experiences you have had or tricks you might have picked up. Talk about your ideas and dreams. Just by sharing your ideas and dreams, by simply saying them aloud to someone who knows and loves you, you will make them more viable, more real.

Visualize Your Future

One of the goals of this book is to help you create the life you want. So let's imagine what that life will look like. All set? Whether meditating or simply contemplating, start to form a picture in your mind. Imagine yourself fifteen years from now. How do you look? Where are you living? What are you doing? Who are you with? How do you feel? Happy? Anxious? Try to make the picture as clear as possible and then hold it in your mind. Conjure up as much detail as you can. Fill in any blank areas. If you can't, just leave them blank for now. You can always fill them in later.

Don't be afraid to be playful. Did the four things in this world that make you happy show up in this picture? Or did other things jostle for position?

Now jot down in your notebook, on a piece of paper, or on an index card what the picture looked like. We like to call this the "dream cake." Put the card in your jewelry box or in a desk drawer. Take it out every so often as you work your way through this book.

Kate's Dream Cake

I am sitting at a large wooden table. The picture window before me looks out on a horse paddock. I don't see a barn, but I do see a small, simple shelter. There are three horses grazing in the paddock.

The house I live in is a large one-room structure. It is simple and organized, like a houseboat, with a place for everything and everything in its place. There is a nice galley kitchen with painted tiles along one wall. Elsewhere in the room, there are shelves of books. There is a big high bed, covered with colorful pillows, that doubles as a lounging area.

My Time: Making the Most of the Rest of Your Life by Abigail Trafford (Basic Books). Trafford, a columnist for the *Washington Post,* believes that you have to go through a second childhood in order to reinvent yourself for the second half of your life. An energizing read.

The Four Agreements: A Practical Guide to Personal Freedom by Don Miguel Ruiz (Amber-Allen). Ruiz, a shaman and healer, dispenses wisdom from his Toltec ancestors. It's grounding to read about the wisdom of the elders. The four agreements in his code of personal conduct are: always keep your word, don't take anything personally, don't make assumptions, and always do your best. Sounds easy. It can be.

> I am writing in a journal in which I periodically press flowers that I have gathered from the fields nearby.
>
> Buffy and another friend are coming over for lunch, and I am thinking about what I should make for us to eat. I'm not sure where my husband is or even if he is still a part of my life, and this troubles me a bit. Will my husband play an integral role in my future or not?
>
> Other than that, I like what I see. I'm excited about it. I want to live here. I want to know how to get here from where I am today.

PUTTING IT ALL TOGETHER

Now it's time to review what we've learned. Take a few moments to look back at the exercises you have completed. What have you learned? What are your hopes and dreams? Think about the challenges you are facing. Focus on the actions you might take to meet those challenges. And remember:

1. *Create time* to breathe and get in closer touch with your inner self. Develop your Personality Thumbprint.
2. *Reflect,* using silent contemplation or meditation. Develop a self-concept.
3. *Practice patience* by analyzing your Edge Behaviors and creating a personal prescription for patience.
4. *Research* by opening your mind and actively listening to your inner voice and the voices of others.
5. *Find role models* who have strong self-concepts.
6. *Write down* your thoughts, hopes, and dreams. Through meditation or reflection, whip up your Dream Cake.
7. *Get together* and compare notes about ways and means of figuring out who you are and what you want to become.

TO-DO LIST

Here is a list of things you might consider incorporating into your plan. We call it a *to-do list*, but you don't have to do everything on it. Just do the things that spark your interest.

- Perform Daily Breathers.
- Practice Out-and-About Breathers.
- Buy, borrow, or rent a meditation tape.
- Join a meditation group; visit an online meditation site.
- Develop a home meditation routine.
- Sand down you edge.
- Write and post your personal prescription for patience.
- Start a dream log.
- Play around with what a strong self-concept means to you.
- Chart your daydreams.
- Visit a therapist.
- Join a therapy group.
- Find a teacher or mentor.
- Commission an astrological chart.
- Go on a silent retreat, or spend a day without speaking.
- Keep a journal.
- Chant.
- Choose and use a mantra.
- Design a labyrinth for meditation in your backyard.
- Create a sanctuary in your backyard using a religious symbol such as a Tibetan prayer wheel, a Celtic cross, an angel weathervane, or a St. Francis statue.
- Make a mini–Zen garden.
- Take up Tai Chi.
- Take up yoga.
- Go alone to the beach, mountains, desert, or backyard, and bring your journal.
- Practice your faith.

KATE'S PLAN

My two biggest challenges are learning to breathe mindfully and creating time for myself. My hectic schedule requires five hours of train commuting each day, and I pack five days of work into four. Apart from the many people who work for me, whose problems frequently become mine, I have a husband, two adolescent sons living at home, an older son living nearby who hasn't quite made it all the way out of the nest, an eighty-plus-year-old mother with health problems who now lives with us, siblings who feel guilty or sullen for not helping more, and not enough hours to get in touch with myself. It seems to me as though I spend a great deal of time caring for other people and not enough time caring for myself.

So what is my plan? I found a therapist near my office so I can minimize my time away from work. I see her once a week, and she has already started to help me sort out what's important to me and how I can create more time for myself. I write regularly in my journal. I meditate when I feel the need, but not compulsively. And in order to listen more actively and to shed some of my practical side, I'm now looking for a good astrologer. I feel it is time to venture into the alternative stratosphere to see if there's anything out there for me. So my program looks like this:

- Visit a therapist weekly.
- Keep up with my journal.
- Practice Daily Breathers and Out-and-About Breathers.
- Research astrology to see whether there is anything in it for me.
- Meditate at least once a week.

BUFFY'S PLAN

One of my biggest challenges is to relax and to let others around me relax. I prefer to keep a running list of things to do—for both the short term, over, say, a weekend, and the long term, over a period of months. This near obsession with getting things done often stifles my ability to enjoy the moment and, well, relax. My work, which was so clear in its demands and stress for more than thirty years, has now transformed into a different set of issues and struggles that I want to meet with energy, insight, and joy. My plan is to:

- Recommit to keeping a journal and commit to putting my fears and dreams down on paper.
- Log night dreams and daydreams.
- Practice meditation, or creative visualization, or both, two times per week.
- Breathe mindfully.

Now that you've developed a critical inner eye and know what areas you want to focus on and change, it's time to get physical. You can wear whatever you like, exercise with whomever you wish, and use your discretion (and your imagination!) to design a program of physical activities that's just right for you and fun. In the second half of your life, gym is not an elective.

2 Whose Body Is This, Anyway?

Making exercise part of your daily life

Dear Buffy: I know you live in the Golden State, but I have to confess: Californians make me nervous. Mostly, they are too thin. Love, Kate

Dear Kate: Yeah, some of the women in my Pilates class are so thin I actually worry about them. There is a rumor that my Pilates studio is stopping classes. My haven for eight years. What will I do? Love, Buffy

Dear Buffy: I've also been thinking of joining a gym. We get a discount at work, but I really need to research it. And you, you are going to have to meet new people and find a new trainer or at least good classes. Argh. Poor you. Love, Kate

Dear Kate: Just don't go overboard. Remember how you hurt yourself with that trainer that time. Love, Buffy

Dear Buffy: I went horseback riding last weekend. Does that count as physical activity? Love, Kate

Dear Kate: Not unless you actually lift the horse, darling. Love, Buffy

---

GYM IS NOT AN ELECTIVE

To gear up for the second half of your life, you must have energy, clarity, imagination, and stamina. That means you need to eat right, take care of yourself, and exercise. Regular exercise will help you stay healthy, mobile, and active for decades to come. And, of course, keeping fit also keeps you looking younger and more vibrant, oh-so-welcome side effects of staying in shape.

This chapter will get you thinking about how to create a personal exercise regimen. First, we'll bring you up to speed on the best way to get moving. Then, we'll use the seven candles to help you put your plan into action. Regular exercise is essential if you want to make your dreams for the second half of your life come true.

If you have a chronic condition or have not exercised in a long time, check with your doctor before starting to exercise. Most older adults, regardless of age or condition, do just fine if they increase their physical activity to only a moderate level, according to the National Institutes of Health.

Before we begin, let's review some exercise basics. There are three principal forms of exercise: aerobic exercise, flexibility, and strength training. Each is good for you and necessary in a different way. Ideally, your weekly program will integrate all three, or they will be carried out in separate weekly sessions. In the second half of your life, gym is not an elective. Participating in these three forms of exercise is mandatory. You can select from a variety of options in each category and are always free to experiment, mix it up, and change your routine. Try to keep it interesting and fresh, and challenge your body in new and complementary ways by cross-training. Cross-training combines several different forms of exercise, such as biking and climbing or swimming and biking. Fine-tune your regimen to find just the right combination to keep you fit, flexible, and strong. And above all, have fun and enjoy yourself.

Aerobic Exercise

This is the kind of exercise the doctors always talk about because it helps keep your heart healthy and lowers your risk of heart disease, stroke, diabetes, and other serious conditions. But what is it? *Aerobic exercise* is any exercise that increases oxygen intake and raises your heart rate for a period of 20 to 60 minutes.

You may already know how to calculate your target heart rate, but here's the simple formula:

(220 − your age) × 0.65 = minimum target heart rate

(220 − your age) × 0.90 = maximum target heart rate

Let's use Buffy as an example.

(220 − 54) × 0.65 = 108 beats per minute at the minimum rate

(220 − 54) × 0.90 = 149 bpm at the maximum rate

(Incidentally, Buffy has never actually checked her heart rate, so she will commit right now to learning how to take her pulse rate and to reach and stay within her target heart rate. She may even ask for a heart rate monitor for her next birthday.)

Flexibility

Muscles should be warmed up and stretched regularly. New studies have flipped conventional wisdom on its head (something we like to see now and then). The newest thinking holds that stretching *before* an activity is not as important as experts once thought, but stretching at some point *during* your routine is an important part of your regular exercise program. The reason you stretch is to gain flexibility and to maintain — and possibly improve — your range of motion, balance, and sense of well-being. Do you want to be able to put on your own shoes in twenty-five years? You should stretch for thirty minutes twice a week, either after a brief warm-up or at the end of your workout.

Strength Training

One of the most misunderstood forms of exercise is strength training. We're not talking about Ah-nold pumping iron, just moderate resistance training with free weights, weight machines, resistance bands — even a push-up is a form of strength training. This type of exercise increases in importance during the second half of your life. After age twenty, most of us lose half a pound of muscle each year. As muscle is lost, metabolism slows and fat is gained. Strength training builds muscle and boosts metabolism.

Weight training increases the strength of your muscles, bones, ligaments, and tendons. And don't worry, this type of exercise will not give you muscles like Ms. Olympia. Ideally, you should do eight to twelve repetitions of six to ten different exercises, two or three times a week. You should use enough weight to fatigue your muscles during each session, but do *not* use weights that are too heavy for you, and do *not* overdo the repetitions.

Dear Kate: Peter is so sweet. He bought me some of those at-home hand weights. Love, Buffy

Dear Buffy: Those cute little ones that come in Barbie pink? What next? Matching sweatbands? Love, Kate

Dear Kate: Actually they are purple. And you know I don't need sweatbands because I don't sweat. Love, Buffy

---

WALK!

There are literally hundreds, probably thousands, of different types of exercise from which you can choose, but one simple activity covers all the bases: walking. It sounds so simple. It *is* simple. We urge you to walk as your principal form of exercise.

Here are a few reasons why walking is terrific:

- *You can walk alone*—as a planned activity or spontaneously.
- *You can walk with others.* Grab your mate, your children, your grandchildren (a great way to spend more time with them and to get them into exercise), or one or more friends. Walk with your pet. Organize a walking club.

- *You can walk specifically to exercise.* Walk on a treadmill, around the block, in a charity fundraiser, or go on a hike.
- *You can get the benefits of walking while doing something else.* Walk from the car to the mall (park on the outermost reaches on purpose). Walk around a museum. Walk to watch birds. Walk upstairs to the office rather than taking the elevator. Walk while talking on the phone. Walk around while cooking dinner or while waiting for the clothes to dry.
- *You can walk as a form of meditation.* Let your mind wander and ponder. Observe your neighborhood. Pay attention to the flowers, the scents in the air, the color of the sky, the pavement beneath your feet.
- *Walking is free!* Help yourself.

So why not sally forth? Start by buying yourself a pedometer. Clip it on in the morning and, for a few days, keep a record of how many steps you take each day. Experts say that if you take ten thousand steps per day, which is approximately five miles, you will most likely get all the exercise you need to maintain your weight and health.

When walking, be aware of your posture. When you stand, your body should be aligned so that the pull of gravity is evenly distributed. Good posture means that your head is straight and your neck is relaxed. If a plumb line were dropped next to you, your ears, shoulders, hips, knees, and ankles would all be in a straight line.

Make sure you have appropriate footwear. Don't spend a fortune. Just get something designed for walking that offers good support. Wear comfortable clothes and socks that breathe. If you plan to walk outside, dress appropriately for the weather.

Pick a route. Pick a time. Stand tall. Keep a picture of your posture in your mind. Pull your navel to your spine, hold your chin parallel to the ground, push off on the ball of your foot, take moderate to small steps, and off you go! When you get back from your walk, stretch, then write down how long you walked and how you feel. Do you feel energized, tired, sore, satisfied? If you keep track of your walking regimen, it's more likely that you will exercise consistently.

> ### Buffy's New Gizmo
>
> My husband surprised me the other day with a pedometer. I had some trouble programming it, but once I asked a YP (young person) to help me, I was on my way.
>
> I consider myself a fairly active person and, given my competitive nature, probably walked a few extra steps that first day. I figured hitting my goal of ten thousand steps per day would be no problem. But when I unhooked myself, I had walked only 2,505 steps. *Gulp!*
>
> My first reaction: I'm so lazy! But hold on. I need to be more patient with myself, try to ensure my success, and set a more realistic goal of five thousand steps per day. Wish me luck.

www.tekosocks.com
Features high-performance, planet-friendly socks for hiking, backpacking, and more.

www.cardiocoach.com
This site offers services and products. The iPod-friendly coaching series may be the buddy you need to get your exercise program up and running. It's rather pricey, so be sure to check out other downloadable options.

www.thewalkingsite.com
For walkers of all fitness levels, this site offers advice on how to use walking to get fit and maintain a healthy lifestyle. It is especially helpful for beginners.

www.walkingconnection.com
This site connects walking and hiking enthusiasts to information of all kinds.

www.walkjogrun.com
This site offers Google earth maps, helps plan your route, calculates distance, and helps you connect with a community of walkers in your neighborhood.

Let's see how the seven candles, our seven recurring strategies, can help you make a commitment to exercise. Remember, the goal is not to wear the same dress size you did when you were twenty-one. Instead, it is to pledge to be physically active, to plan to become healthier, however you define that. Remember that no matter what configuration your exercise regimen takes, by creating it and following through on it you are making an important commitment to yourself and your future health and happiness.

CREATE TIME

We all must create time for exercise. No excuses. But isn't a lack of time the handiest excuse not to exercise? What are your excuses?

- I'm too tired.
- I'm too busy with the kids.
- I'm too busy at work.
- I'm too tense.
- I don't want anyone to see me in my exercise clothes.

- I can't afford a health club.
- I'm afraid of hurting myself.
- I'm so out of shape I don't know where to start.
- I need my rest.
- Exercise is boring

Make a list and read it over a few times. Cross out three excuses right away. Then start to create time for yourself, and you'll find that the other excuses fall away. All it takes is thirty minutes a day—and they don't have to be a consecutive thirty minutes. Once you start exercising, you'll want to keep on exercising because you'll feel so much better. You'll feel energized. And because you feel energized, you'll be able literally to create more time to do what you need to do. Of course, there will be conflicts and challenges to staying on track, but you will be able to meet them successfully when you make exercise a priority.

Also, be sure that when you're scheduling time to exercise, you don't schedule a ridiculous time for exercise, like Kate. She scheduled sessions with a trainer near her office for 7:00 a.m. twice a week, forcing her, given her long commute, to wake up at 3:30 a.m. to get there on time. It seemed like a good idea at first, but it backfired in the end. After a few months, Kate was exhausted and even more sleep deprived than before. She started missing sessions because she hadn't had enough sleep or had missed the early train. She was ready to bail on the whole exercise thing, then she had a flash of brilliance: choose a *reasonable* time instead of a ridiculous time. She rescheduled the sessions with her trainer for later in the day, and suddenly committing to exercise became much easier.

REFLECT

In chapter 1, we learned the right way to breathe. Using your breath as both a calming agent and energizer will help you as you exercise. Breathing fully and deeply provides you with energy, stability, focus, and the potential to push yourself and test your limits. Exhale through your mouth with an energized *whoosh* when you exert yourself. Inhale deeply through your nose to reoxygenate yourself for the next effort. Let your breath propel your movement.

Breathing properly can also protect you from harm. It helps your body relax into the exercise and keeps you in sync with your body's limits. Breathing can become a soft, fluffy net beneath you, keeping you from strain and injury.

Ask professional athletes and Olympic contenders about the secrets of their success, and they will tell you that creative visualization is key. Before you exercise, you might want to take time to meditate and come up with a picture in your mind, whether from a training video or an image of a specific person whose athletic style and form you admire. Of course, you can be your own role model and visualize yourself meeting your goals. Holding a picture of excellence and success in your mind as you exercise can actually enhance your experience and help you get the most out of it. Skiers report that visualizing a successful run down a mountain before a competition prepares them better than taking a practice run.

If you can't decide what kind of exercise regimen you want to undertake, try this exercise.

Meditation: Exercise Is a Beach!

Make yourself comfortable. Close your eyes. Count back slowly from ten to one. As you do so, feel yourself easing into a deeper and deeper state of relaxation. Contract and relax each of your muscle groups in turn. Start with your feet. Scrunch your toes, hold for three seconds, then release. Next contract and relax your calf muscles, then your thighs. Squeeze your buttocks and release. Tense each arm by making a fist, hold for three seconds, then release. Hunch your shoulders forward, then relax them. And last, scrunch your face together, hold, and release with a strong exhalation.

Imagine that you are standing at the edge of the ocean. The sun is rising. It is a warm red disc and its glow is spreading across the sky. The air is fresh and salty. A slight breeze is blowing. Your feet are planted solidly in the damp sand. You stand strong, looking out to sea. You hear the waves gently breaking. You feel confident. Your muscles are warm, like soft wax. You roll up onto your toes, balance, then slowly lower yourself, as though

Chi Fitness: A Workout for Body, Mind, and Spirit by Sue Benton (Collins). These low-impact, easy-to-do exercises will help unblock your energy and get your entire being fit.

Chi Walking by Danny Dreyer and Katherine Dreyer (Fireside). This is an excellent handbook for walking mindfully.

www.standfords.co.uk This British site offers detailed walking maps of unusual places (the Turquoise Trail, the Inca Trail) and walkers' journals.

your heels were marshmallows. You exhale deeply. You can feel your heart beating. Your eyesight is unusually sharp. Your hearing is acute. You are ready to let your body move. To let your mind trail behind. The ocean glitters. You stand poised, ready to do absolutely anything.

Now imagine what it is that you might do next: walk along the beach and collect shells; start to run down the beach digging your feet into the sand; do yoga on a plush towel; lift free weights, using the horizon to help you balance. Or maybe you will ride your bike along a path, or kayak or sail or swim.

Once you have this picture clearly in your mind, slowly open your eyes. Return to the reality of your surroundings, but hold on to that picture of yourself exercising. Whatever it is you are doing, you have endless energy and endurance. You could go on doing it forever.

> Dear Kate: I think my exercise regimen needs a little refining. I'm a bit light on cardio. Love, Buffy
>
> Dear Buffy: I can relate. I'm all strength and no endurance. I hate treadmills, and I hate to sweat. And I'm not even sure the stretching I'm doing when I do yoga at home with my mother is effective. It's not easy doing yoga with someone who is practically deaf. Shouting out the poses is not exactly conducive to yogic serenity. Plus her tiny little incontinent dog keeps running around underfoot. I'm afraid he's going to lift his little leg on me while I'm doing the Downward Dog pose. Love, Kate

PRACTICE PATIENCE

Remember that all things are possible if you are patient. Like other aspects of your life, exercise takes work: steady, daily adherence to your dream of fitness. But know that it is possible to live that dream. Approach exercise calmly and purposefully, not as just another task to be rushed through and crossed off your to-do list. As you continue to increase patience in your everyday life, you also need to develop patience with your body.

Remember your Edge Behaviors from chapter 1? Take a moment now to reread them. Some of the points you made might apply to your body and exercise. Here is part of Buffy's list. She knows that these issues are in need of constant sanding. As you read them, you might find yourself nodding emphatically in agreement or inclined to add a few of your own. Patience is key.

- Works too hard (Buffy once complained to Kate that, try as she might, she was just too competitive with herself, too macho. Kate nodded sagely and noted that Buffy was really too femmo.)
- Is disappointed with the shape of her body.
- Often skips the cool-down period after exercise because she is running late.
- Wears the wrong sort of top and spends an inordinate amount of time sneering at her reflection in the gym mirror.
- Refuses to admit when her wrists are aching and an exercise is too hard.

As you start this journey to better health, you will need to be patient when your body is sore, patient when your muscles are weary, patient when your body fails to live up to the image of how you think it should look. Forgive your body its limitations and *celebrate* your beauty and strength.

Buffy on Ballet

Growing up, my most influential ballet teacher was a commanding six-foot-three-inch Russian balletomane. Igor Schwezoff was rail thin but strong when lifting girls to demonstrate a movement. With a mane of white hair and gorgeous, clear blue eyes, he cut a dashing, charismatic figure with two Russian Wolfhounds sprawled at his feet. He even carried a riding crop! He never actually used it, but I didn't know that at the time. His deep, heavily accented voice would scare the hell out of me one moment, and the next romance me into again trying a complicated series of steps — even though my toes were bleeding inside my slippers. If anyone ever faltered or stopped doing a combination he had asked for, he would halt the class, and signal the person who had stopped, either from fatigue or confusion, to repeat the exercise alone.

www.sportsnationvideo
.com
Eager to learn a new
sport, but need a little
guidance? Sports Nation
offers instructional
videos on almost every
sport imaginable.

We all had a crush on Mr. S., and without him I probably would not have retained the lessons I learned so well so long. I haven't had a ballet class in almost twenty years, yet I still have the ballet mind, the ballet atti- tude instilled in me by many teachers, but none so eloquently as Mr. S. With me are these tenets:

1. Strive to do better each day.
2. Use your memory, both your mental and muscle memory.
3. Relax your face and jaw, and don't forget to breathe.
4. Isolate. If you are doing a leg lift, don't use your shoulders. The only part of your body that can always help is your stomach. Always pull your navel to your spine.
5. Repetition is valuable.

When I exercise, I try to stay focused. I try to stay within myself, and I try hard. When it's over, I feel like I have been given a gift. The gift is not always the same. Sometimes it is the gift of independence, sometimes the gift of energy, sometimes the gift of accomplishment — often the gift of fun. If performed with presence of mind and consideration for yourself, exercise is always, one way or another, a gift.

RESEARCH

It is easy to listen. Why, then, is it so hard to listen well? In order for your exercise regimen to be successful, you need to listen: to your body, mind, experts, friends; you need all sorts of information. That's why, in addition to doing exercise, it's sometimes really helpful to read about exercise.

First and foremost, listen to your body. Don't push yourself beyond the limit of your abilities or endurance. If you do, you will set yourself back weeks or, worse, injure yourself. Many of us are now in our fifties or be- yond. As we get older, it takes longer to heal. It might take weeks to get over a minor pull or strain, but we don't have to risk an injury. Actively lis- ten to your body, and you will do it no harm. If you feel discomfort, stop and ask yourself whether you are performing the exercise correctly.

Here are a few other specific ways you can listen and learn:

- Engage in conversation with your friends who exercise. Ask them questions and really think about their answers.
- Borrow or buy exercise tapes or visit online health and exercise sites.
- Learn about the facilities at your company. More and more companies provide exercise rooms; some even provide well-appointed gyms.
- Visit a gym and at least two exercise studios, and listen to what the practitioner or trainer tells you about exercise.
- Ask yourself—and really *listen* to your answer—what parts of your body you want to focus on and what you want to get out of exercising regularly.

Here are some points to keep in mind as you begin to figure out what type of gym or exercise facility you want to join:

- Location, location, location. Choose a place close to home or work. Don't give yourself an excuse not to go.
- When visiting a gym, or better yet during a free trial visit, pay attention to the cleanliness of the exercise room, locker room, and bathroom.
- How busy is it? How long is the wait for the machines and treadmill?
- Are weight rooms monitored by attendants or trainers?
- If there is a training session in progress, see if you like the style of the trainer. Is the trainer pleasant? Does he seem knowledgeable? Is he certified?
- If you have to sign a contract, read it carefully. Before signing, take it home and figure out if it covers everything you were told verbally.
- Find out how you can cancel your membership if you need to—if you move, are transferred or injured, or fall ill—and whether there are any hidden fees. Pay attention to the terms of the contract.
- Check with your state attorney general's office or the Better Business Bureau (www.bbb.org) to see what people have been saying about this facility (behind their back). Lodge your own complaints at www.it-pays-to-complain.com.

exercise.about.com
This site offers helpful exercise tips, articles, related links, and equipment recommendations for personal health and fitness.

www.fitnessonline.com
Offering fitness information and services, this site includes links to articles on eating healthy and exercise advice.

www.skicentral.com/seniors.html
The number one search site for skiing and snowboarding provides a comprehensive guide to skiing for ages 50 and older.

www.swimsearch.com
Welcome to the world's leading independent resource for swimming.

www.diabetes-exercise.org
The Diabetes and Exercise Sports Association focuses on teaching healthy and safe exercise strategies in the treatment of diabetes.

FIND ROLE MODELS

As you get into the swing of designing the second half of your life, you will want to notice how other people are doing it, particularly those people who are having fun and living not so much *in* style as *with* style.

When Buffy and her husband walk, they routinely see four other people out walking. You might say they are Buffy's walking role models. One is an older, white-haired gentleman, a retired physicist, who walks while doing the *New York Times* crossword puzzle. (How is that for combining a physical and a mental workout?) He stops to chat with neighbors about local politics and whether the new sewer system is a good idea. His walks are long and leisurely. One is an older woman. It's sometimes hard to tell how old people are without asking, but Buffy suspects she is somewhere in her midsixties. She walks with purpose, waves, but does not stop. The other two walkers are a mother and son who walk with flashlights in the early evening. They never miss a night. The son is about forty and may have a mental disability. They smile as they pass and seem engaged and very devoted to each other.

All these walkers provide Buffy with a sense of security, constancy, and community. They are good role models whom Buffy can easily watch and observe. She notices what they are wearing, the time of day they walk, their invariable good humor when exchanging hellos, and the optimism and commitment with which they seem to approach exercise.

Who are your exercise role models? Think about who in your community, neighborhood, gym, office, or church you admire and can emulate.

WRITE IT DOWN

Writing things down makes them happen! Studies show that people who keep written logs of their exercise routines tend to stick with them longer and achieve lasting results. You might even want to keep a separate notebook just for exercise. Write down what your reasonable goals will be, what you want to achieve, and what parts of your body you want to pay special attention to. Write down tips from friends and role models who inspire you, or post a cartoon that sums up your feelings about your new commitment to exercise. Write down the days and times you will exercise and what you will do during each session. If you don't keep a log, you can write at the end of your daily journal entry (or up the side of the page) what you accomplished for your physical well-being. Describe the gifts you gave yourself for better health.

GET TOGETHER

It's lonely being a long-distance runner. Exercise is more fun if it's not always a solitary affair. Experiment with making exercise a more communal effort. Find an exercise buddy and go to the gym together. Start an informal exercise class in your home and take turns being the leader. Start a walking, swimming, trail-riding, or biking group. And remember, two's company; three or more is a group!

Kate has developed a small circle of friends at the barn where she rides. These are not jodhpur-wearing, crop-wielding equestrian divas, just regular women from different walks of life who share a love of horses. Every weekend day, they show up at 10:00 a.m. to tack up. If you know friends are waiting for you, it provides a little added motivation to get out there and do it. When Kate is tempted not to go because she feels sluggish, hates her life, or doesn't like the color of the sky, she knows she will let down her friends as well as herself. And she *always* feels better after a good ride. Exercise makes you feel good.

Our friend Katherine started training for the Los Angeles Marathon with a group of friends last year. They trained together for months. While they were training, they decided they would walk the marathon rather than run it, that walking would be enough of a challenge. And it was. It took Katherine eight hours and thirty-six minutes to finish her first marathon, but she was exhilarated! And she must have communicated that joy—and been a great role model—because her son Nathan is now training for a marathon and he'll be running for charity.

Shape: This magazine is about living healthy and getting fit. Maybe some of the models on the cover are too perfect and a tad too young, but don't let that stop you from reading some of the newest information on nutrition and exercise.

Fitness: The subtitle for this magazine is *Mind, Body + Spirit.* It's a good source for new exercises to keep your regimen fresh and fun.

Yoga Journal: This magazine offers insights into how yoga can play a part in every facet of your life from health to parenting. In a recent article, a doctor at Cedars-Sinai Medical Center in Los Angeles, which is known for its cardiac care unit, spoke about how hatha yoga for stress reduction is a standard offering for its cardiac patients.

www.exercisefriends.com
Search for an exercise
partner by activity.
Friends can help
motivate. Find an
exercise partner online.

Maybe getting together
means exercising with
your pet. Walking is a
good exercise for both
of you, but some people
are now practicing yoga
with their dogs: Doga,
yoga for dogs, and Ruff
Yoga. Check out doga
and see if canine karma
works for you.

PUTTING IT ALL TOGETHER

Now it's time to design your exercise regimen. Keep your goals foremost in your mind. There are so many different kinds of exercise, spanning the spectrum from calisthenics to recreation to hobbies like gardening. Mix it up! Make it lively and interesting.

1. *Create time* for exercise and don't rush through it.
2. *Reflect* on what you want out of exercise, and learn to cultivate meditative breathing practices. Remember: exercise is a gift.
3. *Practice patience* with your body and forgive your body its limitations.
4. *Research* what experts, trainers, and friends say about exercise. First and foremost, listen to your body.
5. *Find appropriate role models,* not necessarily the twenty-two-year-old, spandex-clad, six-pack-sporting Nautilus Goddess at your local Y.
6. *Write down* your goals, your regimen, and any tips you've read or heard. Keep notes on your progress, setbacks, concerns, and successes.
7. *Get together* and exercise with a friend. A friend helps you keep your exercise commitment because you are making a commitment to her, as well as to yourself.

TO-DO LIST

Don't be alarmed by the length of this list of suggested activities. Keep in mind that one activity can incorporate the three forms of exercise—aerobic, flexibility, and strength training—so consider these groupings of convenience rather than rules. There's something here for everyone. Also keep in mind that exercise should be fun.

Aerobic exercise

- Walking
- Spinning
- Exercise boot camp
- Swimming

- Tennis
- Racquetball
- Jogging
- Tango or swing dance

- Kick boxing
- Cycling
- Hiking
- Mountain biking
- Rock climbing

- Dancercise
- Golf
- Volleyball
- Badminton

Flexibility

- Walking
- Yoga
- Pilates

- Ballet or modern dance
- Stretch classes
- Resistance bands

Strength training

- Walking
- Bowling
- Free weights
- Rowing

- Fly fishing
- Surf casting
- Gymnastics

Combinations

- Walking
- Snorkeling
- Scuba diving
- Tae Bo
- Tai Chi
- Rent/buy exercise videos in lieu of hiring a personal trainer

- Aquatic aerobics
- Playing tag
- Playing football
- Juggling
- Wobble board
- Medicine ball
- Stability ball

KATE'S PLAN

I have a history of exercise bingeing, frenzied periods of committed exercising that come to a crashing halt when I injure myself. So it's important for me, at least initially, to have a teacher or trainer on hand to protect me from my overzealousness. It will cost me a little bit more, but once I've learned patience and self-restraint from a trainer, I will know how to exercise properly without harming myself and can do so alone for the rest of my life if I want. But I also need to make sure I find the right trainer. A trainer who doesn't understand my inability to say no when an exercise is too much for me has the potential to hurt me.

I also need to get outside more during the winter months. The stingy winter light and frigid temperatures in the Northeast from November to March make me want to curl up in a miserable, tense little ball and not lift a finger, much less a leg. So I need to make my horseback riding, which I currently do only during the warm months, a year-round activity. (Get out the long undies!)

My exercise regimen looks like this:

- Horseback riding twice a week with my trail buddies
- Strength and aerobic training at a gym twice a week with my trainer
- Walking at 4 mph for thirty minutes on a treadmill twice a week
- Yoga twice a week with my mother (maybe find a class for us so I don't have to be the yoga mistress and bellow out directions)

BUFFY'S PLAN

I want to strengthen my upper body. When I studied ballet, strength training was not part of the discipline as it is now. I have fairly strong legs, but my shoulders, arms, and chest are relatively weak. I would also like to spend time with my husband when I exercise. And though I am a relative newcomer to meditation, I have already begun to feel the benefits. I would like to blend silent contemplation with my exercise. I have a recurring neck and shoulder injury I want to manage better.

But my real challenge is that my longtime Pilates studio will no longer offer mat classes, and I can't afford private instruction. I am desolate. I have been going to this studio three times a week for nearly seven years, usually with my dear friend Kathy. Now I must research new places and potentially attend classes on my own. Seems a bit daunting.

So my exercise regimen looks like this:

- Find a new Pilates studio or a new gym and ask Kathy to join me.
- Do yoga with my husband once a week.
- Walk with my husband two or three times a week.
- Tennis with my husband as time and weather permit
- Use free weights at home twice a week while watching television.

Making a commitment to exercise is as important as taking care of your inner self. With a healthy body, you will have the strength, stamina, and agility to soar to even greater heights during the second half of your life. The next chapter addresses the path to health and how to stay on it.

3

When Was the Last Time I Went to the Doctor?

Staying healthy

> Dear Buffy: Confession time: I haven't been to the doctor since Noah was born. Love, Kate
>
> Dear Kate: Are you serious? Noah's what? Sixteen now? Are you nuts? Love, Buffy

THE WHITE-COAT WILLIES

Let's face it. We have come to a vulnerable point in our lives, when age, gravity, and the sundry sins we visited upon ourselves in the past start making themselves known. You might have begun to notice that your back aches in the morning or that your hip rebels during an exercise class. Maybe you are experiencing allergies for the first time or indigestion more often than you used to. Maybe you are having trouble falling asleep at night. At the same time, many of us who were fairly conscientious about getting regular checkups start skipping these appointments just when health maintenance is becoming more important than ever before.

Health maintenance is the ticket. Your goals in this chapter are to devise a set of healthy habits and to create a daily plan for your health maintenance, one that you will be able to sustain willingly and gracefully for the rest of your life.

There are many ways to approach the subject of your health. Some of you may be under a doctor's care. Others may feel perfectly healthy on your own. Still others, like Kate, may suffer from the "White-Coat Willies" —

a severe aversion to medical professionals wearing white lab coats and bearing stethoscopes. However we are living, all of us must make our health a priority. We can all benefit from adopting the ten simple, commonsense rules that follow, the second-half health maintenance checklist:

1. Drink water.
2. Don't smoke.
3. Don't use alcohol to excess.
4. Get fresh air and exercise.
5. Protect yourself from the sun.
6. Eat a healthy diet.
7. Get enough sleep.
8. Stand up straight.
9. Get checkups regularly.
10. Keep your sunny side up.

DRINK WATER

"In aqua salus," as the Romans said, and they were right — in water, there is health. Drinking lots of water is good for your skin, hair, nails, and vital organs, and it flushes waste material from your cells and body. For proper hydration, some experts recommend dividing your body weight in half and drinking that number of ounces of water daily, more if you exercise. That means if you weigh 160 pounds, you need to drink eighty ounces (ten eight-ounce glasses) of water per day. That seems like a lot of water to us but, hey, do the best you can.

Drinking water is a little like walking. Think of Buffy and her pedometer. It will be a rare day that she actually reaches those recommended ten thousand daily steps, but that doesn't mean she won't try every day, right? Take the same approach when drinking water. Here are some tips to help you:

- Use additives like lemon or fruit flavorings if you must, to make the water more palatable, but remember that additives can slow down the absorption of water into the bloodstream.

- Make your plan a habit. Your plan might be: drink one glass of water with breakfast, two before lunch, two with lunch, two in the afternoon, two with dinner, and one in the evening. Go with the flow. Drinking plenty of water also keeps you active and moving, skipping to the loo on a regular basis.
- Get yourself a fun glass, jug, bottle, mug, or flask. Bring it with you everywhere. Wash it daily so it doesn't get funky. Replace it when you get sick and tired of the look of the thing.

Are all waters created equal?

Not according to Kate's eldest son, Aaron, whom she jokingly calls the "boy in the bubble" because he's so sensitive to pollution and impurities. Aaron, like an increasing number of people these days, prefers to drink ultra-purified water, and he believes it's worth the extra expense.

Because minerals and impurities in water can slow its absorption into the bloodstream, ultra-purified water is ideal. Makers of ultra-purified water filter out nearly every possible impurity, including arsenic, bacteria, chlorine, chromium-6, fluoride, lead, and pesticides. If the water you drink is important to you, you might want to check it out. On the other hand, you might want to consider buying a good-quality water filter and turning on the faucet instead.

DON'T SMOKE

According to the Centers for Disease Control, smoking is the number one preventable cause of death in the United States. If you've been having trouble quitting, get help. See a doctor, try the patch, join a group, try hypnosis. Do anything to break your addiction.

DON'T USE ALCOHOL TO EXCESS

Keggers, shots, and martinis were OK (sort of) once upon a time, but no more. Drinking dehydrates you, depresses you, and saddles you with tons of empty calories. Limit your alcohol intake to a drink or two a day. Make a point of drinking one extra glass of water for every glass of alcohol.

GET FRESH AIR AND EXERCISE

As we learned in chapter 2, it is important to get out and walk every day or include an outdoor sport as part of your exercise program. Make exercise part of your life every day. If you have a desk job, don't sit for extended periods of time. Make sure that you get up at least once an hour, shake your bootie a little or stretch, and walk around. Whatever you do, it's a good idea to take a minibreak for five minutes once an hour. It will refresh you and improve your focus.

www.realage.com
This site helps you calculate the biological age of your body based on height, weight, exercise regimen, blood pressure, cholesterol levels, and other personal data.

www.yourdiseaserisk
.harvard.edu
Determine your level of risk for the five most important diseases in the United States. Prevention tips are provided by the Harvard Center for Cancer Prevention.

Kate Comes Out

At one time in my life, my idea of getting fresh air was baking out in the sun like a lizard, cultivating my melanoma. I'm over that now. But I'm still not a big fan of walking. Even when the weather is balmy, walking makes me impatient to get where I'm going, even if I'm going nowhere.

After I took up horseback riding, I began to enjoy being outside. I liked to look at the scenery. I liked the smell and the feel and the rhythm of the horse beneath me. I liked to trot and gallop and ride and jump. I looked forward to getting some fresh air. But I was a fair-weather equestrian. I rode from March until November, or whenever the first frost hit the hay bales. Then one day my riding instructor told me I would never get really good if I didn't ride year-round. So I gritted my teeth and started riding in the winter. I hated it at first. It was cold, gray, and nasty. Then someone brilliantly suggested that I get some serious winter clothing: warm gloves and socks and long underwear. That made all the difference. Lo and behold, it was fun being out in the cold. Winter scenery has its own special beauty, and the colder the weather, the better I feel afterward. In fact, my whole being is suffused with a sense of warmth and health. I sleep really well. I feel as if I have left my stress somewhere back there in the woods. Horse or no horse, I highly recommend breathing fresh air, year-round.

Strong Women, Strong Bones by Miriam Nelson and Sarah Wernick (Perigee). This book on osteoporosis is the third in a great series of books that includes *Strong Women, Stay Young* (how strength training can delay aging) and *Strong Women, Stay Slim* (how strength training can help control weight). Take the assessment test.

www.healthycomputing.com
Includes some great stretching exercises you can do during a five-minute break to counter-act the deleterious effects of sitting at a computer all day long. Also gives sound advice about ergonomic workstations.

www.skincancer.org
This comprehensive site is maintained by the Skin Cancer Foundation, a group that seeks to raise public awareness about skin cancer and the importance of prevention, early detection, and treatment.

PROTECT YOURSELF FROM THE SUN

To minimize sun damage, follow these tips:

- Avoid sun exposure between the hours of 10 a.m. and 2 p.m.
- Shop around to find a sunscreen that you really like and don't mind slathering on your skin. A good sunscreen will moisturize your skin without clogging your pores.
- Wear sunscreen with an SPF of at least 15. Thirty minutes before you go out in the sun, apply sunscreen liberally. Reapply often.
- Sunscreen alone is not enough. Get a wide-brimmed hat and learn to love wearing it.
- Cover your arms and chest. Savor the shade.
- Learn to cultivate and find joy in your radiant healthy skin, rather than tanned skin, which is unhealthy.

Skin damage is cumulative and irreversible, but that's no reason to make it worse. What if, like so many of us, you are a recovering tanaholic? There are some effective, but expensive, treatments to help your skin look better. Administered by a licensed aesthetician, dermatologist, or plastic surgeon, facial peels use fruit, glycolic, or even stronger acids to burn away the damaged outer layers of your skin. The skin revealed underneath is softer, clearer, tighter, and may even have fewer wrinkles. If you undergo such a treatment, you must be careful to protect your skin with sunscreen, hat, and clothing, and make a commitment to avoid direct sun exposure.

A less expensive option is to use a skin cream with retinol in it. Derived from vitamin A, retinol thins the surface layer of your skin. It is best applied at night and, like the peel, will make your skin more vulnerable to harmful ultraviolet rays. Use your sunscreen!

EAT A HEALTHY DIET

This is not a diet book, but we both firmly believe that a diet is a way of life, not a thing you go on. If you eat a proper diet, day after day and year after year, you will be the right weight for you. If you fast in order to lose weight and look like Kate Moss, your body will go into survival mode, slowing down your metabolism and storing up energy in the form of body fat. Avoid fasting. Keep the food pyramid in mind. The food pyramid you learned about in high school health class has fallen out of favor. The divisions are now vertical wedges, rather than stacked groups from top to bottom. And — good news! — we each get to design our own personal food pyramids based on our unique requirements. Work with your doctor or a dietitian to come up with a plan that suits your body, metabolism, and nutritional needs. Everyone's pyramid should include these five basic food groups:

1. *Grains.* Wheat, rice, oats, cornmeal, barley, and other cereals. Grains can be whole or refined. Whole grains — including whole wheat, oats, and brown rice — still have the full kernel which contains the fiber and minerals. Refined grains — like white flour and white rice — have been processed to remove the fiber and, although minerals have been added back in, the nutritive value is no longer as great. Whenever possible, use whole grains. A diet rich in fiber and minerals helps you fight heart disease and cancer.

2. *Vegetables.* The subgroups are green; orange and yellow; starchy; dry beans; and everything else. Mix it up and give yourself a nice variety of veggies, but try to favor the green and the orange/yellow. Green vegetables are rich in iron and high in fiber; orange/yellow vegetables are high in antioxidants, which help your body fend off cancer.

3. *Fruits.* Keep in mind that fruits such as bananas, prunes, dried apricots, and peaches are high in potassium, which helps cut cholesterol. Fruits rich in vitamin C, such as oranges and grapefruit, are good for your teeth and gums. Again, mix it up. Avoid fruit juices as they tend to have too much sugar.

4. *Oils.* Try to get your oil from fish, nuts, and vegetables, and minimize your intake of butter, margarine, lard, and shortening.

5. *Milk and dairy.* This group includes ice cream, cheese, eggs, and yogurt. Learn to love the taste of fat-free or reduced-fat milk products. And avoid egg yolks whenever you can.

6. *Meat, beans, nuts, and seeds.* Stick with lean meats, chicken, and fish. Select fish such as salmon, trout, and herring, which are high in omega-3 fatty acids.

www.mypyramid.gov
Put out by the original pyramid architects, the U.S. Department of Agriculture, this site explains the food groups and their nutritive value. It also gives tips on how to design a pyramid that's right for your body and your life.

www.environmental nutrition.com.
This excellent Web site is independent (no sponsors or advertisers) and aims to "open your eyes to what you put in your mouth."

www.wholegrainscouncil.org

Switching to whole grains — that is, unrefined breads and cereals — can absolutely help with diabetes, heart disease, and weight control. But not all whole grains are truly whole grains. What? The Whole Grains Council issues three different stamps to indicate whether food is a good (a half serving), excellent (a full serving), or 100% excellent (a full serving using only whole grains) source of whole grains.

www.edap.org

This site is dedicated to expanding public understanding of eating disorders and promoting access to quality treatment for those affected, along with support for their families through education, advocacy, and research.

Whatever your pattern of meals, if you're not getting everything you need through food, consider taking a good multivitamin or a vitamin supplement. Some vitamins and supplements to think about are calcium, vitamin D, fish oil, selenium, lutein, magnesium, zinc, and vitamins B12 and E. If you have achy joints, look into glucosamine with chondroitin. If you are like Kate, and pills make you *gack,* get a powdered vitamin supplement, and mix it up with yogurt and frozen fruit. Instead of coffee and a Danish for breakfast, make yourself a power shake and notice the quality of energy it brings to your day. Whatever vitamins or supplements you choose, we recommend that you consult with your physician or dietitian, especially if you are taking prescription drugs.

GET ENOUGH SLEEP

Although individual sleep requirements differ, eight hours is the general recommendation. Studies have shown, however, that eight out of every ten adults are suffering from sleep deprivation. Let's blame it on Thomas Edison and his electric light. Back in the days of firelight, most of us went to bed naturally when the sun went down. Nowadays, all-night TV, work, stress, and a plethora of stimulants keep us up. Late nights and early mornings have conspired to create a sleepless society. Lack of sleep makes us crabby, depressed, forgetful, and prone to illness. It's a good idea to try to maintain a consistent sleeping schedule, going to bed and waking up at more or less the same time every day, even on weekends. Figure out how many hours of sleep refresh you and try to get them. Naps and power naps are also a good bolster.

What If You Can't Sleep?

Don't despair! If you have trouble sleeping, here are some suggestions to help you find sweet release in slumber:

- Don't just lie in bed and fret. Count your blessings instead of counting problems.
- Practice your breathing exercises.

- Draw a warm bath and put lavender oil in it. Studies have shown that lavender oil works as effectively as sleeping pills to make you relaxed and drowsy. Light a candle, turn off the lights, and watch the shadows dance on the tiles as you soak.
- Drink warm milk with vanilla.
- Listen to soothing music.
- Read a book, preferably one that's not very stimulating. Hegel or Plato or Kierkegaard work well. Henry James does it for Kate every time. Reading those long sentences is exhausting.
- If your sleep problem is chronic, examine your daily routine. Are you getting enough exercise and fresh air? Do you eat a heavy meal too close to bedtime? (When you eat too close to bedtime, your stomach begins working to digest the food and that can keep you awake.) Could the sleep disturbance be related to menopause?
- Do a little exercise after eating your evening meal. Nothing strenuous. Walk the dog, do some yoga, walk on the treadmill — or, as we call it in Our Own Private Iowa, the hamster wheel — at a low speed.
- Talk to your doctor. He may suggest that you go to a sleep clinic, where your sleep will be monitored to determine the cause of your problem before a remedy is recommended. While sleeping pills can do the trick, they also can cause adverse side effects and you may become dependent on them.

Your Present: A Half Hour of Peace (Relax . . . Intuit). On this best-selling CD, Susie Mantell's voice is soft and so soothing it puts you to sleep one body part at a time, from head to toe. Why worry? Be sleepy!

Let Uncle Johann lull you to sleep. Try *Bach for Bedtime* (Philips).

www.posturepage.com Provides practical information about methods for improving posture, such as the Alexander technique, Feldenkrais, somatics, yoga, Rolfing, and physical therapy.

STAND UP STRAIGHT

At this stage of our lives, chronic bad posture, including how we stand, sit at the computer, and drive, can cause serious problems such as scoliosis and chronic neck, shoulder, or back pain. Good posture and mindful breathing are the foundations for a healthy body and a beneficial exercise regimen. You can maintain an erect bearing. Here's how:

- *Be mindful of your posture from moment to moment.* Don't pinch or clench your shoulder blades. Drop your shoulders. Think of your chest and your upper back as being wide open and smooth. To avoid hyperextending your back, pull your navel toward your spine.

- *Uncross your arms.* Many of us cross our arms. When you stand, let your arms dangle loosely from the "coat hanger" of your shoulders.
- *Uncross your legs.* Almost all of us cross our legs almost as soon as we sit down. Why is this? Are we protecting our naughty bits? Are we trying to look suave or casual? More feminine? Who knows why. But it is as if we were tying ourselves in a knot. This knotted pose is bad for the circulation and constricts the flow of blood to your heart.
- *Use a small pillow or no pillow at all.* Sleeping with your head jacked up high on pillows reinforces bad posture all night long. Instead, place a pillow behind your knees when you are lying on your back or between your legs when you are lying on your side to support your lower back.
- *Make sure your workstation is ergonomically correct.* When working at your computer, sit up straight and avoid craning your head toward the screen. Your keyboard should be on a height-adjustable tray so your shoulders and elbows do not strain upward. To avoid wrist strain, your space bar should be higher than your keyboard.
- *Avoid extremely high-heeled shoes.* Fashionistas have convinced us that three-inch and even higher heels make us look well dressed and, yes, sexy. In fact, high heels throw off our center of balance and cause the tendons and muscles on the backs of our lower legs to shorten. If you must wear high heels, try to limit the number of hours you walk in them to two or three. Better yet, shop around for low-heeled or flat shoes that give you support and still make you feel like a stone fox. If you simply can't resist those Manolo Blahniks, try this exercise:

High-Heel Relief Stretch

Every day that you wear stilettos, try to do this exercise. Take off your high heels and climb halfway up a set of stairs. Lightly hold the railings on either side of you, and rest the balls of your feet on the edge of the step. (Your heels will hang over the edge of the step.) Drop your weight into your heels, and hold that position for a count of ten. Feel the stretch! Now lift up on your toes. Alternately stretch, pushing down into your heels, and lift to increase flexibility and strengthen your lower legs.

GET CHECKUPS REGULARLY

Got the White-Coat Willies? Do doctors make you nervous, paranoid, defensive, fearful, or angry? Do your fears sometimes keep you from going to the doctor when something doesn't feel right or from getting essential tests like mammograms, bone density, and colonoscopies? Make your health a priority. Find a doctor and a dentist you like and trust. Get regular checkups. And don't forget to have your eyes checked.

At this stage of our lives, it's important to address health issues through diet and exercise when possible. All too often, when we reach a certain age, we find ourselves on slippery pharmaceutical slopes. Our symptoms are masked, and all too often replaced by harmful side effects. More important, the drug we are taking simply enables us to continue with destructive habits such as overeating and underexercising. True, there are wonder drugs today that save lives and improve the quality of life for some, but drugs are not the answer to all your ills.

www.livecomfortably.com The Comfort Council (does anybody else love this name?) addresses various issues relating to physical, emotional, and psychological comfort and the importance of feeling relaxed. Helpful articles, FAQs, and expert advice.

Dear Kate: I was in for my physical five days after I had an "incident" with the nurse. I'd asked her to refill a prescription that had expired, and she refused. It was for my headache medicine, and I was going on a two-day business trip and didn't want to leave home without it. So I'm sitting on the table in that lovely gown, and I'm not even thinking about the recent dustup, but when this same nurse takes my blood pressure it's sky high. When the doctor — a lovely woman wearing a gray sweater — comes in, she looks at my BP and says, "This doesn't look like you. Is something wrong? Let's take it again." Of course, it was still high. She joked, "Maybe you've developed white-coat syndrome." I joked back and said, "Gray-sweater syndrome, you mean." But the fact was, I was too embarrassed or proud to tell her about the fight I had had with her nurse,

Heal Thy Self: Lessons on Mindfulness in Medicine by Saki Santorelli (Harmony/ Bell Tower). This book offers inspirational stories and helpful exercises as it tries to bridge the gap between patient and practitioner.

www.allaboutvision.com Useful information about eye health and vision correction. Buffy used this site when she researched her LASIK surgery. Kate used it to find more effective eye drops for her itchy allergic eyes.

www.betterhearing.org Eh? What's that you say? This site educates the public about hearing loss and what can be done about it, offering prevention tips and treatment solutions.

> which certainly would have explained the anomaly. So my punishment is that I have to go to the drugstore twice a week for the next three weeks to monitor my own blood pressure. Aren't I ridiculous? Love, Buffy
>
> Dear Buffy: It's called human. I love it when you're human. Love, Kate

KEEP YOUR SUNNY SIDE UP

We've placed this one last, but it might just as easily have been first. We all have our ups and downs but if, for the most part, we maintain a sunny outlook and believe that all things are possible, our days will be more energized, productive, and enjoyable, and we will experience a higher level of physical well-being.

What about the Winter Blahs?

Do you find that you feel more depressed during the winter months? Do you crave starches and sweets from late August until early March? Do you just want to roll over and hibernate until that first robin comes bob bob bobbin' along?

Years ago, Kate's mother, Sandy, would have told the kids to quit moping around the house and go outside and play in the sun, even if there had been three feet of snow on the ground. In those days, we called it the winter blahs. Today we call it SAD, or seasonal affective disorder. The brain's pineal gland produces more melatonin, a biochemical closely associated with depression, during the dark winter months than at other times of year. Phototherapy—that is, exposing yourself to concentrated bright fluorescent light or natural sunlight for one to two hours per day, any time of day—can slow the body's production of melatonin and effectively take the edge off your SADness.

A few years ago, Kate suspected that she and one of her sons might be struggling with SAD, so she sprang for what her family now jokingly refers to as the "bummer light," a rectangular box of fluorescent lights that she hauls out in October to ward off those dark winter mornings. She likes that it is, in a roundabout sort of way, a natural remedy. At Kate's suggestion, Buffy bought a similar light for her mother, although Buffy isn't at all sure whether her mother even opened the box.

Replacing lightbulbs in your kitchen and bathroom with bulbs of stronger wattage can be effective, too, as can taking a ninety-minute walk in the winter sun. (Don't forget your sunscreen!) You might want to consider hanging a crystal in your window so you can enjoy rainbows dancing on your walls. Wearing yellow-tinted sunglasses can also give you a boost, as can indoor plants or fresh flowers.

Review the ten points of the second-half health maintenance checklist. Rate yourself on each item, using a scale of 1 to 10, with 1 being poor and 10 being excellent. How do you rate? Begin by acknowledging your current habits of behavior, then identify where there is room for improvement. At the end of this chapter, you will address these areas with a plan. Resist the temptation to be hard on yourself; it's an energy sucker. Instead, be mindful and acknowledge, identify, and address.

Now, let's light our candles and look at our seven recurring strategies to find ways to put this health maintenance plan into practice.

CREATE TIME

Drinking enough water, getting enough sleep, going to the doctor when something doesn't feel right, making and keeping regular doctor's appointments, flossing your teeth, rubbing lotion on your body—all of these activities require time. You must make time and take time to care for yourself. Taking care of yourself is your number one priority for the second half of your life.

Many of the ways you can take care of yourself need to be scheduled; a specific time needs to be set aside. Just as you are beginning to create the time for contemplation, meditation, and regular exercise, you need to find time for feel-good therapy, such as massage, hot tubs, saunas, and steam baths. In the past, you might have considered such activities as luxuries,

Landscaping Indoors: Bringing the Garden Inside by Scott Appell (Brooklyn Botanic Garden). Includes practical advice for growing indoor plants.

Cold Weather Cooking by Sarah Chase (Workman). Offers recipes to brighten even the darkest days. Chase says early fall is the time for stronger flavors such as dried figs, black olives, and smoky ham. She tempts us with a recipe for Ribollita — a vegetable stew served over bread and sprinkled with parmesan cheese.

Aging with Grace: What the Nun Study Teaches Us about Leading Longer, Healthier, and More Mindful Lives by David Snowdon (Bantam). The author of this fascinating and thoroughly charming book is an epidemiologist who has spent more than twenty years with elderly nuns of the School Sisters of Notre Dame to study the effects of aging. The secret of a long and healthy life? Antioxidants and optimism!

www.outsidein.co.uk/sad info.htm
This British site offers free information about SAD and products for purchase.

Aromatherapy A-Z, revised edition, by Patricia Davis (C. W. Daniel Company). Geared to professional or potential aromatherapists, but accessible to anyone interested in this fun, fascinating, and time-tested practice. Davis tells you about the history of aromatherapy, how the oils work, and which oils to use for minor and serious ailments.

www.amtamassage.org Sponsored by the American Massage Therapy Association, this site is useful in helping you find a place to get a massage in your area. It also posts a feature explaining the types of massage therapy available, how to choose the kind of practitioner you need, what to look for in a massage therapist, what to expect in a session, and questions to ask.

evidence that you were pampering yourself, but no more! These are health maintenance activities of the highest order. Give yourself permission to create time for any or all of these:

- Take a massage class with your friend or mate, and learn to give each other gratis massages.
- If you have a unique skill or product, shop around for a massage therapist who will barter with you. We know a woman who cleans a massage therapist's office in exchange for monthly massages or facials.
- Got knots in your shoulders? Put a couple of tennis balls in a knee sock and fling it over your shoulder. The impact of the tennis balls will help to work away those knots.
- Use your tub for home-based hydrotherapy. If you have muscle aches, draw a hot bath and squeeze the juice of a fresh lemon into it. If you have trouble sleeping, take a hot bath with lavender oil sixty to ninety minutes before getting into bed. Studies have shown that lavender oil relaxes more effectively and induces a better night's sleep than most prescription and over-the-counter sleep medications.
- Consider purchasing an aromatherapy shawl that you can pop into the microwave and then place on your shoulders, back, or legs for a warm and nearly instant stress and ache buster.
- Consider using aromatherapy to alleviate everything from headaches to bad moods.
- Turn your shower into a spa by giving yourself a salt-glow scrub.

Salt-glow scrub

2 cups fine sea salt
4 cups oil (macadamia, olive, safflower, almond, sea algae, or a mixture)
20–30 drops essential oil (lavender, orange, rose, palmarosa, or peppermint)

Combine ingredients in a glass jar. Mix well.

Dampen yourself in the shower, then turn off the water. Starting with your feet, rub the salt-glow scrub all over your skin (but do not use it on your face or on any open cuts or scrapes). Rinse thoroughly. The salt exfoliates, the oil hydrates, and your skin will feel like a million bucks.

REFLECT

Before you go to the doctor for your regular checkup, ask yourself how you feel. Do you have any aches or pains or chronic complaints? Are you feeling fine? No current complaints? Sometimes, our bodies are like cars. Those funny bumping noises that they make occasionally go away when we get into the shop to have them looked at. But just because your body feels good right now doesn't mean it won't start making that weird knocking noise as soon as you leave the doctor's office.

Take a head-to-toe inventory of yourself and ask yourself how you feel. As you tick off each body part, ask yourself if you have a feeling, question, or concern that relates to that part of your anatomy. Take your notes with you to your appointment, and discuss your findings with your doctor.

PRACTICE PATIENCE

Impatience is the most common cause of stress. We are not suggesting that you should eliminate stress from your life. That would be impossible! Stress, in and of itself, is not bad for us. In fact, stress can often be a great short-term motivator for productivity, provided we don't become addicted to the adrenaline rush and lose ourselves in the process.

Certain things we ingest and certain things we do, usually to excess, to cope with stress are not always good for us, however. Things like drugs, alcohol, tobacco, caffeine, food, sex, TV, shopping. Our stress response has a sneaky habit of manifesting itself in the most unhealthy ways. Exercise can be a great buffer to stress, but even exercise, if you throw yourself into it, can do more harm than good. Practicing patience helps us to manage stress and avoid behaviors that are deleterious to good health.

It's important to set some goals for improving your health. As you review the health maintenance checklist and begin to acknowledge what your current habits are, identify areas where there is room for improvement, and address them with a health maintenance plan of your own design. Whatever you do, don't go overboard. Health maintenance, when approached in a radical fashion—such as a stringent, semistarvation diet

Self-Healing Cookbook: A Macrobiotic Primer for Healing Body, Mind, and Moods with Natural Foods by Kristina Turner (Earthtones). This book has been around for fifteen years and is full of good recipes, prevention checklists, and low-guilt desserts.

Anatomy Coloring Book by Wynn Kapit and Lawrence M. Elson (Benjamin Cummings). Originally created to help medical students learn anatomy, this nifty book illustrates how the body works and its interconnectivity.

www.aapb.org
If the subject of the mind's influence on the body (and vice versa) is of interest to you, visit this site, sponsored by the Association of Applied Psychophysiology and Biofeedback, an international society for mind-body interactions in research, health care, and education.

or three hours a day at the gym or such resolutions as "Absolutely no sunbathing ever again as long as I live!" — is simply impossible to sustain. Eventually, you will abandon your impossible plan and take refuge and comfort in your old, less than healthful habits. You want a reasonable plan, a balanced plan, one that you can live with every day for the rest of your life.

Be mindful of the following:

- *Address things on the checklist one at a time.* Roll out your plan, bit by bit, over a period of weeks or even months. Don't initiate a new set of goals until you have successfully met and incorporated the last set.
- *Be flexible.* If elements of your plan turn out to be unreasonable, tweak them.
- *Forgive yourself if you don't always comply 100 percent.* Being hard on yourself doesn't help improve your health. It's a morale sucker. It just makes you feel lousy about yourself and prevents you from making progress. Practice patience.
- *Remember that health maintenance is a plan and also a process.* Progress one step at a time, and stop to congratulate yourself for every single baby step that you take along the way.

RESEARCH

Open your mind, then research and explore traditional and nontraditional forms of health care and body work. Studies have shown that, increasingly, medical doctors are combining traditional health care with alternative medical therapies. Read about the potential benefits of these alternatives for healthly living, and discuss them with your doctor. Wait for the dialogue to begin! You might want to consider:

- *Breathing therapy:* Breathing therapists use yoga breathing and the altered states of awareness it brings to heal and to reduce stress.
- *Yoga therapy:* Practitioners provide yoga exercises specifically designed to complement traditional medical treatment for conditions ranging from arthritis to asthma to stroke.

- *Rolfing:* Sometimes called *structural integration,* these treatments involve deep-tissue, structurally integrated body work based on the idea that injuries and stress can throw the body out of alignment and cause muscles and connective tissue to become rigid and inflexible. Therapists use fingers, thumbs, knuckles, elbows, and even knees to apply pressure that brings about deep-tissue releases and eventual realignment over a series of treatments.

- *Medical intuition:* Practitioners work side by side with doctors and use intuition to scan the body for areas of imbalance that may need realignment and treatment. Believe it or not, some doctors are themselves medical intuitives.

- *Homeopathy:* Originally developed in the 1800s as an alternative to leeches and bloodletting, homeopathy is based on the theory that like heals like. If you have an allergy to tree pollen, for instance, you take an infinitesimal, diluted dose of tree pollen to cure it.

- *Acupuncture:* This ancient Chinese practice, said to be the oldest medical procedure in the world, uses needles to stimulate certain points in the body in order to bring about healing and balance.

- *Craniosacral therapy:* The craniosacral system comprises membranes and cerebrospinal fluid that encase, protect, and nourish the brain and spinal cord. When the system gets blocked due to injury or stress, therapists use a gentle touch to detect the location of the blockage and to assist in relieving it.

- *Alexander technique:* Practitioners show you how to rid the body of tension caused by awkward movement and posture by reeducating your mind and body so you move with greater ease and balance. This practice is popular with actors, dancers, and athletes.

- *Reiki:* This Japanese technique is based on the principle that Reiki, or energy forces, flow throughout the body. The therapist uses a very light touch to channel this energy and bring about relaxation and healing.

- *Reflexology:* This science holds that there are reflex points on the hands and the feet that correspond to organs and systems of the body. By rubbing the hands (or feet), the organs and systems of the body receive indirect stimulation and relief from stress or congestion.

www.pitt.edu/~cbw/altm
.html
The Alternative
Medicine Homepage,
sponsored by the
University of Pittsburgh,
is a good example of an
online index for
researching alternative
medicine.

www.asch.net
Hypnosis is one way of
exploring the mind-body
relationship. Check out
the site of the American
Society of Clinical
Hypnosis for more
information.

- *Aromatherapy:* Essential oils (sandalwood, peppermint, lavender, orange, rosemary) are used to treat—via massage, inhalation, or compresses—muscle aches, chronic fatigue, arthritis, and mood disorders.
- *Chiropractic treatment:* Practitioners use manipulation, physical pressure, and the application of electrical impulses to release pressure between vertebrae and joints and relieve muscle aches caused by misalignment and injury.

These are just some of the mind-body practices you can research and sample to obtain valuable insight into your personal health and well-being. Review the particulars of your medical insurance policy. You might be pleasantly surprised at the number of alternative therapies your health insurance policy covers.

If you are having a medical problem, listen to your doctor, but also read everything you can lay your hands on. Think of your doctor as a member of your personal care team, and consider yourself the coach and star player. The more open you are to exploration, the more profound your self-knowledge will become.

Buffy Goes Alternative

One sunny April day four years ago, I was sitting in my office when I felt a strange pain in my left arm. I looked down at my arm and it looked the same, but with each minute the pain was increasing, and it began to move up toward my biceps, then down into my hand. My fingers began to tingle and then went numb. I looked over at Kathy, my business partner and friend for more than twenty years, and asked, as casually as I could, if pain in the left arm meant a heart attack.

We determined that I wasn't going into cardiac arrest, but I took a tiny yellow half of a Valium to calm me down. I was calm, but the pain persisted. It persisted for days, which turned quickly into a week. I was so uncomfortable I started keeping a diary of my discomfort, knowing that I would probably need the data when I finally broke down and went to the doctor. At night I would lie in bed and wonder if I would always feel like this. Was this a preview of things to come? Was chronic pain something I would just have to learn to live with?

In the end, when I finally turned myself over to the medical authorities, I was diagnosed with a pinched nerve. My doctor thought it might be related to my use of the computer, so I spent time and money making sure my workstation was ergonomically perfect. Still no improvement. Then she thought maybe it was the way I held the phone. I ruled that out quickly, since for years I have worn earphones in the office and when using my cell. A series of ever-increasing doses of painkillers, an MRI, and a neurological consult did not relieve my pain. It was then that I decided that I had to take control of my injury and my recovery.

After consulting with my doctor and doing some research on the Internet, I started a series of alternative treatments, a combination of acupuncture and aggressive (no, *painful* is a better word) massages called structural integration. My gentle therapist, Jason, would tell me to rate my pain, from 1 to 10, as he worked on me. During the first massage, I whispered in a quiet voice because I didn't want to scare him, "Fifteen!" I have to continually work to manage my shoulder-neck injury, which afterward gave rise to tension headaches, but for me, going outside the traditional medical establishment helped to alleviate my chronic discomfort.

FIND ROLE MODELS

At the end of summer 2001, Buffy's business partner, Kathy, was diagnosed with breast cancer. Buffy learned about many things during this period: how to detect breast cancer, various treatment options, recovery and post-operative care, nutrition and exercise regimens. But far and away the biggest lesson Buffy learned was about grace. There are countless ways in which Kathy demonstrated grace, but two stand out.

Kathy and Buffy knew that she had a tumor in her breast. The day Buffy traveled to Maryland to take her son, Jesse, to his first year of college, Kathy had a biopsy. Buffy was torn between Kathy and her son, and on emotional overload about both. Kathy got the news her tumor was malignant

*Survivor: Taking Control
of Your Fight against
Cancer* by Laura Landro
(Touchstone/Simon &
Schuster). A memoir, at
once moving and prac-
tical, about the author's
battle against leukemia.
It is about the blessings
of a supportive family
and Landro's journalistic
determination to tackle
her illness as if it were a
difficult news story.

www.supportpath.com
This comprehensive
listing of online com-
munities, message
boards, and events
brings people with
similar health-related
interests and needs
together to find healing
and recovery through
friendship and support.

the very day Buffy and Peter moved Jesse into his dorm, but Kathy waited to tell Buffy the outcome until she was having a recuperative weekend in New York. Kathy gave Buffy a forty-eight-hour window to focus on her son and then to summon the wherewithal to focus on her. Kathy's ability to place her friend's needs first—and at such a time—overwhelmed and touched Buffy.

Kathy went in for her surgery and was back home on the mend but feeling a bit blue—depression was the anticipated by-product of the oper-ation and the fact that she had cancer. She woke up Tuesday morning, 9/11, and saw the World Trade Center collapse, then called Buffy to say, "Those people are facing a real tragedy. I will be fine."

Kathy was open about her illness and, more important, about her re-covery and health regimen, but she never hijacked the situation. It's so easy, when you are undergoing a life-threatening crisis, to put yourself at the center of the universe and demand that everyone participate in your drama. Kathy never placed her illness above her friends' problems. She was graceful during a very trying time and her grace comforted those around her. For Buffy, she became a clear, and dear, role model.

WRITE IT DOWN

Start a health maintenance notebook, and write in it the names, numbers, and addresses of your doctors, dentist, and other health care profession-als. Maintain a log of the dates of your appointments, the reason you went, and the outcome of each visit. Record vital statistics there, too, like your weight, blood pressure, pulse, and cholesterol level at the time of each visit. Keep a scrupulous listing of your prescriptions and how you react to them. Also keep a list of the medications you are allergic to or react badly to. Jot down the major events in your medical history so that if you have to provide them on a form, you'll have the information, including dates, at hand.

Prepare your questions and concerns in advance before you go to your doctor. You might think that you have them firmly in your mind, but there's something about that divine gown that opens up in the back and that wonderful paper-covered examination table that sucks all intelligent thought from your brain. Take your notebook in with you to jog your memory, and write down what your doctor says and recommends to you during your visit. While you are sitting there listening to him, you might think you'll remember everything he says, but afterward you rarely do with any accuracy or clarity. Write it down.

You can also use your notebook as a therapeutic tool. For instance, if you have the White-Coat Willies, as Kate does, you might want to explore why this is so. Writing down positive thoughts gives them power and helps us to follow through. Likewise, writing down negative thoughts, like situations or feelings having to do with fear, anxiety, and anger, can strip them of their power and even bring about a process of healing. Beyond hypodermic needles, there are plenty of reasons not to be particularly fond of going to the doctor. Write down yours. By acknowledging negative thoughts, rather than letting them skulk, ratlike in some dark corner of our minds, terrorizing us, we take an important first step in diffusing and conquering them.

Kate's Plan for Overcoming the White-Coat Willies

- I will not approach the doctor like the Scarecrow in the presence of the Great and Powerful Oz. I will not salaam on wobbly legs of straw. I will keep my dignity.
- My doctor and I are peers, participating in a professional dialogue that concerns me deeply.
- I am serving in two capacities: I am both patient and patient advocate. I will be persistent in my efforts to ensure that the doctor joins me in my cause.
- If I have been experiencing symptoms, discomfort, or pain, I will not leave the doctor's office until I have articulated it fully and honestly and have received guidance, direction, and remedies.
- I will remember to bring my insurance card.
- I will wear comfortable clothes that are easy to get in and out of.

We recommend these sites as tools and resources, not as solutions to your problems or questions. Do not attempt to diagnose yourself, and avoid spending too much time reading about diseases and disorders lest you succumb to the dreaded "medical student's disease" and imagine you are suffering from any or all of the conditions you read about.

www.healthfinder.gov
www.nih.gov
medlineplus.gov
www.webmd.com
www.healthweb.org

Laura Landro, who writes on health for the *Wall Street Journal*, notes that doctors, nurses, and health practitioners have joined the blogging revolution. Here are some Web logs she thinks may be of most interest to consumers:

www.shrinkette.blogspot.com
Addresses mental health issues.

www.codeblog.com
Nurses share personal stories.

www.bioethicsdiscussion.blogspot.com
A retired California doctor discusses ethical issues.

The Wisdom of Menopause by Christiane Northrup (Bantam). The physician-author writes, from her own experience, about going through menopause, how it feels, how it can wreak havoc on relationships, and how it brings about life changes that aren't just physical.

www.power-surge.com One of the best Web sites going (on this or any other subject matter). The folks at this site offer advice, survival tips, chat rooms, guest lecturers, and have coined (and trade-marked) what we think is one of the more outrageous modern neologisms: *hormotional.* Gotta love it.

www.menopause-online .com Here you'll find up-to-date, easy-to-use information to help you transition through the change.

- • I will not be glib, nor will I leave my sense of humor at home. I will not be afraid to make small talk with other people in the waiting room.
- • I will practice my breathing techniques.
- • If, after my visit, I feel that the doctor was less than thorough, less than caring, less than honest with me, or a flagrant shill for the pharmaceutical companies, I will immediately seek recommendations for a new doctor from friends and family.
- • I will find a doctor with whom I feel comfortable, confident, safe, and free to ask questions.

GET TOGETHER

Get together with a friend or friends and go over the health maintenance checklist. Compare notes and grades. Take turns acknowledging your current habits, identifying areas where improvement is needed, and planning how you will address those areas. In a friendly, helpful way, monitor your friends while keeping a careful eye on yourself. If you have a friend who has the White-Coat Willies or who may be ignoring an obvious health problem, offer to be her advocate or hand-holder when she finally gets it together and visits a health care professional. Too often premenopause, menopause, and postmenopause are phases we experience in isolation. There's no need! We all go through it. Share the hideous, often hilarious, ups and downs of this major life change.

PUTTING IT ALL TOGETHER

Now it's time to address your health maintenance plan. For each of the ten points on the second-half health maintenance checklist, come up with at least two habits you plan to implement in order to live a more healthy life. Remember: acknowledge, identify, and address. Be sure to let the candles guide you in the process.

1. *Create time* to take care of yourself. If you are due for a checkup, make the appointment now.
2. *Reflect* on your physical, mental, and spiritual health. If something's bothering you, do something about it.
3. *Practice patience* by being kind to yourself. Be aware of any negative behaviors you resort to when under stress and avoid them.
4. *Research* traditional and nontraditional forms of health care and body work.
5. *Find role models* who know how to take good care of themselves or who have gracefully and successfully met the challenges of an illness or injury.
6. *Write down* in a health maintenance notebook details about your health issues and health team.
7. *Get together* with a friend or friends to go over the health maintenance checklist and to offer support as you navigate some of the trickier issues that need addressing.

TO-DO LIST

Here are some suggestions to help you take charge of your health. Don't expect to roll out these new healthy habits all at once. Stagger the process and let it evolve over time. This will be your health maintenance plan, a lifelong plan for a healthier you.

- Buy a special water glass or bottle.
- Drink more water more often.
- Plan a water-drinking regimen.
- Get a water filter.
- Research bottled waters and buy them in bulk.
- Buy nicotine patches.
- See a hypnotist about quitting smoking or drinking.
- Join Alcoholics Anonymous.
- Walk around the block on your lunch hour.
- Research and buy a sunscreen with moisturizer, and wear it every day.

- Keep a pair of sunglasses in your car or bag, and wear them.
- Choose healthy snacks — a handful of unsalted almonds, apple slices, low-fat yogurt.
- Design your personal food pyramid.
- Read up on nutrition and determine whether you are getting the nutrients you need.
- Sleep eight hours a night.
- Try a lavender bath.
- Maintain good posture.
- Take a yoga class to improve your posture.
- Practice the high-heel relief stretch.
- Shop for sexy shoes with lower heels that give your arch support.
- Change your pillows.
- Improve your workstation at the office and at home.
- Start a health maintenance notebook.
- Buy an anatomy chart and study it.
- Talk to your friends about doctors they like.
- Make an appointment for a full checkup.
- Write down your fears and anxieties about medical visits.
- Take a notebook with you to your next doctor's appointment and take notes.
- Take a small tape recorder with you to your next doctor's appointment.
- Bring another pair of ears with you to your next doctor's appointment.
- If you are diagnosed with a serious illness, create a support team; find an advocate and a communicator who can keep friends and family updated if you cannot.
- Have an eye exam.
- Have an ear exam.
- Have a skin-cancer screening.
- Have a colonoscopy.
- Have a bone-density screening.
- Find a massage therapist, and schedule regular appointments.
- Try acupuncture.
- Breathe mindfully.
- Minimize stress.
- Meditate while you commute.
- Do yoga on your lunch hour.
- Research aromatherapy.
- Buy a SAD light and use it daily from late August until early March.
- Replace the lightbulbs in your house with ones that simulate natural light.
- Read funny novels.
- Rent DVDs of stand-up comedians.
- Make a list of your blessings and post it where you will see it every day.
- Rent funny movies.

KATE'S PLAN

I acknowledge that I'm inconsistent about my water intake. I admit that some days I guzzle gallons of water and others I drink like a Bedouin with a leaky canteen — mere droplets. I don't smoke, but I admit to using wine as a decelerant at the end of the stressful workday. I acknowledge that I sometimes drink as much as half a bottle of wine before bed and feel sickly and dehydrated in the morning. I get plenty of fresh air on weekends when I horseback ride, but I admit that I seldom venture outdoors during the week. I admit that I love the sun and acknowledge that I use an SPF 4 tanning oil. I admit that I try to keep my weight down by skipping meals, which can lead to bingeing at night. I do not take vitamins because I hate to swallow pills.

I have chosen to live far, far away from my workplace because I prefer a rural setting. The train ride into the city is more than two and a half hours long and, for twenty years, I have been waking up to catch the first train of the day. When I get home at 8:00 p.m., it takes me hours to unwind, so I don't get to sleep until 11:00 p.m. Net result: I average four hours of sleep a night. I am chronically exhausted and grumpy, so much so that on weekends I often disappear into my bedroom and binge on sleep.

I admit that I have slouched most of my life to conceal my large breasts. I acknowledge that I feel undressed unless I am wearing high heels. My desk chairs in my home office and workplace are uncomfortable and hurt my shoulders and neck and aggravate my chronic hip injury. I admit that I haven't been to a doctor in fifteen years. I acknowledge that I suffer from the White-Coat Willies. I am pretty good about going to the dentist, but I don't floss much.

So this is my plan:

- *Drink water.* I will sleep with a glass of water by the bed and drink a glass of water when I wake up in the morning. I will line up water bottles on my desk and make sure I have guzzled them all before I leave the office for the day. If I fail to drink enough water on a given day, I will just try again the next day.
- *Reduce my alcohol intake.* I will work to reduce my wine intake to one or two glasses a day. I will drink one glass of water for every glass of wine.
- *Get fresh air and exercise.* I will go horseback riding once a week year-round instead of hibernating during the winter months. I will get outside at least three times a week during my lunch hour, if only to take a walk around the block.

- *Beware of the sun.* I will invest in a chemical peel and start fresh. Because my skin will look so good, I will be loath to bake it afterward. At a minimum, I will wear an SPF 15 sunscreen, daily.
- *Watch my diet.* I will eat three meals and two to three small snacks a day instead of fasting. I will worship my food pyramid.
- *Get more sleep.* I will try to be in bed by 10:30 p.m. every night. I will keep to the same six- to seven-hour sleep schedule over the weekend as well. I will soak in a lavender oil bath before bedtime instead of drinking wine to make myself drowsy.
- *Stand up straight.* I will sleep with a smaller pillow under my head and place a small bolster between my legs. I will wean myself off killer high heels. Whenever I can't resist wearing them, I will do the high-heel relief stretch at least three times a day. I will research ergonomic chairs and buy one for my home office. I will convince my office manager to invest in one for my workplace.
- *See doctor and dentist.* I will make and keep regular doctor and dentist appointments. I will take all those tests that I'm supposed to take (mammogram, bone density, colonoscopy). I will brush at least twice a day and floss and use mouthwash daily.
- *Work with my therapist to stay focused and positive.* I will keep on using the bummer light, especially in the dark winter months.

BUFFY'S PLAN

I admit that I am inconsistent about fulfilling my water quota each day. I do better at work than I do at home. I usually have a small glass of wine at dinner during the week, but find this makes me extremely tired and I often fall asleep before I have fully digested my dinner and before I have accomplished what I would like to at night, whether that be reading, relaxing, or making love. Living in Southern California has helped me to exercise regularly and wear sunscreen religiously. I admit that for convenience I sometimes eat cereal at night for dinner instead of a real meal. Rather than keeping the weight off, it has had the opposite effect. Because my body isn't getting enough calories, it holds on to those it gets, storing fat around my middle.

I usually sleep enough hours, but I need to experiment with different pillows to help relieve the aches in my lower back and neck that I often wake up with. I do a fair amount of work at a computer and have noticed that my posture starts to erode when I get tired. My shoulders, particularly, start to round and hunch. I am good about seeing my doctor for my regular appointments (once a year for a checkup), but for some reason I'm not as good about making an appointment when I feel sick. I could be much better at flossing and should take more time to brush my teeth.

So this is my plan to address our commonsense health rules:

- *Drink water.* I will be more mindful of drinking water on the weekends and will use a refillable bottle or pretty glass to keep with me.
- *Reduce my wine intake.* (Though I have to note that when I was on vacation recently, drinking wine with dinner did not make me sleepy.)
- *Get more fresh air and exercise.* I will keep up with, and try to increase, my walking regimen.
- *Stay out of the sun.* I will stay current with improvements in sun protection technology.
- *Improve my diet.* I will try to eat a regular meal each night and not resort to cereal. I will also try to eat more fresh fruit.
- *Get more consistent sleep.* I will try to have a more regular sleep pattern, avoiding sleeping to excess on the weekends.
- *Stand up straight.* I will try various pillows at night to see if I can improve my sleeping posture and alleviate my lower back and neck pain. I will be mindful of my posture while sitting at the computer and will experiment with a cushion under my forearms. Whatever I'm doing, I will keep an image in my mind of my head up, my shoulders back, and my heart opening up to the sky.
- *See doctors/dentists.* I will invest in a sonic toothbrush to encourage me to take more time cleaning my teeth. I will try to wean myself off the prescription pain medicine I take to manage my tension headaches.
- *Maintain good thoughts.* I will keep a positive attitude and be aware when I or anyone else indulges in mental malpractice.

Now that we have addressed our spirits and our bodies, from both the exercise and the health maintenance points of view, it's time for a mind fix. Are you suffering from memory lapses? Do you feel that your mind is less razor sharp than it was when you were a sweet young thing? The last time your office updated its software programs, did you feel just a little bit slow on the uptake? If you answered yes to any of these questions, you're ready to move on to the next chapter.

What's Your Name Again?

Keeping your mind and memory sharp

Dear Buffy: My biggest problem is names. This is my classic nightmare situation: I'm at a party or a convention and I'm talking to three people that I've known for years. Three more people walk up who know me but don't know the three people I'm talking to. I'm the only one who can make the introductions, and I can't remember a single person's name, not even my own. I just want to run screaming from the room. Love, Kate

Dear Kate: So you throw your hands up and say, "Everybody? Meet everybody!" And you leave them to it. They won't remember each other's names anyway. But everybody has that nightmare. What gets me is that I lose the names of really common items. I'll say, "I have to put my gloves on," and then when I see the look on Kathy's face, I realize I meant to say "glasses." Love, Betty — I mean Buffy

MIND GYM

The mind, like the spirit and the body, needs attention, care, and love to keep it going and growing. The brain is nerve tissue, but it's also very much a muscle in the proverbial "use it or lose it" sense. We may mistake our oh-so-modern ability to multitask as evidence of an agile mind, but this is not, strictly speaking, correct. Multitasking often results in sloppy or addled thinking and, more often than not, slipshod work.

As you move into the second half of your life, you need to prepare and maintain your mind with focus and precision, in much the same way you are preparing and maintaining your spirit, your body, and your health. You will be calling on your mind to function at peak capacity so you can

Word Freak: Heartbreak, Triumph, Genius, and Obsession in the World of Competitive SCRABBLE Players by Stefan Fatsis (Penguin). Offers a riveting look at the colorful and eccentric world of tournament Scrabble, but also explores the nature of intelligence, memory, language, and creativity.

en.wikipedia.org
This is a free online encyclopedia to which anyone can contribute. Search for information or share your own knowledge. See the entry for *whilm* to learn a new word coined and defined by Buffy's son, Jesse. It's a doozy.

www.reference.com
Search an online dictionary, thesaurus, and encyclopedia.

www.refdesk.com
A great source for facts, news, and family-friendly resources.

www.ask.com
A good all-purpose search engine (formerly Ask Jeeves).

develop new skills, sharpen your thinking, enhance your memory, and teach yourself to perform at the highest level possible.

In this chapter, you will design a plan to keep your mind active, useful, and fascinating to both yourself and others. By building your mental muscle, by improving your mental strength and stamina, and by stretching your mental capacity, you will live a richer, fuller, and more enjoyable life. Think of exercising your mind in the same way you think about exercising your body. Three principal types of training are needed: mental aerobic training, mental flexibility training, and mental strength training.

Mental Aerobic Training

This includes any form of activity that engages and improves the mind's speed and attention span. Reading a newspaper, doing Internet searches, playing bridge or chess, watching a hockey game — all offer the mind an "aerobic" workout. It's easy to get lazy, to sit down in front of a television set or plug ourselves into an iPod and let the sensations wash over us without processing any of it. It's easy to start an article or a book and not finish it, to channel-surf rather than watch a single show in its entirety, to not bother following what's happening on a football gridiron, and to toss aside a Sudoku puzzle because it's too much trouble or just too darn hard. But every time you commit yourself to finishing one of these activities or tasks, you are increasing and strengthening your attention span. You are giving your mind an endurance test, an extended workout. Every time you finish a puzzle or connect seemingly disparate pieces of information, every time you solve a mystery, you are helping to improve your mind's agility and speed.

Mental Flexibility Training

This form of mental training includes any activity that keeps the mind flexible or fine-tunes the memory. Activities that challenge the memory — for example, doing puzzles, memorizing songs, recalling events or data we read and knew long ago — make our minds more supple. Imagine that your brain is capable of doing a yogalike spinal twist or of easily holding an inverted posture. Now, imagine how you will keep your mind flexible enough to do those things in the years ahead. As we grow older a lively, accurate memory often becomes a gauge of our mental health. Our mental acuity serves as a standard, whether fair or not, by which others may judge and treat us. It is vital to exercise your mind every day.

Mental Strength Training

This encompasses any activity that requires some special effort, either because we are learning something new, seeking an answer to a problem we are facing, or renewing an interest in something we may have set aside during our middle years. Learning a new language, learning to play a musical instrument, embarking on the novel you have always wanted to write, starting a new career or business—all of these challenge our mental strength. Over the past twenty to thirty years, we've all become experts at one thing or another. However, we seldom venture outside our realms of expertise because doing so makes us uncomfortable and puts us off our footing. That's precisely why now is a good time to cast your mind about and find something completely new to learn from the ground up. It's empowering, enriching, heightens our self-confidence, and reminds us that we're never too old to learn something new.

MEMORY TIME-OUTS

How many times have you said recently, "Oh, gee, I forgot." Usually we forget little things—the keys, a quart of milk, the letter we were supposed to mail—but sometimes we forget bigger things, like the names of our friends, pets, and coworkers or boss. Why does this happen? Is it menopause? A midlife crisis? Stress? Overwork? Sleep deprivation? Depression? A lack of fish oil in our diets? Worn-out brain cells?

There are any number of reasons why we forget things. We like to call these forgetful moments "memory time-outs." (You might have heard them referred to by the less savory term "senior moments.") Let's face it, as we get older we are increasingly prone to having moments when we forget the name of someone we've known for years or where we put the check we were just about to deposit.

Brain Food:

The Western Canon: The Books and School of the Ages by Harold Bloom (Harcourt Brace). The controversial professor explores the Western literary tradition by concentrating on the works of twenty-six authors central to the canon. Centermost, he places Shakespeare, the fastest gun in the west.

The Practical Cogitator or The Thinker's Anthology, selected and arranged by Charles P. Curtis Jr. and Ferris Greenslet (Dell). A sentimental journey through the world's great literature.

D'Aulaires' Book of Greek Myths and *D'Aulaires' Book of Norse Myths* by Ingri D'Aulaire and Edgar Parin D'Aulaire (Doubleday). Both books were written for children, but we highly recommend them to grown-ups as well, as they offer lively, concise, and highly readable stories of the Greek and Norse gods and goddesses.

History of Art by H. W. Jansen (Abrams). From the Old Stone Age to the modern age, this book presents the history of art in words and pictures.

Herodotus Histories translated by George Rawlinson (Book of the Month Club). The *Histories* have fascinated readers for centuries, offering a detailed picture of life in the ancient world during the period when the city-states of Athens and Sparta held off the westward sweep of the Persian Empire.

Walden by Henry David Thoreau (various editions). Near the end of March 1845, a young man in Concord, Massachusetts, borrowed an ax from a friend and went into the woods a mile and a half from the village to build himself a cabin on Walden Pond. Read it in high school? It's worth reading again.

We tend to remember more easily the things we *need* to know. For example, we remember, without effort or prompting, how to drive a car, how to use a telephone, how to swim. Details that are of particular interest to us seldom slip our minds for any length of time: the name of a favorite movie star or how much your daughter spent at the mall. We also tend to remember firsts: first kiss, first lipstick, first car, baby's first steps. As we get older, these memorable firsts may be harder to come by. Perhaps that is why our memory starts to click off more frequently, as if to say, "Been there, done that." It is our responsibility, our obligation, not to allow our memories to click off. It is our job to make things important enough to remember. That's worth repeating: make things important enough to remember.

Having a good memory is another way to express love to those most important to us. It goes beyond remembering birthdays, favorite colors, and blouse sizes. It is about remembering the triumphs, the sadness, the challenges of others; remembering how to make them happy; remembering what a particular look on his face means. Do some "memory toe touches" to strengthen your memory.

Memory toe touches

Here are some exercises to keep your mind limber:

- Memorize or rememorize the names of all the presidents of the United States.
- Memorize all the states and their capitals.
- Memorize a poem.
- Learn a new language. Learn American Sign Language or Braille.
- Play bridge. Play solitaire on the computer.
- Memorize the names and characteristics of all the trees and wildflowers in your area.
- Start with last year's Christmas/Hanukkah/wedding anniversary/Fourth of July celebration, then think back, year by year. Remember each holiday and special occasion as far back as your mind can reach, in as vivid detail as you can muster. Write it down.

🕯🕯🕯

Now let's turn to the seven candles and explore how, in the context of expanding your mind and organizing what needs to be done, they can help you devise a plan for your mental workout. Remember, your plan should include activities that routinely build the endurance of, stretch, and strengthen your mental muscle.

CREATE TIME

Create the time to simplify your life by getting rid of external clutter. After all, isn't external clutter simply a reflection of internal clutter? Remember senior year of high school when everyone cleaned out their lockers? Remember the halls being ankle deep in papers, notebooks, and gym socks? Remember the sense of freedom you had when you cleared out all that stuff? Of starting over fresh? Well, it's time to roll up your sleeves and clean out your locker!

It is hard to take in new ideas, plan for the future, and start to develop new interests when we are burdened with too many things. Believe it or not, the sheer abundance of things in our lives may serve as a roadblock to clear thinking. Now is the time for you to clean out your house and home. Thirty years of accumulated stuff needs to be sorted — go through everything in your drawers, cubbies, closets, spare rooms, attic, basement, and garage. Now is the time to clear the decks.

This exercise is not just about getting rid of stuff. It's also about taking an emotional inventory of your belongings and figuring out what is important to you and what you want to keep. Do you need to keep the physical manifestation of a memory, or is it OK to give away or even throw away certain things if the memory is safe in your heart? Keeping your kids' baby clothes in boxes in the attic where you never see them is not as meaningful as choosing a little piece of each garment and making a quilt, or dry-cleaning and framing a single perfect smock or onesie with a photograph of your child wearing that very item, or snipping the tiny buttons and sweet little designs from sweaters and T-shirts to create a collage or a

Committed to Memory: How We Remember and Why We Forget by Rebecca Rupp (Crown). An easy book to dip into to learn about the complexities of memory and practical tricks for improving your memory.

Blink: The Power of Thinking without Thinking by Malcolm Gladwell (Little, Brown). An illuminating, entertaining book about jumping to conclusions and training the mind to focus on relevant and important facts.

www.queendom.com/mindgames
Exercise your brain, flex your mental muscle, and stretch your mind with these boggling online brainteasers, games, and puzzles.

www.brainbashers.com
Online puzzles, crosswords, games, and brainteasers to keep your mind sharp.

www.allstarpuzzles.com
This premier puzzle site offers the world's largest collection of free online puzzles.

shadow box. Favorite items have much more resonance when they are out on display.

Few of us exercise much discrimination when it comes to belongings — we keep everything. Hoard it, pile it up, squirrel it away. We even rent spaces to keep more of it. When you reduce your inventory of possessions and make choices between essential stuff and clutter, between important papers and all other papers, you engage your mind, memory, and powers of discrimination. And you do yourself and your loved ones a huge favor. Anyone who has helped parents downsize knows that when we wait to share our treasures and declutter our lives, possessions begin to have an unnatural hold on us. But with a little planning, our possessions can be enjoyed, shared, and, over time, handed down.

Buffy's "Bin" There, Done That

Though I don't put a lot of stock in astrology, I do tend to believe that some Virgo characteristics are integral to my personality, specifically organizational skills and practicality. I have other, sexier, facets to my personality, too, but I do enjoy organizing things.

For instance, because I live in Los Angeles, in case of earthquake I keep a set of "freeway-free" directions to my daughter's school in my car. I start my Christmas shopping after Labor Day. Also, I have placed most of our family photos in scrapbooks. I have a whole closet full of them: each scrapbook is labeled, and each photograph in each scrapbook is labeled. I also regularly frame and display pictures of my family. I try to change them to reflect new milestones, such as getting a new hairstyle or sitting behind the wheel of a car for the first time. And believe it or not, people still like me. Even if I am a bit of an organization nerd.

My habits give me a sense of serenity and convey a certain level of security and predictability to my family. But mostly, these habits provide me with a deep feeling of inner calm. Finding moments of calm and wholeness in our frazzled, splintered world is important. Organizing our lives can be crucial to a successful second half. I know not everyone will find this chapter as satisfying as I do, but I promise that it will be incrementally rewarding.

REFLECT

Lighten Up! Free Yourself from Clutter by Michelle Passoff (Harper). The only book we've found that views busting clutter as a near-religious experience. Amen to that.

Now that you have started to clean out your locker and have created some free space, both psychic and actual, for yourself, you can start to reflect on the big questions that face you as you enter the second half of your life. Your answers and the plans that evolve from them will depend to a great degree on your willingness to address the questions with imagination, energy, and optimism, much as you did when faced with other major life decisions when you were graduating from high school, deciding on a career, or getting married. What do I want to be when I grow up? Where do I want to live? What are my skills and talents? Will I love this boy forever? Now the questions run along these lines:

- Where do I want to live during the second half of my life?
- How old will I be if and when I make the decision to move?
- How much longer do I want to continue working at my current job?
- What transferable skills do I have that may lead to other forms of employment?
- What do I want to do for a living?
- Will I need to study or go back to school?
- If I don't want to live where I do now, should I plan weekend getaways or vacations to places I might want to move?
- How do I go about researching what amenities, such as health care, cultural events, public transportation, and recreational facilities, are available in these communities?
- If a close friend or my parents become ill or disabled, are my dreams and plans realistic and flexible enough to allow for the care of my loved ones?

Consider these questions, then formulate some of your own. It may seem premature to ask some of them, but it isn't. The questions are timely. Answering them or just reflecting on them will provide you with a mental map that will help you navigate your way through the second half of your life. And you will achieve something else that is equally, if not more, important. By asking yourself these questions and beginning to formulate your

www.spiritualityhealth
.com

*Spirituality & Health:
The Soul/Body
Connection* is a
magazine that reports
on the people, practices,
and ideas of the current
spiritual renaissance
and provides a forum for
the active exchange of
ideas among various
faith traditions and
communities. Consider
a subscription or enjoy
the extensive site.

answers now, you are providing the most loving gift of all to your children, your nieces and nephews, your mate, friends, siblings, godchildren, pet — you are taking responsibility for your future. Talk about being a role model!

PRACTICE PATIENCE

When planning the second half of your life, you are bound to feel overwhelmed from time to time. Deciding to enroll in a class, read a plumbing manual, or change jobs may seem like daunting tasks. Have patience with yourself. Relax. There is plenty of time, and the great news is that you are starting now. You are practicing patience in your health and exercise regimens and in your daily communications with yourself. Now be patient as you set reasonable goals to realize your plan for mental fitness. Answers will come to you gradually in fits and starts and at surprising moments — maybe in a dream, during a brainstorm at work, or while you are washing the dishes — but come to you they will if you remain open and listen actively for them. Being open requires patience.

When those memory time-outs set in, no matter where or when they hit you, *relax*. Sure, it can be plenty embarrassing when they happen in a business setting or in social situations. They may even bring on a panic attack or depression. It's OK. It's not the end of the world. Take a deep breath and relax. When you relax, your mind more easily stretches and reaches for that stray bit of misplaced data. Fair or not, people often judge us by our mental quickness. Never judge yourself. It's a time sucker.

When you try to learn something new, remember that you are venturing out of your safe sphere of experience and plunging into the unknown. By doing so, you use parts of your brain that have not been accessed recently. You find resources and talents you never knew you had. You may feel like a klutz and you will probably make plenty of mistakes. Try not to call yourself names, and remember that we learn by making mistakes. Learning keeps us fresh and moving forward.

Be kind to yourself. Go with the flow of life. Embrace each new day. Don't criticize. Don't long for how it used to be. This is how it is now, and now is perfect. Be here now.

Kate on Learning in the Slow Lane

For the past twenty years, my husband and I have lived in the country — as it happens, horse country. I spent a great deal of that time gazing out the car window at horses gamboling in fields and saying, "You know? I should learn how to ride those things." I guess my husband got tired of hearing me say that. Not long after my fiftieth birthday, he stopped at a nearby teaching barn and made an appointment for me to take my first lesson. (Actually, I took two lessons when I was in junior high, but they were so long ago, I figure they don't count.)

Oh, how I secretly cursed my husband! How I did not want to go to that first lesson! I hoped and prayed something would come along that would make me cancel but, alas, no crisis arose, and on the day of the lesson I pretty much had to drag myself kicking and screaming to the barn. The teacher, a woman about fifteen years my junior, must have sensed my nervousness because she was very gentle with me. She asked me why I wanted to take lessons. I thought for a second and then I said, "I always dreamed of riding a horse. It would be nice to ride one for real." She smiled in such a way that I actually felt proud of my incredibly lame answer.

During that first lesson, she led me around on a horse like I was a six-year-old at a birthday party. It was just about my speed. She had me close my eyes and feel the motion of the horse beneath me. She had me breathe away my nervousness. I learned that she had been a kindergarten teacher. I also learned that she taught Tai Chi and something called Centered Riding. The idea of combining principles of a "soft" martial art with riding a horse intrigued me. I signed up to take a package of ten lessons and learned what equipment I would need to buy and what I could do without.

For me the hardest part of riding was the tacking up. I got it bass ackwards every time. It was as if I suffered from some radical form of spatial dyslexia. I often put the bridle on upside down, the saddle on backward, the saddle pad on inside out. Sometimes, I could swear the horse actually curled his lip at me in derision: two-legged, ten-thumbed fool! Once, I had the horse all saddled up except for the bridle. I couldn't get the bridle buckled. The horse gave up and cantered away. If a horse could

The World According to Mister Rogers by Fred Rogers (Hyperion). A sweet inspirational book by a favorite neighbor.

Endurance: Shackelton's Incredible Voyage by Alfred Lansing (Carroll & Graf Publishers). *Incredible* is the word for this true account of one man's bravery and determination to save his crew after his ship is destroyed in the Antarctic. A breathtaking account.

Centered Riding by Sally Swift (Trafalgar Square). This revolutionary philosophy of riding, derived from classical riding principles, emphasizes body awareness, relaxation, proper breathing, centering, and balance.

www.bobjeffreys.com Bob Jeffreys specializes in training rider and horse in partnership and offers classes, clinics, training, books, and DVDs.

thumb his nose, that horse would have done it. I sat down on the ground and wept, holding out a carrot, hoping he would take pity on me.

I leased a horse to see what it was like to almost own a horse. Leasing a horse was great because I could go over to the barn whenever I liked and practice by myself between lessons. I knew I didn't always look great, but I kept at it. I continued the lessons. I read books. I bought videos. I went to exhibitions and demonstrations. I began going out on the trail with more experienced riders. They gave me tips. I signed up for clinics. Weekend clinics. Trail-riding clinics. Jumping clinics. Weeklong clinics. Two-weeklong clinics.

Sometimes I wanted to quit. Often my dignity was wounded. Sometimes I would cry in frustration and say, "This is what I do to relax? I must be crazy!" Somewhere along the way, although I cannot say exactly where, I began putting it all together. I relaxed and began to enjoy myself. Gradually, little eight-year-old equestrian divas stopped making fun of me. Gradually, I learned how to do something new. Suddenly, newcomers were looking at me and seeing, if not an expert, then at least what seemed to be a bona fide old hand.

Now I own a horse and cannot imagine living a life without horses. More important, perhaps, I now know, as I look around at all the wonderful things there are to do in this world, that there is almost nothing I cannot learn to do, if only I put my mind to it, practice patience, and keep at it. Nothing.

RESEARCH

What walking does for the body, reading does for the mind. Like walking, reading combines all three kinds of mental exercise: it builds stamina, flexibility, and strength. And just like walking, reading is easy to do, inexpensive, and infinitely rewarding. Walking the mind is an activity vital to the success of the second half of your life.

You'll begin by making a list, a reading list. But before you do that, ask yourself what the first book was that someone read to you. And what the first book was that you read all by yourself. Buffy remembers her mother reading aloud to her and her sister when they were little girls. *The Country Bunny and the Little Gold Shoes* is about a single mother bunny who has twenty-one children and divides up all the household chores by two. Two bunnies paint pictures, two sweep the floors, two garden, and the last little boy bunny pulls out the mother bunny's chair at mealtime. Buffy knows the story well because she read it many times as a child and many times to her own children.

What are some of the books you remember from your childhood? What was your favorite picture book? Your favorite novel in high school? Your favorite comic book or nonfiction book? Do you still own these books? If not, you might want to order some of them and keep them as part of your library. They are as important as having photographs of good friends. They remind you where you have been and how you have grown and represent your progress forward. As you compile your reading list, the books you have read and loved in the past will help inform your decisions about the future.

If it's been a while since you've sat down to read a book, don't sweat it. There will be no tests or book reports. Reading regularly is like exercising regularly. Any time you start is the right time. You may be out of shape, but reading gets easier the more you do it. Your reading list can include anything and everything: fiction, magazines, selections from Oprah's Book Club, nonfiction, histories, cookbooks, mysteries, self-help, how-to, pot-boilers, biographies, and tell-alls. Your reading list is not about quantity or even about quality, so much as it is about your making a commitment and opening yourself up to the benefits of reading. And—hey!—you might even learn something!

Reading will help you get reacquainted with an important part of yourself. You will begin to see what interests you and what you want to know more about. If you're starting to plan a transition from a nine-to-five job to something part-time, you might want to read a book about financial planning or psychology. Perhaps you want to learn how to tie a fly or design an English garden.

What do you do if you have no time to read or if your eyes are too

Good Books: A Book Lover's Companion by Steven Gilbar (Tichnor & Fields). The author recommends and reviews thousands of good books on a vast range of subjects.

Off in Zora: A Modern-Day Tale of a Traveling Bookseller by Alan Armstrong (Booksellers House). The author periodically takes off from his day job in a beat-up van called Zora that is filled with used books and sells them in small towns throughout New England. Includes a list of books that Armstrong carries and feels are necessary to a well-stocked library. Kate had the pleasure of working with this Newbery Award-Winning author who loves nothing better than to recommend a good book.

For the Love of Books by
Ronald B. Shwartz
(Grosset/Putnam). Book
recommendations from
one hundred major
contemporary writers. A
fun book to help you
decide what you might
want to read.

*Beethoven for Book
Lovers* (Philips). The
perfect CD to
encourage reading,
balance your
concentration, and
kindle your imagination.

tired? Listen to books on tape (or CDs) while you commute by car or public transportation. What do you do if you have no budget for books or CDs? Get a library card or buy them secondhand online.

A book of commonplaces

What do you do if you can't remember the plot of the book you read just last week? Start a book of commonplaces, an old literary tradition. Once upon a time, readers kept commonplace books to record striking or inspiring passages from their reading as well as their responses to them. It's like keeping a written collage of everything you read, and it's interesting to look back at these pages and trace the path of your reading and the interplay of the authors' ideas with your own. You might start with *A Book Lover's Diary: The Reader's Companion* (Firefly), a small notebook in which to keep your lists, remind yourself of your favorite books, and keep track of books you lend. Or use a blank journal to create your own.

FIND ROLE MODELS

The poet William Butler Yeats, the composer Giuseppe Verdi, the conductor Leopold Stokowski, the artists Louise Nevelson, Georgia O'Keeffe, Henri Matisse, and Pablo Picasso were all still performing and creating well into their eighties and nineties. You might say they outran old age. Older people who demonstrate determination, creativity, and productivity are inspiring and can be useful to us as we design the patterns of our future lives. Consider your parents or grandparents as role models.

Joan is seventy-two. She worked as an attorney until she and her doctor husband decided to retire. Her husband enjoyed his leisure time, but Joan retired for just six months. Feeling dissatisfied, she enrolled in college in order to become a teacher. Sadly, Joan's husband passed away in his sleep just two weeks after she started her classes. She grieves, but she is more committed than ever to her new teaching career and thankful her courses were under way before her husband died.

To support himself and his family, Francis worked as a commercial artist for thirty years, but not once during all those years did he cease doing his own artwork. When he reached seventy, he began to do less commercial work and started devoting more time to his own artwork. Now he does large, grant-financed public works, exhibits in galleries all over the world, and even publishes articles and books about the theory and philosophy behind his work. Although the art world is generally considered the domain of the young, Francis continues to work at his art and demands attention for it. At eighty-five, he still rides his bike uptown from his loft in Greenwich Village to his studio in Midtown Manhattan.

WRITE IT DOWN (AND FILE IT!)

What concrete steps must you take to plan the second half of your life? Now is the time to collect your wishes and dreams and figure out what you need to do to get there. Navigating this new territory will require that you write things down and keep a file. Let's call it the "file of important things." If we're not careful, most of us will not get around to compiling it until we are in our seventies and eighties, by which time it will be too late for us to do an adequate job. The File of Important Things has two goals: (1) making your life easier and simpler as you move into your fifties and beyond, and (2) helping you focus on what's important to you.

Most of us already have files of some sort, but now we must start to be a little more discriminating about what we keep in them. We talked about this earlier in the chapter. For example, by now we hope you've already dumped every report card of your married-with-children daughter, the out-of-date manual for the lawn mower, and all the canceled checks from 1981. Because that's not what this file is about.

What is in the File of Important Things? Personal information that will be of infinite help to your mate, children, and most especially you. Write it down at fifty when you are clear headed and not particularly threatened by the onset of the years so you can actually do it at seventy. Finding out what's important to you is crucial if you are to have a successful and satisfying second half. Your files won't be perfect. Repeat: won't be perfect. Perfection is not our aim. Mindfulness is. Responsibility is.

www.teach12.com
The Teaching Company is a treasure trove. Invite the best professors in the world to teach you while you drive to work or sit quietly and attentively on your Adirondack chair in your backyard.

www.booksense.com
A collection of independent booksellers' Web sites.

www.literature.org
This online literature library features full and unabridged texts of classic works of English literature now in the public domain.

www.gutenberg.org
Choose from more than 180,000 free eBooks of classic literature and famous essays.

www.audible.com
Home of premium digital audio entertainment and information, such as digital audiobooks, radio shows, audio versions of popular magazines, newspapers, and more.

Buffy started her File of Important Things with this question: What will it take for me to teach school in the second half of my life? What started as a fantasy—one that she had kept alive since she and her girlfriend Susan Pickrel played pretend school as seven-year-olds—led her on a surprising journey. She started her research online. How do I go about getting a teacher's certificate? Could I go to night school? Should I start as a substitute? Can I afford it?

She ordered a couple of books to read. Then she went even further and attended a three-hour seminar held at St. Mary's College of California, which excels at turning out new teachers in an accelerated fashion. The class was filled with people of all ages and from all walks of life. Some wanted new careers; others wanted to advance in their current teaching careers. Many, like Buffy, were clearly sizing up what a career change might mean. As it happened, the commitment required for class time, homework, fieldwork, and tuition seemed too much for her just then. Does this mean that Buffy won't one day become a teacher? Not necessarily. It just means that she has taken a wish of hers, a desire, and explored it a little more deeply. Now she knows what it will take to teach in the public school system in the Los Angeles area. Next, she plans to research requirements for teaching in private institutions, college or secondary. Just recently, Buffy was asked to teach a marketing course at a nearby college. She believes that her early research helped make her more open to the opportunity when she was asked to teach.

Buffy's next file item began with the question, How do I want to be treated when I'm eighty-five? She started this file when she realized that her parents would not be forthcoming with information about their health benefits, health care wishes, or medical histories. Buffy figures that she cannot change her parents or how they have chosen to share information, but she can conduct herself in a different fashion. She can spend time now thinking about how she wants to be treated when she is eighty-five, and then she can take that thinking and turn it into an action plan. Her kids and her spouse will not have to guess what she wants if she is unable to tell them. If you confront now some of the issues that you will face in years to come, you will give yourself a gift of ease and calm. Your efforts will demystify some of the challenges that lie ahead.

Formulating Your Own Questions

In the pages that follow, we share some more specific questions you might want to consider. They are basic nuts-and-bolts questions, questions we can *all* probably benefit from answering. We will delve into many of them in upcoming chapters, but these will get you thinking about what's important to you.

When creating your own questions, consider grouping them together. Imagine you have four beautiful wicker baskets on the floor in front of you or on the dining room table. Each basket is big enough to accommodate all your papers, files, and DVDs, and each is a different color. Let's imagine fire-engine red for everyday living, cool blue for a comfortable future, pumpkin orange for health, and lovely lilac for dreams and what it will take to make them come true.

Everyday Living (Red Basket)

- *What credit cards and important papers do I have?* Make a copy of credit cards, insurance policies, PINs and passwords, financial accounts, and put a copy in a safe deposit box or send it to a sibling or close friend.
- *Do I really need all these credit cards?* Consider using only one credit card, keeping one for emergencies, and cutting up the rest. Create files that make it easy for you to access your financial paperwork, especially your bills. There are hundreds of books and sites on this topic; www.realsimple.com has some practical ideas for all budgets.
- *What are the important items in my home? Should I videotape or photograph them for insurance purposes?* Yes. This will simplify your life and give you an opportunity to take a real inventory of your possessions. Consider videotaping and photographing your possessions.
- *What are my home, car, and health insurance needs now, and in five-year increments, and what is the cost of it?* Call your insurance person and start the dialogue now. She should be willing to do some cost

analysis for you. Visit www.ace.uiuc.edu/cfe/insurance for a simple reference guide to insurance terms.

- *How do I go about tracking down my Social Security statements?* You should receive a Personal Earnings and Benefits Estimate Statement every year. If not, contact the U.S. Social Security Administration and ask for it, or do so online at www.ssa.gov. This report provides projected Social Security earnings based on your income.

- *What's my FICO (credit rating) score?* Go to www.myfico.com and for a fee you can access your credit history and rating from three different sources. You can get a free report by going to www.annualcredit report.com.

- *What is the status of my 401k and other retirement vehicles? How can I make sure they are being managed effectively?* Contact your company's human resources department, or call the phone number provided on your quarterly statements.

- *What is the amount of my pension, its rate of distribution, and the date it becomes available?* Your human resources representative should be able to tell you these details.

Comfortable Future (Blue Basket)

- *What about a living trust? How does it work? Is a living will better?* There are many sites and many books on these topics. Doing research is a good way to start. A lot of FAQs are answered, and there is state-specific information.

- *Consider writing down your beliefs, important life events, what you are grateful for, and your hopes for the future.* These may become treasured reflections for you and your family. Read *Women's Lives, Women's Legacies: Passing Your Beliefs and Blessings to Future Generations* by Rachael Freed (Fairview Press). You might also want to consider writing an ethical will, a document in which you share your values. *Ethical Wills: Putting Your Values on Paper* by Barry K. Baines (Perseus) helps you "clarify and communicate" the meaning in your life to your loved ones. Or visit www.ethicalwill.com

- *How do I go about making my husband/partner/sibling/friend my health care proxy? How do I find the right time to tell him or her how I want to be treated if I am unable to make my own health care decisions?* You might want to consider broaching the topic with your spouse, partner, or good friend as a way of starting to sort out your feelings about death. Consider researching both the practical side and the spiritual side of this issue. *How We Die* by Sherwin B. Nuland (Vintage) talks about both the biological and the emotional details of dying. *Final Gifts: Understanding the Special Awareness, Needs, and Communications of the Dying* by Maggie Callanan and Patricia Kelley, two hospice nurses (Bantam), shares insights into a complex and often scary time.

- *Who do I see about home equity loans?* Although you may not need this, you will be better off walking yourself through the process now than when you are in your seventies. Start by researching what a home equity loan is and how to get one approved. At www.ehow.com, search using the keywords *home equity loan* for answers to some very basic questions.

Health (Orange Basket)

- *What's the lowdown on long-term health care insurance? Should I buy it now or wait until I am older?* Talk to your insurance representative and start to clip and read articles as you see them. Ask your friends what they are planning. This is a serious issue, so spend some time thinking about it. Do your best to get a second opinion, an objective opinion and information that aren't provided by someone selling you a policy. A good place to start is www.consumerreports.org.
- *When will I qualify for Medicare? What forms do I need? How do I fill them out?* You must be sixty-five or older and you or your spouse must have worked for at least ten years in a job that had Medicare coverage to qualify. The Social Security Administration provides many forms online at www.ssa.gov. You will need your birth certificate, a driver's license, your social security card, and proof of other insurance if you have it.
- *What is Medicaid?* Medicaid is a state-run program that provides

www.lifetips.com
Features a large
network of sites that
offer more than 68,000
tips on a wide variety
of topics ranging
from business and
entertainment to
personal growth and
health to home repair.

www.infospace.com
Find people and places
using this online
directory of white and
yellow pages, map
directions, phone and
e-mail search, and more.

www.findlaw.com
Find a lawyer, find
answers to your legal
questions, and
download forms and
contracts.

www.lawyers.com
Find qualified legal
counsel; research legal
topics for personal and
business needs.

medical insurance for low-income people. You can contact your state's department of social services for more information.

- *Will my current doctor continue to see me if I am on Medicare?* Buffy's won't, and when she used to see the sign years ago, it was completely unimportant to her. Well, it's important now. Start researching a senior-friendly doctor.
- *How do I go about creating a medical family tree?* A medical family tree traces the generational history of a family's health. In order to make your tree as complete as possible, record births and deaths, and for each family member research answers to questions such as: Did she smoke? What were her dietary habits? What diseases did she have? Did she have any surgery? If yes, for what? What environmental factors were at play? What kind of job did she do? Did she have any allergies, depression, postpartum blues, miscarriages? This is not as morbid a task as it seems. It's a way of developing communication with your family and informing you and younger ones of medical risks. Go to www.geneweaveronline.com to learn how to create a medical family tree.

Dreams (Lilac Basket)

This particular basket will get lots of attention in the upcoming chapters. For the time being, toss in any and all ideas that come to you about the second half of your life; any career idea, no matter how fleeting; any articles, magazine clippings, photographs of places you might want to live; any article about an organization whose philanthropic works you admire. In fact, toss into this lovely lilac basket anything whatsoever that might pertain to your future dreams—your Dream Cake!

GET TOGETHER

Join or form a reading group. Challenge your comprehension and your comfort levels. Help to choose the topics and then participate in the discussions. If the Sunday crossword puzzle is too much for you to do on your own, find someone to do it with. Two heads are frequently better than one. When you are considering taking up a new interest, see if you can find a friend to join you in the adventure. Help a friend clean out her "locker," one section at a time. Then have her help you. Have a joint garage sale or, better yet, donate it all to a local charity store. Develop a list of questions for your red, blue, orange, and lilac baskets. Many of your close friends are probably starting to ask themselves these questions, too. Why not figure it out together?

www.readinggroupguides
.com
An online community
and resource guide for
reading groups.

www.readerscircle.org
Search the online book
club and reading group
directory to find a local
group near you.

PUTTING IT ALL TOGETHER

Now it's time to design a plan that will keep your mind active, useful, and fascinating. We've covered a great deal in this chapter, so be sure to light those candles.

1. *Create time* to begin to simplify your life, clean out your locker, and focus on what is important to you, emotionally and materially.
2. *Reflect* and develop questions about how you might live the second half of your life.
3 *Practice patience* and set reasonable goals for strengthening and stretching your mind and increasing your mental stamina.
4. *Research* by reading. Find out what interests you and how to transform interests into actions.
5 *Find role models,* people who live a vigorous life of the mind. Look for people who have already answered many of the questions you may be just starting to ask about your own life.
6. *Write it down* as you start compiling your File of Important Things.
7. *Get together* with a friend to enjoy books, pursue new interests, and work on your File of Important Things.

TO-DO LIST

Here are some ways to strengthen your mind and your memory, begin your file of important things, and launch your reading program.

- Make a list of favorite childhood books, track them down, and purchase them for your library.
- Start a reading list; get ideas from the book review section of the Sunday paper.
- Visit a secondhand bookstore.
- Visit amazon.com, barnesandnoble.com, or bookwire.com.
- Start or join a reading group; remember, it takes only two to make a group.
- Read aloud to your mate, parent, child, or friend.
- Listen to audiobooks while driving or relaxing.
- Clip and file articles that interest you even if you don't have time to read them right now.
- Do crossword puzzles or brainteasers; build models.
- Make an emergency first aid kit for your home and your car(s).
- Join a theater group and land a part; memorize your lines.
- Enroll in a continuing education program.
- Unclutter a kitchen drawer; clean out your makeup bag; empty out your purse.
- Assemble jigsaw puzzles.
- Write letters regularly to friends and family.
- Become a blogger; start a Web site.
- Decide if you want to be an organ donor, and if so note it on your driver's license; also communicate your wishes to your family. Your family may overrule donation if they don't know of your wishes.
- Memorize a poem a month.
- Pick a meeting place for your family in case of an emergency.
- Commit to memory the names and appearance of trees, leaves, wildflowers, and identify them as you walk.
- Roll out a plan for reducing your inventory of possessions; for example, plan to clean out one closet or one drawer each week.
- Frame pictures of your loved ones to display or to give as gifts.
- Create a memory box out of old clothes or toys.
- Start your File of Important Things.
- Spend a day using your nondominant hand to perform everyday tasks like eating and brushing your teeth.
- Visit Web sites to download newspapers, magazines, and radio programs that interest you.

KATE'S PLAN

I've noticed, with mounting panic, that my memory is getting a little fuzzy. I already read a lot, both professionally and for pleasure, but all of it falls within my comfort range. I keep no files whatsoever, let alone a File of Important Things, so I have lots of work to do there. My life is full of clutter, both actual and mental. My plan looks like this:

- Complete the *New York Times* crossword puzzle at least twice a week.
- Read one book a month on a topic out of my range, such as Plato's *Republic.*
- Start my File of Important Things with gusto.
- Go through every room in the house and do a knickknack sweep. Create some breathing space.

BUFFY'S PLAN

I've noticed that I often can't remember the name of someone I know or even the name of some common everyday item. Sometimes I can't remember *fork,* or I improvise and say "kitchen linen" when I want my husband to hand me a dish towel. It usually passes quickly, but it is alternately concerning and infuriating. Being true to my Virgo traits, I have a pretty good head start on my files but still feel there are gaps to close. I am currently working in a feast-or-famine line of work and may have to find another job to augment my income. Job hunting at my age is a big challenge for me. So this is my plan:

- Get out of my comfort zone, familiarize myself with the continent of Africa, and start to memorize the names and locations of the countries.
- Read poetry, a literary form I have not explored outside of school.
- Videotape (or more probably use my daughter Daisy's digital camera to record) important and meaningful things in my home for insurance purposes and for my memories.

- My husband and I already have a will, but I would also like to write an ethical will.

$\overset{\curlyvee}{\mathbf{Y}}$

The chapters in this section focused on your inner spirit, your body, your health, and your mind—in other words, on you. Now it's time to expand your focus upward and outward to include your mate (or date), your children, your parents, and your friends.

My Family and Friends

In a van down by the river — not!

Face it, you are not a hermit living in a van down by the river. You are a social being. You probably live in a family unit of some description. You may have married and had children. And even if you haven't gotten quite that carried away, your parents have probably started calling on you more frequently for help, support, and possibly even your hard-earned money. And then there is the sibling-sibling relationship. With them you will need to find a way to assist your aging parents while keeping your relationship vibrant, honest, and loving. And let's not forget friends! In the second half of your life, friends will play a more crucial role than they did in high school or college. In these next four chapters, you will explore how coming of age all over again affects the important people in your life.

Who Is This Person Sleeping Next to Me?

Assessing and strengthening your primary bond

Dear Buffy: Harry and I are going away together without the kids this weekend. I should be happy about it, but mostly I am dreading it. This marriage needs serious work. In fact, recommitting to this marriage is the most difficult work I've ever faced. Sometimes I just want to turn away from it, hop on the Love Boat, and start out fresh. Love, Kate

Dear Kate: *The Love Boat*'s been canceled for about twenty seasons. Just work on it every day. Day after day. Love, Buffy

Dear Buffy: Hah! That's easy for you to say. You have the world's most perfect marriage. No offense. Love, Kate

Dear Kate: None taken and besides, it's not perfect, just awfully good. I'm lucky. And Peter and I work on it every day. I think it's those Mama Annie genes. I never knew my grandfather. Mama Annie lived most of her life without a partner, but she was so positive about love and life. She said she felt like Sparkle Bright, a doll she had as a child. Every day, I strive for Sparkle Bright. Love, Sparkle Buffy

TABLE FOR ONE OR TWO?

Imagine for a moment that you are in a restaurant and blessed with an all-knowing, all-seeing eye — in other words, you're a complete voyeur.

- *Sparkle Bright.* Here's a woman sitting alone. She's asked the waiter to remove the plate across from her so she can spread out: newspapers, a book, a folder of work, a notebook. She sits there, so at ease and serene in her solitude, so self-contained, that you feel something very nearly like envy. When the waiter comes, she takes her time perusing the menu, asking him what he recommends, bantering with him a little. When the food arrives, she greets it with enthusiasm and eats with such slow deliberation and obvious enjoyment that someone from another table decides he wants what she's having and leans over to asks her what it is. She strikes up a brief, friendly conversation with her fellow diner, then returns to her meal. Later, she opens the notebook, and while she lingers over coffee and dessert she writes. Whatever it is she is writing, she is fully engaged. With a bow to the late great Mama Annie, let's call her Sparkle Bright.

- *Eeyore.* Over in the corner, near the kitchen door, sits another woman, also alone. She orders as soon as she is seated and sits staring into space while she waits for the waiter to bring her meal. As soon as he does, she bolts her food while staring at her plate and calls for the check before she has even finished. Clearly, she can't get out of there fast enough, so mortified is she by the spectacle of herself, out in public, amid all these happy families, alone with no one to talk to or keep her company. Did the meal satisfy her? Perhaps it filled her stomach, but essentially she is still a little empty, longing for that indescribable something or someone to come along and bless her with completeness. She is convinced that whatever or whoever in the world can make her happy is *out there* waiting for her, if only she could find it (or him); if only it (or he) could find her. Mr. Milne probably wouldn't mind too much if we call her Eeyore.

- *The Golden Duo.* They sit, hand in hand, a beautiful white-haired couple in their seventies or eighties or older. Just one look at them and you know they've spent a lifetime in each other's company. Why, they've grown so close over the years they've actually started to look alike! But time hasn't doused the fire. The spark is still there. He is as attentive to her as a man on his first date, and she is clearly more deeply in love with him than ever. They are a couple, yet somehow they are something greater: they are a living work of art, the result of years of love, continuous effort, and mutual care. They are linked, as if by an invisible golden cord. It is apparent in the things they say to each other and in the things that are not said, that don't need to be said because their communication is almost telepathic, so attuned are they to each other's moods and thoughts. It is a sight beautiful, uplifting, and inspiring to behold, like watching a pair of exquisitely skilled dancers move across a polished ballroom floor to the glorious strains of a full orchestra. We'll call them the Golden Duo.

- *The Cranky Crones.* A few tables over, there sits a second couple, looking very much like the first, snowy-haired and handsome, but as you pay closer attention, it becomes apparent that they are not at all like the Golden Duo. You see it first in their eyes. There's a certain coldness there, a dissatisfaction with present company and with the world around them. Or else there's a dejected look of quiet desperation that says, "This is it." They might be ignoring each other or bickering, taking potshots at each other or carrying on some half-hearted argument that they've been waging almost since their courtship, as if the main business of each day were to tear each other down, as if the marriage license were, in fact, a license to nitpick. They are like a couple of inmates, condemned to serve a life sentence in the same cell. You shudder and turn away and you say to yourself, "Jeez, what's kept them together all these years?" Let's call them the Cranky Crones.

Start by choosing the scenario that you think might describe you in the coming years. Will you be Sparkle Bright, Eeyore, the Golden Duo, or the Cranky Crones? Actually, that was a trick question. We'll devote space to each of these profiles in the coming pages. In this chapter, you will learn how to assess and strengthen your primary bond, whether that bond be with yourself or a partner. Fanning or perhaps reigniting the flame with yourself or your mate is important if you want a stimulating, satisfying future life.

We acknowledge that, whether by chance or by circumstance, we are not all linked with a mate. The sections in this chapter are therefore directed to single people ("if you are one") and to those who are part of a couple ("if you are two").

REMEMBER THE SELF?

Let's talk a little bit about the power of self. Everything in your life begins and ends with you and you alone. You will recall that in chapter 1, we discussed the importance of cultivating a self-concept—a clear and thorough understanding of yourself, what brings you satisfaction and what brings you unhappiness. Your self-concept is your personal operating manual. Equipped with a clear self-concept, you will be more likely to make informed and mature decisions about relationships.

Let's review the happy outcomes of having a clear self-concept, keeping in mind that these apply whether you are living as one or two. They are:

- *Self-appreciation:* being in touch with what makes you lovable to others, without becoming a raving egomaniac or a seedy solipsist.
- *Self-acceptance:* loving and accepting yourself without reservation.
- *Self-enjoyment:* being able to spend a day with yourself with nothing else on the agenda but doing your nails, reading a book, or watching C-SPAN, and finding your own company an absolute joy.
- *Self-confidence:* having faith in your own strength and wisdom.
- *Self-sufficiency:* being able to support yourself without leaning on someone else.
- *Self-comfort:* if you are not self-conscious around your mate or date, you'll be engaged in the relationship, rather than standing outside it.

Quickly go through this list of *self* words and rate yourself from 1 to 10, with 1 meaning *needs improvement* and 10 meaning *darned near perfect,* to see how you do. Do you rate yourself consistently low or high or do you go up and down, depending upon the category? Can you draw a connection between a low rating and any chronic problems you are having in your relationships? Do you recognize any patterns of behavior?

Now let's illumine the seven candles, our trusty strategies, to see what focus we can bring to bear on your primary bond. Being single and being part of a couple actually have a great deal in common, because they both start with you. You can skip over the sections that don't pertain to you, but you might want to take it all in. Who knows what might spark your interest.

CREATE TIME

If You Are One

Create time to get out of the house, whether to meet new people, find a mate, or simply be out and about. Some of us are alone and lonely because we are divorced or separated or because our partners have passed away. Others of us have chosen to be alone because we enjoy our own company and our own rhythms. It may be that the compromises required when living with another person exact a price higher than we are willing to pay. No matter the circumstances, it's important to get out and interact with something other than your own reflection.

Online dating and franchised singles groups are now fixtures of modern life. If you are comfortable searching for a mate that way, good luck and good hunting. Our friend Shawna met Ned at a dinner party. The hostess—a dating service guru—had arranged the dinner for eight, figuring she knew each of the people well enough for couples to form naturally. And she was right. That night Shawna and Ned fell into a lively conversation that is still going on. But for some of us, such agencies are stress- and cynicism-inducing enterprises that too often force us into all-out obsessive searches for Mr. or Ms. Right. Precisely because we are trying so hard, we are prone to failure and disappointment. How much more enjoyable to

If the Buddha Dated by
Charlotte Kasl, PhD
(Penguin). Wise, funny,
fun, and sensible. What
would it be like if you set
out to find true love
armed with the wisdom
of the ancient Buddha?

*Falling in Love for All the
Right Reasons: How to
Find Your Soul Mate* by
Neil Clark Warren with
Ken Abraham (Time
Warner). Written by the
founder of the howlingly
successful online dating
site eHarmony, the book
discusses the twenty-
nine dimensions that
determine compatibility
and long-term success in
marriage.

meet a mate when we are concentrating on doing something else, pursuing an interest, or learning about something engaging and new.

Anna Marie wants to meet someone. She jokingly calls him her Intellectual Cowboy. So she got the idea to take up horseback riding again. She
was raised in Texas and spent a lot of time around horses, so by simply renewing an interest she will be looking for a man in the right place.

Don't worry. You don't have to get on a horse to find a mate or companion. You just have to remain open-minded and consider actively pursuing an outside interest. Don't wait for life to come knocking at your door.
Spend time exploring interests you might pursue. It might be a cooking
class, a chamber music concert series, or a spinning class. It all depends
on who it is you see yourself with, who your version of Anna Marie's Intellectual Cowboy might be, and where you'll most likely meet.

If You Are Two

As the ratio of leisure time to work time begins to shift in the second half of
your life, it will be increasingly important for you and your mate to recommit to your relationship, and recommitment requires time. During this
transition, some long-married couples experience anger, unhappiness,
dissatisfaction, a sense of having drifted apart. All of these feelings are
nothing more than bad habits, and bad habits can be transformed into
positive actions. Creating time to renew and reenergize your marriage or
partnership is crucial to a successful second half of your life.

One way of recommitting is to build a rich store of interests to pursue
when time becomes increasingly available to you and your partner. Don't
wait until you are swimming in an ocean of time before you learn how to do
new strokes. Come up with interests that are yours alone, have your mate
come up with some, then come up with some that you both can share.

It's important to cultivate separate interests, for they take you away
from each other and immerse you in worlds and interactions with people
outside the relationship. When you return to your home base, you return
reinvigorated, full of stories and information and ideas to share. But cultivating a common interest permits you to grow together, to work together,

and sometimes take risks together. What are your mate's current interests? What are yours? Is there any potential for sharing?

Some people find it uncomfortable to share hobbies. If you belong to such a couple, then consider simply spending more time together, time you have specifically scheduled for each other. Go to the movies every third Friday, cook a meal together, rent a movie and take in dinner, go to church together, read aloud to each other, go for a walk, do joint meditations. Just make a point of creating time to do something together.

Go for a sleigh ride

Just like when you first met, preparation for an evening together can be half the fun. Take your time getting ready. Put on the music you might have listened to when you were dating. Take a long, leisurely bath or shower. Dress in something that makes you feel and look great.

When you meet your date at the front door (you'll both be on the same side of it, but hey), say what a knockout your mate is. Date manners will extend to the entire evening. Be gracious and polite, maybe even a little nervous. Make an effort to keep the conversation going. If necessary, think of topics in advance, something you saw on the news, a book you've read, something you've been thinking about a lot lately, yourselves. Try not to lapse into humdrum discussions about the kids unless it is to celebrate them.

Being a good conversationalist is an art. A good conversation is like a sleigh ride: there are easy parts, thrilling dips, surprising twists and turns, and gentle companionable coasting. Keep it fresh. Think of your special date as a communication date. If lovemaking happens afterward, great, but that is not the goal of this exercise.

Forty million people are currently reaching out to meet other people via the Internet. Following are some of the sites they frequent. While we're not endorsing any one of these, we urge you to check them out to see if one or more of them suits you.

www.perfectmatch.com Features a "duet compatibility" system to help people find each other and fall in love.

www.eharmony.com The eHarmony "personality profile" system successfully matches couples.

www.match.com The world's largest online dating, relationships, singles, and personals service.

www.matchmaker.com Has been helping to introduce people to each other and build real relationships for eighteen years.

Kate's New Riding Buddy

My husband, Harry, took up riding rather suddenly, five years after I did. I recently bought a horse, a fourteen-year-old Appaloosa called Mississippi Mud Pie, and owning a horse really deepened my interest. Harry says he took up riding mostly because it was the only way he could see me, because I was spending so much of my time at the barn.

The barn across the road where I board and ride is not a jodhpurs, high boots, and flower boxes kind of place. It's country, as Loretta Lynn puts it. You may not be able to eat off the floor, and the refrigerator in the tack room has alien life forms growing in it, but the people who run it know horses and love horses and love teaching people what they know. When Harry started taking lessons, he didn't really talk about it or involve me very much. He just did it. Occasionally, some of my friends from the barn would say, "Hey, I saw Harry in the arena taking a lesson the other day! He looked great!" And I would feel a small surge of pride. It's not always easy to start riding, and I know my first year of lessons was sometimes pretty grim going. But Harry seemed kind of mellow about it. When his teacher, Bob, saw me, he'd say, "Harry's got himself a pretty good seat. He's doing all right."

About six months later, we learned that one of the horses at the barn was on sale, for a dollar, to a good home. Max was a twenty-four-year-old Paint that had been ridden too hard and put away wet. Now he needed a little loving care in his sunset years. Bob asked Harry if he was interested. Harry thought about it for a day before he took that dollar out of his wallet. Harry and I now try to trail ride together every weekend. We enjoy the weather and the scenery and we get to talk.

Riding has shown me another side of Harry. When I see him brushing that old horse or taking him out to graze or for a roll in the dust, when he calls Max "Sweetheart" or "Good Old Boy," I get kind of misty. I have been married for almost thirty years, but I have never before seen this tender side of Harry. Now we share a dream — for later on in our second half — of living where we can keep horses on our property. We also want to trailer our horses to all the national parks and tour them from their backs. Has a shared interest brought us closer together? You bet it has.

REFLECT

If You Are One

It may very well be that you are comfortable with yourself and self-sufficient enough to have chosen not to live with a mate. It may be that you know yourself well enough to understand that for you the compromises required to live as a couple are simply not worth the pleasures of constant human company. If this is the case, then more power to you. The virtues of solitude are multitudinous and largely unsung. But if being alone is starting to get to you, or if being alone is a stand you have taken as a defense against potential relationship failure, or if you are alone because of divorce or death, now is the perfect time to find a mate. Begin with this refresher:

- Imagine you are meeting someone for the first time. What would you say?
- Imagine meeting up with a flame from the past. Are your feelings still burning brightly? If not, where did the flame go?
- Imagine you are traveling by ship. Consider what you would do if you stayed on board and what you would do if you debarked at this or that port.
- Imagine what sounds you like to hear. Which sounds excite you? Which comfort you? Which colors? Which smells?

When we're younger, we often link up with a mate, whether consciously or unconsciously, in order to have children. As we get older, that drive tends to recede into the background. Dating, when you're older, wiser, more centered, more settled in your career and don't have that biological imperative of children prodding you forward, can be a civilized and intriguing enterprise. Just think about how much you have to give.

If You Are Two

We've discussed the importance of breathing in our lives. Breathing deeply and mindfully is important during exercise and for taming and reshaping

Outermost House by Henry Beston (Owl Books). In prose that soars, the author chronicles the year he spent alone in a little house on Cape Cod with nothing between him and the ocean but the dunes. This wonderful little book speaks volumes about the beauty and peace of solitude.

Living Alone and Loving It: A Guide to Relishing the Solo Life by Barbara Feldon (Fireside). Feldon, the actress best known for playing Agent 99 on TV's *Get Smart,* got married, got divorced, got over it, got set to find another mate, then discovered that she actually preferred to live alone.

My Boyfriend's Back by Donna Hanover (Hudson Street Press/ Penguin). After her acrimonious and very public divorce from former New York mayor Rudolph Giuliani, Hanover met up with the high school boyfriend who had dumped her during her first year of college. He apologized, they rekindled, they married, and Hanover set out to find other women with the same experience. A charming collection of true-life stories about true love rediscovered.

our emotions. Breathing can play a vital role in our relationships, too. Kate's very wise riding instructor says that she can always tell when Kate is holding her breath while she's riding around the arena. If Kate's not breathing while she watches, she finds that she suspends her own breathing. That's what is known as a *sympathetic response*.

Do you ever sense that your partner is tense and breathless? Next time it happens, try this. Take a big, deep, audible breath within his or her hearing range. Seconds later, see if your mate responds with his or her own deep breath. If it doesn't happen right away, keep at it. Eventually, it will. You can actually influence others to breathe more deeply by breathing deeply yourself. Breath is an influencer, and playing with breath is fascinating and powerful stuff.

Here are two exercises for you to try. The first will help you cultivate sympathetic breathing with your mate. The second takes dual breathing even deeper into meditation. Both will help to shine new light on the power of projected moods and feelings and the potential for nonverbal communication.

Breathing Duet

Sit facing each other in a comfortable, cross-legged position. Start breathing deeply and naturally. Attune yourself to the other's breathing. Breathe in sync. Do it until it feels natural, relaxed, and normal to breathe as one. The next time you sense that your mate is tense or out of sorts, ask him or her to sit down and breathe with you. See if you can influence your partner's breathing with your own deep breathing.

Meditation Tango

Try doing simultaneous meditations on the subject of the two of you. Lie down side by side or sit cross-legged facing each other. Close your eyes and begin the relaxation process together. Consider using one of the suggestions that follows to trigger your emotions and seed your images. See what bubbles up. Afterward, maybe over a pot of tea or glass of wine, write down or share any thoughts, pictures, epiphanies, or solutions you saw or felt during the meditation.

- Imagine yourselves on a desert island together.
- Imagine you are both a certain kind of animal, the same animal or different animals.
- Imagine that today you are meeting for the first time.
- Hold a color in your mind and see what color surrounds your partner.
- Imagine a conversation with your mate about a subject that has been difficult to broach.

PRACTICE PATIENCE

If You Are One

Living with another person is about compromise. When you live alone, there isn't much call to make concessions. As a consequence, when you *do* need to compromise, it may not come easily. Your skin may be a little thin and your patience with and tolerance of others a little less as the years pass. Consider instituting some anti-Eeyore measures, ways to keep yourself flexible and sociable. Consider a roommate or an extended visit from a niece, nephew, or a friend's YP (young person) who could use some help and companionship. Consider getting a pet. Caring for a member of another species will help you perfect your patience.

Are you setting your standards regarding prospective mates too high? You say you've made your peace with the fact that no one is perfect, but have you really? Do you hold your dates to unreasonably high standards? Love comes in when you let go of your expectations, let down your guard, and declare a moratorium on being judgmental. If you stop being judgmental, chances are your dates will sense that it's OK to relax and be open. Only then can honest communication begin. Make sure that any expectations you have are reasonable and not tainted by unfair comparisons to some romantic ideal.

Feline Therapy

Natalie, a close colleague of Kate's, suffers fools not at all and made the choice, in her late thirties, to live as a single person. One night, she invited guests for dinner in her lovely and carefully decorated apartment, where there was a place for everything and everything was in its place. She cooked osso bucco and served a fine Tuscan wine. It was a delightful evening, but a long one, and toward the end her guests pitched in and helped her do the dishes and clean up. She fell into bed, pleasantly tipsy and exhausted as only a hostess can be.

When she woke up the next morning, she went to the kitchen to fix herself some eggs. She couldn't find the salt and pepper shakers or her favorite cast-iron skillet. They were not in their assigned places! Could one of her guests have filched them? Impossible! She banged the cupboard doors open and shut, searching for these items, seething. Eventually, she found the shakers and the skillet, stowed away where one of her well-meaning guests surmised they belonged.

That very week Natalie went out and bought herself a cat. Why? Because living alone was clearly turning her into a creature of unreasonable inflexibility, used to always getting her own way, resistant to change, and fearful of losing control. She got a cat because even though a cat can't talk or move a cast-iron skillet, a cat can hawk up hairballs, sometimes misses the litter box, and likes to sleep with you, even when you want to be left alone. A cat reinforces ongoing compromise.

If You Are Two

Living with another person is about compromise, and this can sorely tax our patience. We try not to take it out on our coworkers. We try not to take it out on our kids or our pets or our friends or the guy who bags our groceries. Why, then, do we feel that it is all right to take it out on our mates? It may not be apparent in the things we say to them; it's all in the way we say it. Try to listen for your impatience. You're tired and aggravated, and your mate asks if you've deposited such and such a check in the bank yet.

Instead of saying, "No, sorry, I haven't gotten around to it yet," you grit your teeth and snap, "If you're so bent on getting the money into the bank, why don't you do it yourself?"

It's natural to feel impatient with the behavior of others, particularly those closest to us. A good percentage of daily behavior falls into the category of habits and quirks. When someone's habits and quirks get under our skin, the result can be a slow-burning anger that builds to the point of venting. Some people think venting — complaining, yelling, throwing temper tantrums — is good because at least it gets the anger out of your systems and avoids toxic buildup.

But by accepting bad behavior as OK, we give people permission to act out. This is the rocky road to becoming a Cranky Crone. Other people take the martyr's route and prefer to swallow anger. That can make us lifeless and weigh us down with hidden grudges. It can also make us downright ill. Still others aren't very good at swallowing anger and so just a little bit comes out before we bite it off. But, in any case, who are we kidding? We're angry!

Think back to chapter 1 and your personal prescription for practicing patience. Now consider amending that list. Write down the things that make you habitually angry or short-tempered with your partner. The more specific you are, the easier it will be to resist making a big deal of them, manage them, and get past them. Here are a few examples to get you started:

- My mate is overly critical.
- My mate gets angry over small things, like not reloading the toilet paper dispenser.
- My mate is always fifteen minutes late.
- My mate always has to be asked to help around the house.

Think about how much of your anger, on an ongoing basis, derives from frustration and disappointment in your mate's behaviors because they are not what you want them to be. Remember: the only behavior you can control is your own.

If the Buddha Married
by Charlotte Kasl, PhD
(Penguin). The last thing
Kate wanted to do was
turn her wounded
marriage over to a
counselor. (They already
had enough therapists in
their lives, thank you
very much.) At the
suggestion of a friend,
she bought this book
and found it to be a
wise, witty, practical
guide to living life as a
married person.

*The Bitch in the House:
26 Women Tell the Truth
about Sex, Solitude,
Work, Motherhood, and
Marriage* edited by
Cathi Hanauer (Harper).
Not a how-to so much as
a bracing, ballsy, funny
read, mostly about
balancing life and work.

www.tickle.com
Your online destination
for self-discovery,
providing guidance with
your relationship,
lifestyle, mind and body,
and matchmaking needs.

Learn to articulate to your mate—without anger, snideness, or whining—how his behavior is making you feel. Try to be as concrete and specific as possible. For instance, if your partner is perpetually late, don't snap at him and say, "Can't you ever get anywhere on time?" That just sets him on edge and fosters defensive behavior that may lead to a fight. Instead, in a neutral and straightforward manner, try saying, "When you're late, I get so nervous that I have trouble settling down and having a good time when you do arrive." This is a simple example, but the same technique can be used in a more serious situation. For a marriage to be good, you must be able to talk about anything and everything.

If you and your mate are already a couple of Cranky Crones, it's possible that you are not meant to carry on together. You may be destined to part. If that is the case, be aware of your feelings and thoughts. It is equally possible that together you can resolve your problems and go on to share a better future. Either way, now is the time to act.

A hundred years ago, when our great-grandparents came to an unhappy pass in their marriages, they simply sucked it up and made the best of it. Today, divorce is an option that is, in many ways, all too available and convenient. Rather than doing the hard work necessary to resolve our differences, we simply opt out. While many of us go on to embark on happier marriages, just as many of us simply repeat the same mistakes the next go-round.

Imagine for a moment that you are on a desert island with your mate. You are all the other has. Then you really have to make it work, don't you? Before you bail out for another island, make sure that you make a genuine effort to fix what's not working.

One of the reasons relationships are hard to keep on track is that they require daily work. You and your mate are like athletes in a never-ending Olympiad. You must practice, strive, break your own records. You must do everything a gold medalist does. In short, nothing is more important than you and your partner. Don't let each other get away with carping, snapping, falling silent, or sulking. You must be your own shining role models, behaving always in a straightforward, respectful manner. Be considerate and kind. Remember that the work you do now is a precious investment in your future as the Golden Duo.

How do you know you need marriage counseling?

- You have lost the habit of talking to each other and speak only to criticize.
- You are no longer friends. You spend very little time together.
- Your main form of communication is arguing, even in front of the children and in front of friends and out in public.
- You can't remember the last time you made love.
- You feel anxious or depressed. You are having difficulty sleeping.
- You have trouble seeing each other together in the future.

If you agree with any of these statements, it may be time for you to consider talking to someone about your marriage, someone who is a professional in dealing with complicated interpersonal relationships. Helpful resources might include:

www.aamft.org

The American Association for Marriage and Family Therapy can assist you in locating a marriage counselor, therapist, or mediator near you, as well as recommend books and resources.

www.pairs.com

Devised and founded by the late Rabbi Morris Gordon and his wife, Dr. Lori H. Gordon, Practical Application of Intimate Relationship Skills is an educational system designed to enhance self-knowledge and develop skills to sustain a successful relationship.

www.equalityinmarriage.org

If you are seeking to avoid a messy and expensive divorce, visit this site. Instead of suing, try mediation. The Equality in Marriage Institute's goal is to educate men and women about the importance of equality in marriage and divorce. In the words of institute founder Lorna Wendt: "Even if you can't resolve everything through mediation, you can limit what is left for the courts to decide."

Gee, this particular section of our bookshelf is groaning. What do you suppose *that's* all about?

The Delta of Venus by Anaïs Nin (Harvest House). To make ends meet, Nin wrote pornography for an unknown patron, and the result is this wild collection of erotic and exotic stories. Sure, lots of us ate up this torrid little tome in college, but it's yummy fun to reread.

The Complete Illustrated Kama Sutra by Lance Dane (Inner Traditions). Yes, Virginia, there *is* tasteful pornography. This offers some great ideas about positions, too, if you and your mate are feeling particularly gymnastic.

Sex over 50 by Joel Block (Prentice Hall). This guy got into hot water in the media for suggesting certain naughty sex acts be performed while operating a moving car, but give him a break. You will be happy (and perhaps shocked) to learn from this book that sex is not only for the young.

RESEARCH

Whether you are a *one* or a *two,* how is your sex life? Changes in our bodies brought on by time, menopause, childbirth, weight gain, job stress, concerns about money, even the proximity of adolescent children, can take a toll on the quality of our sexual relationships. When we were younger, many of us took our active sex lives for granted. Just as we can fall into certain daily habits, so can sex become a habit—a biological one, but a habit nonetheless if you are doing it by rote. It's important to try to restore to sex some of its old energy and mystery. After all, for many of us, sexual attraction was what drew us to our mates in the first place.

One of the best and most powerful prescriptions is a romantic weekend away together. Plan a weekend where you will have privacy and enjoy pleasant surroundings. You'll probably be spending a lot of time in bed, so make sure the bedroom is one of the finest features of the place. In advance, go to the library or a bookstore and get some books on the art of making love and improving your sex life. There are several very good books about tantric yoga, the ancient art of making love, as well as some excellent books that will direct you through a course of sexual therapy. Videos are available on these same subjects. Take the books and videos you like best with you. Bring along massage oils, finger food, candles, flowers, music, soft sexy clothes, and anything else that will enhance your mutual pleasure.

As preparation for the weekend, you might want to make a list of unfinished statements or questions to fill in with your mate or partner. For example:

- What I like best about our sex life is . . .
- What I really love and wish you would do more is . . .
- What I love best about your body is . . .
- It would really help me to relax if . . .
- The best sex we ever had was when . . .
- I sometimes feel that the biggest obstacle to my ecstasy is . . .

Have fun with this. Contrary to what some people say, humor and lightheartedness do play a role in happy, healthy sex. What play unwanted roles are uptightness, nervousness, negativism, and shallow breathing, all of which can block your energy and prevent you from achieving orgasm. Many of you, sadly, may even have given up on having consistently orgasmic sex. Revive your hope. Orgasmic sex is possible for everyone. Pass the word. All you need to do is commit to letting it happen. Before your romantic weekend away, make sure you both commit to discovering or rediscovering ecstatic lovemaking.

Your Long Erotic Weekend: Four Days of Passion for a Lifetime of Magnificent Sex by Lana Holstein, MD, and David Taylor, MD (Fair Winds). This one's kind of fun. It's full of exercises and great anecdotes collected by the authors, sex therapists and managing directors of the Partners, Pleasure, and Passion retreats at Miraval Life in Balance, Catalina, Arizona.

The Joy of Sex by Alex Comfort (Crown). Remember that big juicy book and those wonderful line drawings? It's been updated, and it's still a great resource. Go back to it and have fun.

The Art of Tantric Sex: Ancient Techniques and Rituals That Enhance Sexual Pleasure by Nitya Lacroix (DK Publishing). Lots of pictures and great ideas, like creating a space for your love-making and exploring the "gateway to ecstasy." Sounds like a worthwhile destination to us.

Sexual healing

Here are some ideas to help you rediscover your passion:

- Learn how to give each other back rubs, foot massages, and hand massages.
- Use massage oil. Lubrication is sexy!
- Learn about tantric yoga; this could be the key to renewing your sexual relationship.
- Seek out tasteful pornography. (Yes, it does exist.)
- Watch a sexy movie together.
- Visit a sex shop together, and have fun speculating about what some of those weird gizmos do.
- See what happens when you abstain for a month.
- Keep it fresh. Don't do it the same way every time. Try to make each time unique.
- Learn to make love *slowly*. Quickies are for hot-sheet hotels.
- Don't be bashful about introducing sex toys. A good vibrator can be the ideal third party in a ménage à trois.
- Don't expect to do it every day!
- Talk about what's not working. Talk about what's working. Talk!
- And while you're talking, share your fantasies.
- Sometime when there's no one home but the two of you, try walking around all day long bare nekkid.
- Masturbation is nothing to be ashamed of. Pleasuring yourself can enhance your sexual energies and desires.
- Commit to making ecstatic lovemaking part of your ongoing relationship.

Traveling Solo by
Eleanor Berman (Globe
Pequot). Almost 25 per-
cent of the U.S. popu-
lation (thirty-five million
travelers) has taken a
vacation alone in the
past few years. This
book suggests trips for
the solo traveler to suit
all budgets, ages, and
interests.

FIND ROLE MODELS

If You Are One or Two

Anna Marie lives by herself and has perfected the art of solitary travel. She first traveled alone several years ago when her marriage was coming apart at the seams and she simply had to get out of the house. She chose to take a trip to the south of France all by herself. She planned every detail of the trip in advance. She amassed maps and brochures and guidebooks and lots of recommendations from friends who had made the trip before. She booked a two-week stay at a little inn near Saint Paul de Vence, and spent her days exploring the Riviera, tooling along the dramatic curves and switchbacks in her rented sports car, and navigating the side roads of southern France.

In the years since then, she has taken many such trips alone—a safari, a cruise, a tour of Scottish castles—and prides herself on her chutzpah and ability to derive pleasure from visiting places on her own. If friends are traveling to the same places she wants to visit, then of course she will go with them, but she would rather not go someplace she has already visited or has no particular wish to visit simply to have company for the trip. Her own company is sufficient.

If You Are Two

Buffy and her husband, Peter, have been together for more than thirty-four years. She is a little reluctant about writing down what specifically makes her marriage sing, but sing it does, and she has agreed to share some thoughts about it. (She is curious about what ten thoughts her husband would write down. Maybe they will go away for a weekend and find out!) She agrees with all that we have explored in this chapter, but important ideas cannot be stated often enough. Buffy and Peter believe that their marriage is like a barn door: a beautiful, sturdy, weathered barn door. And every time they have a fight or say something mean or thoughtless to each other, they imagine pounding a nail into the wood of that barn door.

When the fight is over, the nail gets wrenched out. But a hole is left where the nail was. Pound too many nails into the barn door and eventually it will be riddled with so many holes it will collapse. Buffy and Peter have been careful over the years not to pound too many nails into their barn door.

- We were friends before we became romantically involved, and we are still best friends. We enjoy doing many things together and enjoy many things separately.
- Peter makes me laugh.
- Peter has an extraordinary memory, so he remembers my stories, my likes and dislikes, our history together.
- We listen to each other. We try to hear what the other person is saying and feeling. We talk all the time.
- We celebrate our love constantly and continually with little gifts, phone calls, notes, and e-mails. We don't wait for the calendar to tell us it's time to celebrate.
- Rituals are romantic. Having little things or big things you always do together, like building a fire on a cold Sunday morning, or Christmas Eve dinner with family and friends, or a trip to the Botanical Gardens on the first day of spring, or getting up first to get the newspaper for the other person. These repeated moments of sharing are real and important.
- We bring out the best in each other. I would not want to disappoint Peter, so I try to behave in a way that will make him proud whether we are together or apart.
- We try to have sex every single day. Obviously, we don't, but we talk about it. We hold hands, kiss, flirt.
- We display our life together in photographs throughout the house, in collections we have created over the years together, in mementos from the trips we have taken.
- Music is a nearly constant presence in our life and accompanies our relationship in surprising and lovely ways.

Here are some sites that may take the sting out of going solo:

www.osolomio.com
Matches you up with a compatible traveling companion and books packages around the world.

www.solodining.com
This charming, quirky Web site is devoted to "taking the bite out of eating alone." Gives the lowdown on solo-friendly restaurants, how to ingratiate yourself to the management, how to make a reservation, how to cultivate the Sparkle Bright in you.

www.goingsolotravel.com
Going solo doesn't have to mean going alone! This is not a dating club, but rather a fun way for singles to enjoy traveling with others, making new friendships along the way.

www.cstn.org
An international organization of individuals interested in sharing going-solo trips, news, and tips about single-friendly trips, cruises, and tours.

www.webreference.com/
authoring/languages/
xml/rss/intro
RSS stands for "real simple syndication." It's a way for a content provider to "syndicate" information to anyone who wants to access that particular RSS feed. Think of it as the front page of your personal newspaper: it offers headlines and links to the complete stories.

WRITE IT DOWN

If You Are One

Consider celebrating the special people or animal companions who have come in and out of your life in scrapbooks, displayed photos, or a variety of other thoughtful ways. If you're dating, keep a journal of your experiences. Even if you're not dating, you might want to start a blog. A *blog*—in case you have been living under a rock—is a personal Web log you set up on the Internet on your own Web site. It's easy to get started, and you don't need technical support to do it.

While blogs can have serious applications, such as journalism, marketing, public relations, research, and education, there are lots of blogs that are just plain entertaining, in which the blogger shares the adventures of his or her daily life. Your site can be simple text or an elaborate illustrated chronicle of your life. Your blog can be a form of performance art if you have exhibitionist tendencies, or it can be a place to post a daily journal you don't mind sharing with others.

If You Are Two

Celebrate your history and write it down! Remember how you first met? Did you "meet cute," as they say in the movie business? There's something adorable and memorable about the way all of us met as couples. It's the story of us and it's precious. Do your kids know about it? If you haven't— or haven't lately—tell your kids the story of how you met because it's their story, too.

Start a photo album of just the two of you. See if you can hunt down photos of yourselves from every year of your life together. Do this as a couple. If your mate is reluctant to take part at first, give him space, but try to work on it when you are in the same room together. Select photos, write captions, and have some fun. Think about what your lives were like when each photo was taken. Reflect on the rocky years. Discuss your darkest moments as a couple, even while you celebrate the brightest. Think about what your lives are like now.

When Harry Met Sally, er, Katy

It was the summer of 1976 in New York City. I lived in Greenwich Village, but I worked for a children's book company, of all places, in the South Bronx. To get there, I used to ride the subway all the way from Sheridan Square to my office way uptown. Each weekday morning at 14th Street, a tall, dark, handsome man got on with his tie hanging down loose. A few stops before he got off at 125th Street, he would start to execute a near-perfect Windsor knot. I couldn't help but watch, and he couldn't help but notice that I was watching. After a while, we developed a little dual pantomime, in which he would finish and give me a look that asked, "How do I look?" I would nod or smile or give him the OK sign or the thumbs up. It became enough a part of my daily life that I began to speculate about him in my journal. Who was this man? What did he do? What was his name?

One Friday, I was scheduled to fly out to Pittsburgh to have a meeting with Fred Rogers on the set of *Mister Rogers' Neighborhood*. That meant that I was going to the airport. That meant no subway ride. That meant no Mr. Windsor Knot. My flight wasn't leaving until 10:00 a.m., so I made a decision. I would take the subway as I always did, and at the stop after he got off I would turn around and ride the train back downtown to Times Square, where I would catch a cab to the airport. I felt a little foolish doing it, but I just couldn't help myself.

When I switched trains at 14th Street, I didn't see him. I thought, "What a jerk I am!" Then I saw him coming through from the next car. I flashed him a big smile. He came and sat beside me. "What's your name?" I told him. He told me his name was Larry. I wasn't so crazy about the name, but I'd get over it. Then he told me he had accidentally gotten on the wrong subway car and for a minute, he was afraid I wasn't on his train. "I'm breaking up with this woman I've been living with in her West Village apartment. This is the last morning I'm taking this train."

He took my number and said he'd call. All that day I was elated but also blown away by the awesome power of fate. What if I'd skipped the train and gone straight to the airport? I even told Fred Rogers about it as we sat at the table on set and drank apple juice. "You know what we call that?" he asked me, in that gentle, sweet voice of his, which my colleagues and I would come to call Freddish. "That's Kismet."

My subway mystery man called me that same night and came over. I discovered, to my delight, that his name wasn't Larry after all. It was Harry. I have always loved the name Harry. It is lovable and at the same time glamorous, like something out of an old movie starring Ginger Rogers. We've been together for almost thirty years. I won't say they have been an easy thirty years. There have been times when I have wanted to end the marriage. But every time I do, I think of this story — of how much our sons love it, of how much I love it — and I just can't bring myself to do it. Because, after all, it's Kismet, isn't it?

GET TOGETHER

Ones and Twos

If you find you have developed a tendency to shun groups, ask yourself why this might be. Is it because you are shy, agoraphobic, a little depressed, tired, or misanthropic? Whatever your reasons, make a strong effort to overcome your reluctance, and link up with someone or some group in or out of your home. Take a course at a community college or a university extension. With your mate or date, see if you can find an activity that involves other couples, whether it be giving dinner parties on a regular basis; taking swing, tango, or ballroom dancing lessons; playing bridge at someone's house; kayaking on a local river; or Texas two-stepping at the local VFW post.

Consider having a movable feast. Buffy's sister-in-law, Alison, says that in her neighborhood four couples volunteer to prepare and serve one course in a four-course dinner: cocktails/hors d'oeuvres, appetizer, main course, dessert. Then they invite other couples in the neighborhood to join the movable feast. Going from house to house creates its own kind of celebration and people get to know each other. Keep an open mind, get involved, and see what happens.

PUTTING IT ALL TOGETHER

Now it's time to come up with a plan to strengthen your primary bond for the second half of your life, keeping in mind your specific challenges in this area. But first, let's review.

1. *Create time* to cultivate interests with your mate and apart from your mate. Create time to get out and about alone.
2. *Reflect* on the role breathing plays in your relationship. Open yourself to a deep examination of your emotions and the manner in which you project them.
3. *Practice patience* with your mate, and resist snapping or venting. If you have no mate, consider bringing someone or something into your life that will require you to practice patience and the gentle art of compromise.
4. *Research* ways to improve your sex life.
5. *Find role models* of both the Golden Duo and Sparkle Bright.
6. *Write down* what's great about your primary bond. Write down what's great about yourself.
7. *Get together* with an individual or group outside your home and see what happens.

TO-DO LIST

Here's a list of some activities for ones and twos. Mix and match, and try to incorporate at least two or three of them into your life.

- Take up ballroom, swing, or tango.
- Sign up for a cooking class.
- Go to the movies once a week, take a movie cruise, or get season tickets for a sports team, opera company, or ballet.
- Join a gym or walking group.
- Make a weekly date with your mate. Go to the movies, a museum, out for dinner.
- Sign up for an online dating service or let a friend fix you up.

- Join a singles group.
- Do a meditation tango.
- Declare peace talks in the chore wars; reassess the division of labor or make a chart.
- Adopt, rescue, or foster a pet.
- Find a roommate.
- Commit to couple's therapy.
- Start a blog.
- Start a scrapbook, audio tape, or collage.
- Spend a romantic weekend away with date or mate.
- Sign up for tantric yoga classes.
- Take a couple's massage class.
- Read *The Joy of Sex*.
- Buy an erotic video or a sex toy.
- Eat out by yourself.
- Plan a solo trip.
- Redesign your bed area to make it more romantic (scented candles, incense, satin sheets).
- Take up a new hobby with your mate.
- Take up a new hobby and open yourself up to new relationships.
- Share one of your mate's hobbies or interests.
- Share a friend's hobbies or interests.
- Invite friends over for dinner.

KATE'S PLAN

Menopause seems to have pretty much robbed me of my libido, so I need to work to get it back. Until recently, my husband and I had few interests in common, so on weekends we used to disappear into our separate lives and were apart on weekends as much as we were during the week. This apartness has, understandably, undermined our communication. When we're not communicating, we fall out of sync and out of sympathy with each other. We need a plan to enliven our sex lives and bring us closer together on a regular basis. Last Christmas, we went to a dude ranch and it was great for us.

My plan looks like this:

- Redesign the bedroom, and buy incense, candles, and pink satin sheets.
- Buy a book on tantric yoga.
- Continue to trail ride with Harry.
- Commit to daily downloads, conversing regularly with him so we can keep in touch with events, moods, and feelings.

- Get together with people at the barn and go to the movies, see summer stock plays, try local restaurants.
- Plan and go on a romantic weekend.

BUFFY'S PLAN

My challenges somewhat mirror Kate's. While I have not yet officially gone into menopause (perhaps I am a candidate for the *Guinness Book of World Records*), my sex drive has decreased. I need to do two things. First, explain this to my husband, and second, push myself, erotically speaking.

Both of our children were supposed to be away at college and graduate school, leaving the nest empty. I planned to be a good empty nester. My daughter went off to college, but it's close by so I see her a lot. My son deferred graduate school and moved back in with us. I will create time to understand my feelings about this transition period in my life, which so far is going amazingly well. I also plan to reflect on ways to be sure our marriage continues to flourish. My plan looks like this:

- Learn to give a massage.
- Tap more deeply into my sexual self, energies, and desires. Talk with Peter about my fluctuating levels of interest in sex.
- Wear that sexy lingerie Peter gives me, even if it is cold and I feel more thermal than lace.
- Peter has done the lion's share of cooking during our marriage, and I would like to teach myself or take courses in cooking so I can help more and maybe surprise him and myself.

For many of us, the biggest challenge in the second half of our lives is that just as our nest is beginning to empty of children, our aging parents begin to descend on us, literally or in ways that test our love, budgets, and patience. The next chapter deals with this often upsetting phenomenon and will help you formulate a plan for coping with it.

What about Mom and Dad?

Coping with "Super Seniors" and Siblings

Dear Buffy: I learned everything I know about cooking from my mother, and now, of course, I wouldn't dream of leaving her unsupervised in the kitchen. Once I caught her cheerfully buttering the wooden tops of my canisters. (Did she think they were English muffins?) Another time, she was helping me unload groceries, and she stashed a whole leg of lamb in the linen closet, which I didn't find until it started to stink. We had dinner guests the other night, and I figured I'd give her a really simple task to do. I asked her to tear the romaine lettuce for the salad. I'm busy braising the veal, and I'm only keeping half an eye on her, and she seems to be doing a fairly decent job of tearing the romaine into strips. The next time I look over, she's tearing the front page of the business section of the *New York Times* into neat little strips and adding it to the salad. Love, Kate

Dear Kate: Oh, no! All the news that's fit to eat! Love, Buffy

THE ROLLER COASTER OF AGING

Getting older conjures up a lot of images, many of them negative and downright ugly. Oh sure, some positive thoughts may cross our minds, but for the most part, our view of aging has been shaped by advertising and ignorance, and it ain't pretty.

We seldom see an older person as the lead in a TV series or a movie. We seldom see an older person in a commercial for buying a car or going on a glamorous vacation. And rarely do we see an older person on the cover of a fashion, beauty, or health magazine, except in AARP's monthly.

We worship youth. We recoil from age and aging. We push older people out of mind, out of sight, out of touch. As a society, we have condemned older people to a place none of us wants to visit. Ever.

It is time to rethink how we feel about older people, about —yes, let's say it —old folks. We have to work hard to overcome a number of cultural biases. Multiple generations living under the same roof is a relatively rare occurrence nowadays. We have taken one of the most natural cycles — growing older —and hidden it away. As a result, few of us have any real experience or skills in dealing with older people. Many of us had no elderly role models growing up. Our grandparents may have visited on holidays and summers or lived across town, but few of us spent concentrated time with them, time in which we could have learned, seen, and accepted the natural changes that occur as we grow older. The changes in your mother or father due to age may occur slowly, almost imperceptibly, or they may be sudden, abrupt, even life threatening. Either way, when they happen you begin your ride on the roller coaster of aging. The dips are without warning, the heights are dizzying, but it is natural and can be absolutely life affirming if we let it.

This chapter will help you get in touch with your childhood feelings about your parents and your feelings about them today. Now is the time to prepare to accompany your parents on their journey into the far reaches of the second half of their lives. Let's call our parents and their generation "Super Seniors." But do we really have to prepare for this? Can't we just let life unfold? We can. We often follow life's lead, a bit breathless and awkward perhaps, but we manage somehow, don't we? We think there is a better way, and that is a more mindful and responsible approach. Remember that you are now in the process of designing the part of your life that your parents are actually living. The lessons that your parents impart to you by their example, whether good or bad, can have a profound impact on the quality of the second half of your life. This chapter will help you address your level of tolerance for change, plumb the depths of your well of compassion, measure your patience, cultivate your memory, and determine how to access help when you need it. We'll share unique ways for you to get ready for the changes in store.

Traveling Hopefully by Libby Gill (St. Martin's) is a candid exploration of how she struggled with her family's painful legacy and how she learned to get past it and "jump-start her life." She explains how you can do the same.

www.elderweb.com
A straightforward, easy-to-navigate Web site that helps you organize what you need to learn more about. Good list of topics, from end-of-life issues to insurance options.

www.50plusmag.com
An online magazine for boomers and young seniors. Sometimes a magazine article is just the thing to start you thinking about an issue that your parents or an older sibling may be confronting right now.

Using our seven handy strategies, let's consider how you feel about your parents getting older and how those feelings will give rise to an intimate dialogue within yourself about how *you* feel about getting older.

CREATE TIME

Create time to think about, and take some degree of responsibility for, the Super Seniors in your life: your parents, an older neighbor, an aunt, a close friend of your family. We are all responsible, in some way, for at least one Super Senior. If you're not, instead of counting your lucky stars, look around and adopt one. Spending time with Super Seniors reminds you to be patient, to slow down, and to appreciate the basic things in life such as a good meal, a nice walk, and an intimate conversation.

How often do you wonder if your parents have enough money to take care of themselves? Do you have any idea how they want to be treated if they become too ill to communicate their wishes? Do you know if they have a will? We could ask dozens of such questions. Wouldn't it be easier if the answers could be magically transmitted from our parents' brains to our own? It's awkward and difficult to ask these questions. Don't you wish they had their File of Important Things all done and taken care of?

Before you ask your parents for personal information, ask yourself whether you have addressed those same issues. When you are asking your mother about her medical power of attorney, it goes a long way if you can say, "I know it's hard for you to talk about this. It is for me, too. But now that I have designated Bill as my medical power of attorney, I feel more secure about how I'll be treated if I ever become really sick or disabled. And I'm glad I arranged these things now when I'm feeling well, rather than waiting until I become sick, confused, or anxious."

Before asking your parents for personal information or giving them advice, ask yourself the following questions:

- Have I done what I am asking them to do? For example, do I have my will in order before I start nagging them about their own?

- Am I bugging them about it? Do I like to be asked the same thing over and over? Do not make the focus of every visit and every call getting them to do something so you can cross it off your to-do list.
- Have I recently asked their advice or guidance on a topic important to my family and me? Don't let advice be a one-way street.

Remember, this chapter is about you, not about your parents. It's about enriching your relationships with the Super Seniors in your life and deepening your relationship with yourself, your mate, and your friends.

Buffy Receives the Envelope

I remember the day — after many months, if not years, of asking — that my father finally gave each of us, my brother and sister and me, an envelope containing the names of their lawyer and their accountant, a listing of their insurance and medical policies, and the numbers of their bank accounts. When my father dealt out the envelopes that night at dinner in a fancy restaurant, he actually had tears in his eyes. Tears!

It has taken me a couple of years to truly understand his pain. Or was it embarrassment? A symbol of his loss of independence, perhaps? What was my father experiencing? Why tears? I felt that this was information that should be made available to members of the immediate family, as a matter of course, without our having to ask for it. After all, wasn't that the information that would help us help our parents if it became necessary? Could I have better prepared my father for this process, this gradual eroding of the parent-child boundary? Perhaps. But one thing I know. I know that I could have prepared myself better. After all, my actions and my reactions are all I have control over. I learned that evening that it's important to recognize what will be asked of us in the years ahead and that we need to be ready. We need to be ready when our son or daughter asks us not to drive anymore. We need to be ready when our niece suggests that we move into a smaller house. Preparation is important. And I learned the importance of sympathetic alignment — a crucial need to deeply understand how hard it is for our parents to admit in any way that they have grown old.

How to Care for Aging Parents by Virginia Morris (Workman). It bills itself as a "complete guide," and we think it probably is one of the most complete, no-nonsense, bring-on-all-the-tough-questions books available.

REFLECT

What might it be like to be older than you are now? Listen to how people talk about older people, how the media describe them, how advertising portrays them, how you sometimes think about them. Let's fess up to our fears. We are all afraid of growing old. In America, there is a sense that our seniors are almost a separate species. They live apart, away, afar, alone. We tend to feel sorry for friends when a mother or grandfather moves in with them. Sadly, we suffer from ageism, and if we are going to be successful in the second half of our lives, we must start to root out this negativity every time we feel it or see it, read it or hear it. There is power in words and images, and we must use care, imagination, and love when speaking to or about our elders.

In previous chapters, we have talked about the need for active listening. In this chapter, we want you to imagine actively. Reflect on what it might be like to live alone when you are older. Try this exercise.

It Fell and I Can't Get It

Imagine you are alone in a small room. You are sitting on a bed and have dropped the remote control for the TV. You start to reach over to get it, then realize that you are unable to move any further. No longer are you able to fold your body in half and reach under the bed. And your eyes are no longer sharp enough to see the remote in the darkness under the bed. Now let yourself say aloud or write down in your journal how you feel. Here are a few reflections to get you started:

- I am afraid.
- I am angry and frustrated that I can't move.
- I feel alone and helpless.
- I am busy trying to figure out a way to get that darn remote, but I keep losing my train of thought.
- I am frustrated that I don't have my eyeglasses, but I can't see to find them!
- I think I hear someone in the other room and that scares me.

- I am tired, so I will lie back down and deal with it after I have a nice nap.
- I am embarrassed and ashamed.

Now go back and think about what you have written. Isn't this how our parents must feel from time to time? Our challenge is to try to put ourselves in their place, to walk a mile in their shoes, so we really feel and understand, emotionally, viscerally, what it is they are experiencing.

Buffy's Sister's Charmed Circle

My sister lives in Mexico City and counts among her close friends more Super Seniors than any of the rest of us at this point. She lives in a community that holds a different view of seniors and a different view of the extended family. She has learned and benefited much from her host country's attitude toward family and aging.

My sister travels a great deal for business and pleasure. Her trips are organized by a couple with whom she is friends. The wife is seventy-two, and the husband is eighty-two. This couple plans and arranges trips for about ten people twice a year. They may go to India or Thailand or Nepal, as my sister did last summer. The trips have complicated itineraries, often involving several planes, trains, and perhaps a short boat ride. No one ever hints that this couple may be too old to remember all the details or too old to know the most interesting hotels to stay in or too old to have the energy to keep up on a three-week tour of India. And perhaps it is because their age is never considered or whispered about or criticized that my sister and her friends have enjoyed so many wonderful trips.

PRACTICE PATIENCE

As our parents become Super Seniors and as we gradually come to stand in their place, all our relationships are brought into a new focus, but perhaps none more vividly than our relationships with our siblings. It is important to practice patience with our siblings. If we live near our parents, we tend to be the ones who help to make the decisions, include them in family and holiday activities, reach into our pockets to pay for things they need, take personal days from work to take them to the doctor. And sometimes — perhaps after a long day of shopping with your mother for a certain kind of paring knife you are pretty sure hasn't been manufactured in fifty years — you might start to feel a little resentful of your siblings because here you are doing all the work, and probably paying for everything to boot, and there they are living the life of Riley, thousands of *lucky* miles away.

Conversely, if we are the siblings living far away, we tend to feel guilty that we are not doing our share, nervous that the decisions being made without us aren't the right ones, unhappy that we only get to see our parents for short periods of time, reluctant to give up our limited vacation time to go back home, sad that all we talk about with our siblings when we see them is our parents, embarrassed that we do not have any more money to send or time to spend, and angry because we feel guilty.

As we said, you can just go along and let life happen to you or you can prepare yourself. You can prepare for this new phase with your siblings so your relationships will stay secure, loving, and compassionate, but to do so you must set reasonable goals, communicate directly, and practice sympathetic alignment.

There is no magic formula to smooth the journey you are sharing with your siblings. You cannot change your siblings any more than you can change your parents, but you can change how you feel and how you express those feelings.

Don't waste time and energy criticizing yourself or your siblings. Always practice patience. Refer to the personal prescription for patience you wrote in chapter 1, or look at the one you wrote to counter the impatience you feel toward your husband or partner in chapter 5. Think about the reasons you are impatient with your siblings and write them down. If you are the child who spends the most time with your parents, you may feel impatient with your siblings when:

- They don't appreciate the sacrifices you are making.
- They forget your mother's birthday and act as though you are the only who knows what to buy her.

- They give you little emotional support.
- They call you on holidays to speak to your mom and don't say a word to you.
- They never suggest or volunteer coming for a weekend to take care of Mom so you can get away.
- They disagree with the way you are caring for your parent.

Here are a few prescriptions for practicing patience with your siblings. Mull them over and add a few of your own.

Sibling Revelry: 8 Steps to Successful Adult Sibling Relationships by Jo Ann Levitt, Marjory Levitt, and Joel Levitt (Dell). Three siblings help you do the work you need to do in order to have a better relationship with your brothers and sisters.

- *Show compassion for yourself, your siblings, and your parents.* Let your mind circle around each of their lives, consider their complicated time commitments and responsibilities, then slowly come back, with renewed empathy, to your own life. This may be the time for you to reconcile with a sibling who has not been in your circle for some time, to apologize to a sibling for a slight or transgression, to thaw frigid relations.
- *Laugh with your siblings.* Diffuse tension between you and your siblings or between them and your parents. Let laughter lighten the load.
- *Be available and accessible to your siblings.* Just knowing that you can talk to a person who is in many ways, and certainly genetically, one of the closest people to you on earth can be soothing, whether you are the nearby child who is wrestling with difficult situations or the child who is far away and feels disconnected from the heartbeat of the family. With e-mail, cell phones, answering machines, and BlackBerrys, there is no earthly reason or excuse not to be in quick and ongoing contact with your siblings. This connectedness can provide each of you with a renewed sense of clarity, energy, and love.

Patience can imbue a relationship with serenity, a gentle peace and calm, an amnesty that allows us the time and space in which to work things out, make mistakes, apologize, and keep moving. Demonstrating patience to your siblings is a priceless gift.

The surefire therapeutic power of the classics: Kate's mother has outlived all her friends and lives in a house that frequently rings with rock, country, reggae, folk, and rap music. Is it any wonder that she sometimes feels cut off and left out? One day, Kate went out and bought the original cast recording for *Guys & Dolls* (Decca). Kate's mother perked up like an air fern in a wind tunnel. So Kate went out and bought more original cast recordings. Before long, everyone in the house was humming and singing those delightfully clever lyrics that they just don't write any more. Here is a sampling of Sandy's collection: *Showboat* (EMI), *South Pacific* (EMI), *Annie Get Your Gun* (Decca), *The King and I* (Broadway Angel), *Man of LaMancha* (Decca), *The Pajama Game* (Columbia), *Carousel* (Broadway Angel), *Kiss Me, Kate* (Broadway Angel), *The Sound of Music* (Columbia), *Brigadoon* (TCM Music)

Caring for a Super Senior

- *Resist the temptation to patronize them.* Just because they are old doesn't mean they are stupid.
- *Respect them.* Don't call them "Darling," "Dearie," "Sweetie pie," or "Hon," unless they specifically ask to be called by this or some other pet name.
- *Raise your voice only if you know that they are hard of hearing.* We tend to assume that all seniors are deaf, but this is not always the case.
- *If you are accompanying them on an errand or to a doctor's appointment, allow plenty of time.* Whether of necessity or choice, seniors can be slow. Rushing them is rude and can even be harmful.
- *Be in the moment.* It's easy to feel held back by the pace of our elders. Resist the temptation to look at your watch and dash off to the next engagement Enjoy your time together.
- *If you suspect they need help, find a tactful way to offer it.* Seniors can be a little slow buttoning their coats, tying their shoes, counting their change. Often, we want to barge in, take over, and do these things for them. It's important that they do for themselves. So take a breather and let them. If they need help, offer gently.
- *Whenever you can, get them to tell you about their childhood and life.* Stories are their legacy, and they are of great value to you and your children.
- *When they visit, play music you know they will love.* That might be Sinatra and the Tommy Dorsey Orchestra or the Ray Coniff Singers.

RESEARCH

One of our jobs as children of Super Seniors is not only to offer to help our parents, but also to actually know *how* to help them when they need us. It's not about caregiving so much as it is about preparing to meet the demands and being open to accept the rewards of attending to our parents.

Start a list. Jot down random things off the top of your head that you might need to figure out at a moment's notice. Your list will be determined to some extent by the age and health of your parents. You may have already started to research some of these questions for your File of Important Things.

Here are some other questions that your parents may need help answering:

- *Who would you call to order a panic button for your mother to wear in case she falls in her apartment?* www.life@home.com is a site dedicated to helping people live independently by providing helpful products and services.
- *Is there a way to help your parents keep their medications straight? Is there a pharmacy near them that will deliver?* Encourage your parents to use a weekly pillbox, and help them to make a medication chart where they (or you) note each medication and which doctor prescribed it. Make a few calls to neighborhood pharmacies and ask about delivery. Buffy found a pharmacy nearby that delivers. They didn't advertise that, but when asked agreed to do it for a fee.
- *They agree they would like to exercise, but is there a senior-friendly gym near them?* See chapter 2 for a list of questions to ask when checking out a gym for any person. To be sure that the facility is truly senior friendly, you should accompany your parents for at least two visits before they sign up. Notice if they take part in the activities and if the trainer treats them appropriately. Try to observe whether there are any other older people in the gym. Are low-impact classes or classes for seniors offered? If you find that the gym is geared to the under-thirty crowd, consider a different gym. If the gym is crowded or the music is too loud, ask the manager if there is a quieter time your parents might come. Encourage your parents to use all the gym facilities, including whirlpool and sauna, but make sure they know how.
- *Who would you call to get your parents some help paying bills? What if they need help getting dressed in the morning?* Buffy doesn't think her dad needs this yet, but in six months he might. She found the site of the National Association of Professional Geriatric Care Managers, which provides care management resources and helps you locate a local care manager: www.caremanager.org.

The Caregiver's Essential Handbook by Sasha Carr and Sandra Choron (Contemporary Books). The reading line says it all: "More than 1,200 tips to help you care for and comfort the seniors in your life." We find the concept of comfort lovely and compelling, don't you?

- *Do you know whether your parents have written a will and, if so, where they keep it?* Buffy's parents have a will. She would like them to write down how they want to be treated if they become too sick to make their wishes known. Maybe they need an elder law attorney who can help them. Caring Connections gives information about options for end-of-life services: www.caringinfo.org.

- *Their eyesight isn't that great anymore and it's hard for them to read, but Buffy's parents are still very much interested in the news. Are there large-print newspapers available in their city?* Research shows that adults sixty-five and older spend more time reading the newspaper than any other group: more than one hour of reading each day. As a gift, give the weekly *New York Times* large-print edition.

- *Which sibling will get Grandma's yellow pie plate?* Buffy would like her parents to designate which heirlooms will be passed down to which child. Or, even better, ask each child which treasure she wants; www.yellowpieplate.umn.edu provides practical information about the inheritance of personal property and helps you and your parents establish a process for deciding who gets what.

- *Is it safe for your parents to continue to drive?* Buffy thinks her father should give up driving, but she is not sure how to raise the subject. Direct communication about difficult issues becomes more important than ever as our parents get older. Buffy might take a test to assess her own driving skills before she asks her father to do the same. That way, she can assess her own driving and familiarize herself with what challenges older drivers face. MIT and Hartford Insurance teamed up to create a brochure called "Family Conversations with Older Drivers," which is available at web.mit.edu/agelab and www.thehartford.com.

Finding the answers to these questions is like learning a new language. How you negotiate your daily life is second nature, easy, somewhat predictable; to a large degree, it is rote. Our seniors are negotiating a new phase of their lives, and it is uncharted territory for them and for you; it is hard going and the landmarks are often unreliable. Go back to chapter 4, and review strength-training exercises for the mind. They will help you here. You will need to research, make cold calls, and read studies and articles that, until now, you might never have been drawn to. It can be helpful and considerate to clip articles or print out Web site information that might be of interest to your Super Seniors. It is often better to make information available than to tell them what's best. They will know what's best if you help them gather the data.

FIND ROLE MODELS

Kate's mother, Sandy, lives with Kate and her family. It's fair to say that Sandy moved in before Kate had a chance to prepare. Kate had to learn on the fly, and she freely admits that preparation would have helped enormously. But all things are possible, and they have found a way to create new pathways of love and cooperation to accommodate the newest household member. Here is Kate's account.

Sandy, Super Senior!

After we were fairly sure that my mother wasn't going to die from a massive subcranial aneurysm, after we had tucked her will back into the file for some future time, after I had secured power of attorney from her the moment she regained consciousness and then closed on the sale of her home, my mother was moved from the hospital where her brain surgery had been performed to a bleak rehab facility on the south shore of Long Island. How I dreaded the trips out there twice a week. I'll never forget that first sight of her out of a hospital bed and detached from the IV. I barely recognized her: tiny and wizened, hunched down in a child-size wheelchair parked across from the nurses' station in a row of other rehab patients, in various states of gray, shrunken, drooling helplessness. This wasn't my mother. This couldn't be my mother. This *was* my mother. Since I barely recognized her and she had no idea who I was, we were, for a brief, very grim time, strangers.

The health care professionals at the facility were most intent on getting my brothers and me to participate in the rehabilitation process. We

www.nho.org
The National Hospice and Palliative Care Organization values the experience of the end of life. It will help locate providers.

www.wellspouse.org
The Well Spouse Association provides support to wives, husbands, and partners of the chronically ill and/or disabled through monthly support groups and education.

www.nfcacares.org
The National Family Caregivers Association promotes education, support, empowerment, and advocacy of family caregiving for chronically ill, aged, or disabled loved ones.

www.caregiving.org
The National Alliance for Caregiving provides support to family caregivers and increases public awareness of issues facing family caregivers.

www.caregiver.org
The Family Caregiver Alliance is a public voice for caregivers, providing information, education, services — including elder-sitting — research, and advocacy to sustain the important work of families caring for loved ones with chronic, disabling health conditions.

did so reluctantly and with a mingled sense of helplessness, embarrassment, and dread. My daughterly instincts, by which I had navigated for more than fifty years, seemed somehow useless under these challenging new circumstances. What the situation called for was maternal instincts, but the idea of mothering my own mother felt unnatural and awkward. What? Mother the woman who was so self-sufficient ten years earlier that she didn't let me accompany her to surgery to remove a melanoma above her eye? But mothering my mother was precisely what the situation demanded. I think I knew then, with a kind of numb recognition, that this was the new order of my life.

Sandy had a team of five: a primary physician, three therapists, and a social worker or patient advocate. My brother Mark (who came up from Philadelphia every other weekend) and I met with them on a regular basis to discuss Sandy's progress. She had a speech therapist, whose job was to help her begin to recover her memory. Her memory was shot. Where her brain had bled, cells and synapses had been destroyed. Only time, and therapy, would tell us how much of her lost memory she would be able to reclaim.

Sometimes she knew my name and who I was. Sometimes she thought I was her big sister Mary. Again, the paradigm shift. I was the older sister. She was the kid sister now. Never mind that her sister Mary, who had been to visit several times, was eighty-seven years old. I was Moo, which was the nickname my mother had come up with for her sister when she was two years old and couldn't pronounce Mary. Moo was in charge now. Moo was me. Move over, Kate.

Sandy hated the hospital food, but she had lost so much weight while on the IV that the nurses who fed her encouraged her to clean her plate at every meal. One evening, she shoved the tray aside and said, in a froggy whisper, "Save it for Pete." My little brother Peter had died two summers earlier, having come home to live (or die, actually) under my mother's deteriorating roof, where he methodically drank himself to death. But Peter had always been a nosher and a picker and an eater of everyone's leftovers. So saving it for Peter made kind of morbid sense.

And then there were the times she'd look me straight in the eye and ask, "Where's Mother?" "Dead for the last forty years," was my usual rather blunt response. I had no wish to humor her in her historical meanderings.

The physical therapy came easiest. Before the aneurysm, Sandy had been an active Super Senior, a daily walker, and nearly a daily frequenter of the gym at the Y. Now, my mother was the physical therapist's pet. She had "muscle memory" from her years of exercising and a will to do the work. And much work lay before her. It was late December. She had been in bed since early October. Her muscles were alarmingly atrophied and she had lost fifty pounds, about forty-five of which she had needed to lose. When she began to joke that she did not recommend brain surgery as a quick weight-loss program, I began to have hope that she would recover. Her sense of humor was intact. And she would need it.

At first, she could barely get out of her wheelchair and onto the large, elevated mat where she did her slow, painstaking leg lifts and hip lifts. Walking was a big fat deal. At first, she could take no more than six steps with a walker. But within a week or two, she could do ten leg lifts and walk clear down the hall, before collapsing trembling and breathless into the wheelchair I pushed alongside her.

For me, the sessions with the occupational therapist were the most harrowing. Occupational therapy is about doing for yourself: feeding, dressing, bathing, going to the bathroom, and eventually, perhaps, even driving, shopping, and cooking. Before the surgery, my mother had been completely independent and very modest. Helping to dress her, helping her to the toilet, wiping her bottom, these were tasks I did for my own children but never imagined I'd do for a parent. Although I no longer have to do this for Sandy, having had to do them for a time has forever changed me.

Just before Christmas, my mother's advocate at the hospital drew me into her office and asked me if I'd made the appropriate arrangements to take Sandy home. I told the advocate that my mother had no home. She had sold it just before she was stricken, and in the past two months I had finished what she had set in motion. We lost the deposit on the second-floor walk-up with the steep staircase. Going back to the town where she had lived, even to a ground-floor apartment, was not an option. And it was clear that she couldn't stay in rehab much longer. The time the insurance company had allotted for her stay was nearly up.

The health care clock was ticking, and I was in a state of panic. "Can't you keep her? I thought she'd be able to stay here longer. She's nowhere near ready to be released. Isn't there some other sort of rehab place we could send her? I have all this money from the sale of her house. We could get her the best rehab money can buy." In that moment, I was behaving the same way with Sandy's money as I do with my own—perfectly willing to throw any amount of it at a crisis rather than cope with it sensibly. I could see a recognition of this in the advocate's eyes as she turned a look of pity on me and said, "Trust me. You don't want to put your mother in one of those rehab places. Those are places people go when there's nobody to care for them. Those are places people go to die. Isn't there room for her in your home?"

My panic ratcheted up several notches at this suggestion. My house? I did have a nice big home with plenty of room on the ground floor. Mentally, I walked the rooms, deciding which one could best be converted to her bedroom without inconveniencing the rest of us. It would either be the den or the dining room, I decided. Having taken it that far, I began, ever so slightly, to calm down and get used to the idea. The advocate was right there with me. "You need to know that there are things you will have to do to your home to make it livable for Mother," the advocate said. "Just like you had to toddler-proof your house, now you have to make it safe for seniors."

Safe for seniors? I nodded grimly at the thought of my dream house marred by yucky medical-supply-store items like shower stall rails, an invalid commode, a walker, a wheelchair, the whole nine rehab yards, not to mention pills and adult diapers. My mother was an invalid now, and she was officially, for the first time, an old person. I shuddered.

"We can make the adjustments," I said gamely as she handed me the state-printed brochure telling me just what I'd need and have to do. But I had another problem. "We can't take her yet, though. We're going to Mexico for ten days. The tickets are all bought and paid for. The house will be empty. There won't be anybody for her to come home to until after the first of the year when we get back."

"Fine," the advocate said, without missing a beat. "I'll get her stay extended by ten days and you can come pick her up the day after you get home from your vacation. Have fun."

Great. Swell. Merry Christmas. Happy New Year! Happy New Life! Somebody shoot me, please. Now.

We decided not to cancel our trip to Mexico, but I was conscious of it as a sort of final fling before my life was transformed to rehab central, my house to an old folks' home. I made frantic phone calls before I left concerning arrangements for personnel: visiting nurses, therapists, and caregivers. It took me countless calls to figure out that her insurance entitled her to about eight weeks of full-tilt service. I was vaguely grateful for the help, but I did not relish the thought of my house being overrun by strangers, well-meaning but probably meddlesome health care professionals. Then I got an idea.

I called my friend James, who had recently been laid off from his job at a magazine. Jim and I had met years ago when we worked at the same publishing house. Since then, among numerous other jobs, Jim had taught exercise to overweight women and ballet to the New York Jets, and had become a licensed massage therapist and a creator of "outsider" art. I asked him what he was doing for the next few months. If he had no plans, would he consider coming up to live with us during the week and undertake my mother's rehabilitation?

"Buy a massage table," he told me. "She's going to need some serious body work."

I did, as I would frequently do over the next weeks and months, exactly as I was told.

Jim prepared for the new job by reading up on senior care and consulting at length with friends who were in the business of elder care, rehabilitation, and physical therapy. The first week on the job, Jim made Sandy get down on the floor to do her exercises, rather than having her do them in a chair or on her bed as the visiting physical therapist had recommended. It was a major production. Thin and frail as she was, I thought we'd need a crane to lower her down and raise her up. Even before the brain surgery, she had trouble getting up and down. Generally, she avoided getting down on the floor to avoid the embarrassment of having to ask for an arm up. I explained this to Jim. He ignored me. "She can do it," he said.

After getting her down there, it took us five very tense minutes to get her back up following the session of floor exercises. I had a few very bad moments. I was so afraid I had made a mistake bringing Jim in. What would I tell my brothers? "Sorry, guys, Jim broke Mom." He was just too aggressive. He was expecting too much of her. He didn't understand how old and sick and frail she was. But he wasn't subscribing to the "pamper Sandy" line. He expected a great deal of her and got it in very short order. After two weeks, she could get down on the floor and get herself up by using the bed.

Each day seemed endless but was marked by improvement that started agonizingly slowly but speeded up by the day. Her balance improved, her speech cleared, her eyes brightened, her coordination improved. It took her five days to switch from walker to cane and another week to do away with the cane altogether. She fell twice — once on her head — and we had a few bad, guilty moments, prompting phone calls to doctors and even an office visit or two.

Sooner than I could have imagined, all the invalid stuff went away: the shower stool, the walker, the commode, the diapers, the wheelchair — all of it. I was only too happy to donate it all to charity and rid my home of the trappings of my mother's rehabilitation.

There were heavy snows that winter. Jim and Sandy would bundle up and go out into the backyard and walk through the drifts, the higher and deeper the better and more therapeutic. The drift striding strengthened her legs and improved her balance.

They practiced walking up and down the stairs. Walking down, he told her, it was important not to look at her feet. That would make her stumble and trip. Look out before you, and wave like you're the queen mother, he directed her, greeting the adoring crowds. Occasionally, even to this day, when she comes down a set of stairs with grace and absolute ease, she'll do the queen mother bit, waving to her loyal subjects.

Jim and Sandy went out in public as soon as she was walking and maintaining her balance. They'd make lists and run errands. He'd get her to write the lists herself and then they'd figure out together where to go to get what was on the list. Their outings were sources of great amusement. He'd encourage her to recount what happened on each little shopping adventure. It sounded casual and anecdotal, but he was prompting her to strengthen her short-term memory.

Jim got me to buy a Gazelle, one of those low-impact exercise machines that work the arms and legs without straining the knees. We set it up in the master bedroom from which she could watch the neighbor's ducks as she put in her hour of gazelling. She'd observe the ducks and discuss what was happening. We called it her duckumentary.

They did art projects together. They painted egg cartons with bright poster paints. She decorated her room, once my dining room but now undeniably her space, with their outrageous and decorative art projects.

Jim and Sandy went hiking in the park. They found walking sticks and took them along each time they hiked. Sometimes she fell. Sometimes he fell. They came home muddy. She called them forced marches, but I could tell that she loved them.

They made oatmeal for my mother's breakfast to combat her naturally high cholesterol. They'd cook up the Irish oats using fruit juice instead of water so that it sometimes came out garishly colored but tasted delicious all the same. They cut up nuts and dried fruits in the oatmeal and sprinkled it with flaxseeds, and sometimes added a dollop of yogurt.

They talked about my mother's marriage to my father, a larger-than-life merchant seaman who had chosen a path that was far different from the staid lawyer or doctor her parents had expected her to marry. Raising five children while her husband was away at sea could not have been easy, and she told Jim things about her life with my father (who died on my thirty-fourth birthday) that I don't think she had ever confided to another living soul.

They sat in the hot tub talking about books, about opera, about the countries they had both visited, about favorite museums and artists, about food, about nonsense, about politics, about his frustrated love life, about her grandchildren — my kids — whom Jim has always loved as if they were his own.

He took her to visit the doctor who had saved her life. The hotshot surgeon was so dazzled by her recovery that he brought her around to see all the nurses who had looked after her. It was a proud day for everyone.

He invited her friends from Sea Cliff to come up and visit. They adored Jim, and it confirmed a long-held suspicion of mine that every woman of a certain age blossoms under the attentions of a courtly and cultivated homosexual.

Jim and Sandy also talked about her brush with death. How the odds had weighed so heavily against her that it really was a miracle that she had survived. One day on a hike, Jim actually asked her, "Why is it you think that you didn't die?"

She grew very thoughtful, then said, "I don't really know. I certainly had every medical reason to. But there must have been something very important that I had to do. Something I had left unfinished."

When Jim related this conversation to me, my mind traveled immediately back to the weekend before my mother's stroke. Harry and I and our boys, as well as two of my brothers and their families, had all converged on Sandy's house in Sea Cliff, the house we had all grown up in, to help her mount the mother of all garage sales. Having just gone to contract on the house, she was now getting rid of anything that she wouldn't be able to use in the small one-bedroom apartment she was planning to move into. All that weekend, while we brought things down from the attic and up from the basement, emptied cupboards and drawers and bookcases, and slapped on price tags, Sandy complained of a headache. Sandy never got headaches or any other kind of aches for that matter. For as long as I can remember, she had been hearty stock. Her doctor told her it was probably tension from selling the house and had prescribed Valium for her. But so far Valium hadn't touched the pain.

I called her on Wednesday of the following week to see if she was feeling any better. Even though she still had the headache, her focus was turned outward, "What's wrong with Harry?" she asked. "What do you mean?" I replied, knowing perfectly well what she meant. "I don't know," she said, "He didn't seem like his old self last weekend. He seemed sad. Like somebody or something had knocked all the stuffing out of him." Harry was sad, all right. Two weeks earlier, I had told him I was packing it in. I wanted a divorce. I was tired of pulling the wet laundry out of the washing machine where it had sat for hours. I was convinced there was somebody better for me, and I wanted a chance to find him while I was still young. But of course, I didn't say anything of the kind to my mother.

She had this vile headache, and besides, from the first day I brought him home, she has always been wild about Harry. She would not want to hear any nonsense about a divorce.

"Probably just a midlife crisis," I told her dismissively.

There would be time enough to break it to her when her head stopped hurting. The next day, she was in the emergency room being rushed into the operating room. Crisis being the great leveler, it banished from my mind and my heart all thoughts of divorcing Harry.

I'm thinking all of this, not saying it aloud, when Jim says to me, "You know what I think?"

I looked at him and nodded. I knew exactly where he was going with this, so I went there first: "Sandy came back to save my marriage."

Some might say that I saved my mother, and with a lot of help from Jim and my family, I did save Sandy in a manner of speaking. But just as surely, Sandy saved me and my marriage.

WRITE IT DOWN

One specific and comforting way to connect with your feelings about getting older is to remember your childhood. Remember the tiny events that make up your life, and remember how you felt. When Buffy's kids were small, she used to lie beside them at night and tell stories from her childhood. Her kids called them "childhoods." They were quick little vignettes featuring Buffy as a little girl. When Buffy started telling these stories, she realized how many she had to tell. She realized how memorable her own mother, Middie, had made her childhood.

Middie is the quintessential homemaker. It wasn't just that she was the best chef on the block or that she could be room mother, head of the car pool, and troop leader all at the same time. She also made each day an adventure. She let her kids roller-skate in the basement, build elaborate tents made from blankets taken off her bed and theirs, skip school now and then when Buffy's father was traveling on business. She invited Buffy and her sister to tea parties, and together they sat in her bed and watched Bette Davis movies.

Choosing Medical Care in Old Age: What Kind, How Much, and When to Stop by Muriel R. Gillick (Harvard University Press). A jargon-free discussion of the many choices open to you and your amply aged loved ones.

Caregiving: The Spiritual Journey of Love, Loss, and Renewal by Beth Witrogen McLeod (Wiley). Offers practical advice and spiritual advice drawn from many faiths and philosophies.

The Year of Magical Thinking by Joan Didion (Knopf). This is a memoir about grieving. Consider listening to the audio-book version, movingly read by Barbara Caruso.

www.ancestory.com
Discover your family
story; search for your
ancestors and genealogy
records online.

www.genealogy.org
Search online genealogy
and family history
databases.

www.genealogy.com
Access historical
records and build your
family tree.

www.familysearch.org
The Church of Jesus
Christ of the Latter-Day
Saints manages this
genealogical database.

www.amberskyline.com
This site has a varied
menu, including how to
decipher old or archaic
handwriting.

Here is an example of a Childhood. It's a story about one Halloween. Buffy's mother made all of their costumes—every Halloween, without fail, she made imaginative, unusual, often outrageous costumes. On this particular Halloween, Buffy and her sister were human fingers. Where they lived, everyone walked house to house trick-or-treating and usually ended up at a circle at the top of the hill where the parents would judge the costumes. Buffy remembers that she and her sister were walking toward the circle slowly because the costumes were tight. Buffy was wearing a sparkly mask that looked like a ring around the finger. Suddenly, she tripped and fell over. She heard a parent's voice sing out, "A finger is down! A finger is down!" But before any grown-up could come to Buffy's rescue, her sister had picked her up and righted her. And through the material of the costume, Buffy felt her sister kiss her cheek. They received the prize that night for most original costume.

These stories brought Buffy's children closer to her, but also closer to their grandparents and aunt. They restored to Buffy intimate, pleasing moments with her parents and sister that she might have otherwise forgotten in the intervening years.

Do you have any favorite stories—any Childhoods of your own? What's the funniest story you can remember about your dad? Picture your mother cooking Thanksgiving dinner. Think back to the first time you saw your mother cry. Was it at a funeral? A recital? When your big brother graduated from college? Start to retrieve those memories now. Those stories, perhaps known only to you, will provide you with a reservoir of good feelings about your parents and, most likely, about your siblings as well. Draw on them to counter any feelings of frustration or anger you may harbor from time to time as your parents get older. When you find yourself running smack up against an unpleasant or upsetting encounter, a moment of maddening impatience, try slipping into one of your cherished childhood memories. It will serve as a welcome shield between you and those prickly negative feelings.

Spend some time retrieving your own Childhoods, or take a moment to write one in your journal. Here are some ideas to get you started. As we learned in chapter 4, "firsts" are sometimes the easiest to recall and maintain. Consider:

- The day you got your first two-wheeler
- Your first day of college
- The first day of your first paying job

Over time, if you keep at it, you will have amassed a treasure chest of child-hood memories to pore over. To simultaneously enhance your memories and expand the circle of participation, include your parents, and ask them to talk about some of their favorite memories. Super Seniors have stored up a lifetime of stories. Let them share their stories with you. Occasionally, your parents might remember a particular event differently than you do. All of us tend to make ourselves the star of our memories, and our parents are no different. Sometimes how they tell a story might hurt your feelings or make you angry and you might be tempted to interrupt—"Hey! That's not what happened!" Try not to. Be patient. Let them remember in their own way.

    Super Seniors want to share their memories. They also want to share things. They need—literally *need*—to share and give possessions, stories, advice, and memories. We need to practice how to receive this legacy of theirs with grace, whether or not we want or need what it is they are offer-ing. When your parents give you something of theirs, take a moment to jot down something special about it: just a couple of specific words—the date, the occasion—on a small adhesive sticker, and secure it to the item. It will bring you and your children joy in years to come.

Your family tree is also about ideas and values. If you need someone to help you write your story or if your relatives are so far away you need focus, visit www .personalhistorians.org. Or maybe you can get started by asking yourself what five ideas or values you want your children to inherit from you. When you are gone, what are the three or four things you want your children to tell your grandchildren?

Legacy and inheritance are not just about money and material possessions. For instance, your legacy might be recipes. Check out *The Black Family Reunion Cookbook* compiled by the National Council of Negro Women (Fireside/Simon & Schuster).

Buffy's Pearls of Wisdom

Last spring, my daughter was reviewing with me what she would wear to the prom. She had bought a sophisticated, long black dress. She looked great in it. We were discussing whether she should wear her hair up or down and what jewelry she should wear. I went and got her my favorite string of pearls, which her father, my husband, had given to me on our tenth wedding anniversary. The clasp is engraved with "120," representing 120 months together, or ten years. I told her to see how they looked on her. They were perfect. It gave me pleasure to see her wear something of mine. Intense pleasure.

Claims assistance. Do you need it? Do your folks need it? Learning how to file claims, deal with Medicare, and better understand your benefits is challenging, and if you are emotionally drained, it can be downright nightmarish. Claims assistance, a relative new but much needed service, helps you file your insurance claims. Start with www.shiptalk.org or www.claims.org. Alliance of Claims Assistance Professionals is a nonprofit organization that helps you understand and obtain your full benefits.

I try to remember that feeling whenever my mother says to me, which is with increasing frequency, "Here, take this, I want you to have it." I have to stop and remember that what she wants to feel is the same pleasure of sharing her treasures with me that I felt in sharing mine with Daisy. I have to stop myself from saying, "No, you may need this. You should keep it." Or, worse, "I don't really need it, Mom. Hang on to it." My mother sent me a set of dishes that I had told her repeatedly I didn't want or need. Looking back, I am not sure why I thought I didn't want them, because after they arrived I realized that I was glad she sent them. I have used those dishes for every Christmas Eve dinner since I received them, and I savor the connection the dishes make between my family's Christmas Eve dinners and those of my childhood.

GET TOGETHER

Get together with a friend and compare notes about the seniors in your lives. Everyone has a story to tell or information to share about caregiving, Alzheimer's, incontinence, dementia, family issues, community resources, even death and dying. These are all pretty dark topics, but however daunting they might be, at some point while talking about them you will find yourselves laughing. Humor, particularly laughter, has absolutely no adverse side effects and is completely free. When you laugh, you positively influence your body chemistry by increasing blood flow, releasing endorphins, reducing stress, and boosting the immune system. It's easy for Kate to feel depressed about having her mother living with her these days, but when Sandy comes up with a classic question like "Whatever happened to that woman who was going to put dog turds in your hot tub?" it's pretty darned near impossible to stay blue. Laughing until the tears run down your face, and laughing so hard you have to dash to the bathroom before you pee your pants? That's therapy.

If you have no seniors in your life, borrow someone else's or see if you can spend some time where you find them—over at the Y, or in the local nursing home or elder day-care center. Without being patronizing, see if you can cultivate relationships and learn to find joy in the company of Super Seniors and in the prospect of your own eventual Super Senior-hood. If you are open, you might be surprised to learn how Super Seniors can touch your life. Buffy's mother-in-law is selling the apartment she bought fifteen years ago. Peter and Buffy decided to track down the real estate agent who had helped them with it initially. They found her, and Jean is on the case. She's now eighty years old.

Getting older isn't scary. It's life.

PUTTING IT ALL TOGETHER

Now it's time for you to design a plan for getting in touch with your feelings about growing older, about how you feel about your parents and your siblings growing older as well. Light up those seven candles, our seven guiding principles, to create a plan that is perfect for you.

1. *Create time* to think about what issues your parents are facing and which ones you have addressed for yourself.
2. *Reflect* on your feelings about getting older and how to combat ageism in both your life and society.
3. *Practice patience* with your Super Seniors and siblings.
4. *Research* and create a file about issues, necessary services, and helpful data that might be crucial to the Super Senior in your life.
5. *Find role models* who have navigated the often tricky waters of being older.
6. *Write down* your Childhoods, and write down something specific about each item your parents give you.
7. *Get together* with a friend and compare notes about the seniors in your lives. Get a humor fix. Get together with a Super Senior or two. Find yourself a senior pen pal.

TO-DO LIST

Here is a menu of ideas for you to choose from. Be sure to add your own ideas for getting in closer touch with your parents and improving communication with your siblings.

- Start a list of material gifts you might want your children to have.
- Send your sister or brother an e-mail or a card.
- Include a Super Senior at your next family dinner.
- Confront ageism when you hear it or see it. Boycott products and companies that are insensitive to seniors.
- Imagine your parents' living conditions and challenges, and meditate on how you would feel in the same situation.
- Get your folks a geriatric assessment.

- In a meditation, reflect on how quickly our lives pass. Create quick one or two word scenarios for each of the following: the baby, the young child, the teenager, the adult, the adult with grown children, the Super Senior.
- Take a tape recorder with you on your next visit to your parents, and ask them to talk about their parents.
- Bring a family tree and ask them to help you fill it out.
- Get a copy of the *New York Times* for the date and year your parents were born or married. Ask your parents to tell you how they met.

KATE'S PLAN

It's easy for me to feel burdened because my mother is living with me. It's easy to lose sight of what a gift having her in my daily life truly is, for both me and my kids. I need to reaffirm that joy on a daily basis and use it to fend off despair, anger, and feelings of being trapped. I need regular humor fixes. In order not to harbor resentment, I need to express clearly to my brothers how I feel about being the principal caregiver of my mother. I need to practice sympathetic alignment. I need to be conscious of ageism in myself, my children, and the media.

So my plan is to:

- Write a letter to each of my brothers expressing my thoughts and emotions about our mother.

- Encourage my mother to tell me Childhoods so I can record them in my journal.
- Confide in my mother and be honest with her about my feelings.
- Invite my mother's friends up to visit my mother more often.
- Take yoga class with my mother once a week.

BUFFY'S PLAN

My parents moved into an apartment almost two years ago. Simplifying their lives did not come easily. My brother, Topper, and my sister-in-law, Alison, live very near my folks, and without them, my parents could never have managed the move. My parents did not want to throw anything away, so I told Topper to send me the stuff. He sent eight large boxes from my parents' house! They pretty much take up the entire garage. Some of the items are gifts to me, but most of them are my parents' treasures — belongings collected over a lifetime together that would not fit into their new apartment. They could not bear to throw them away or give them away to strangers. They were overwhelmed by the move and unable to decide how to divvy up their things. In the end, it was easier to send them all to me. I need to go through those boxes with love and an open heart.

My sister and my brother and I are very close, but lately I think we spend too much time talking about our parents and not enough time talking about our own lives. My father suffers from restless leg syndrome, and I need to find out what I can about it so I can help him better manage this disability. Too often, I am impatient with my parents' concerns and aggravated and saddened by their many trips to the doctor, who seems in many ways to be their new best friend.

So my plan looks like this:

- Go through the boxes in the garage and write down as much as I can remember about what's inside. If I can't recall anything, I will call Mom, and we will figure it out together. I will choose certain pieces to display.

- Go on the Internet, research restless leg syndrome, and send my father a packet of information he can discuss with his doctor.
- Send regular e-mails and call my siblings. Focus on what is important in their lives.
- Spend time sorting through the old photographs that I took from my parents the last time I saw them. Perhaps I will ask Daisy to help me scan them onto a DVD and make copies for everyone.
- Meditate deeply on the nature of patience and, before speaking to my parents, consciously prepare myself by summoning guiding words to remind me to be patient, loving, and sympathetic.

Now that you have spent some quality time thinking about getting older and taking concrete steps to help yourself and the Super Seniors in your life meet the challenges of growing older, let's explore how you will manage parenting nearly adult children. Pretty rough going, isn't it? Don't be afraid to turn the page.

Will My Kids Ever Leave the Nest?

Nudging your offspring into the world

Dear Buffy: Aaron and Luke were not especially outgoing. Baby brother Noah, on the other hand, has many friends, and they are all very important to him. Suddenly, my house is overrun with teenagers. They are perfectly respectable-looking kids but I find myself not trusting them, wanting to kick them out. I feel like those angry grown-ups I knew when I was a teenager. You know those bigoted types muttering: "Long-haired pot-smoking hippies." Last night I counted nine cars. Nine cars in my driveway! Help! Love, Kate

Dear Kate: Both of my kids are very social, so I know exactly what you are going through. It's hard. There were times when our driveway was so full of cars, they were backed up down the street. Neighbors were calling and complaining because they couldn't get out of their own driveways. I remember one particular time right after the pool house was finished — kids were here 24/7. Christmas Eve the doorbell rang, and I clenched my teeth as I went to the door thinking, "Can't we just have a family Christmas Eve?" It was a bunch of Jesse's friends with a present for me. They refused to come in, but thrust a bottle of wine into my hand and thanked me for letting them spend time in the pool house. I almost cried. I know it sounds crazy, but there are days when I kind of miss it. Love, Buffy

BOOMERANG BABIES

Media critic and educator Neil Postman once said that childhood is a modern invention. As recently as the Depression, kids were out in the world, making their own way and fending for themselves, in their mid- to late teens. For today's children, childhood has been extended into the midtwenties and sometimes even into the thirties. Many kids sail out into the world, try to make their way for a few months or years, then—for one reason or another, whether it's money, bad luck, divorce, or emotional trauma—back home they sail. They are "boomerang babies."

Boomerang babies can exercise a negative influence, financially and psychically, on the second half of your life. But you can be aware of this and work to make the trajectory smooth and one way. If it isn't, take a deep breath. Sometimes your kids will need a little bit of help getting out on their own—emotional support and well, yes, sometimes, financial support. Have you thought about how hard it would be to buy a house in today's real estate market if you were just starting out?

Believe it or not, colleges are now offering courses to the parents of incoming freshmen, advising them about how to let go. Letting go seems to be difficult for us baby boomers. Letting go is about love, but it is also about control. We've taken our roles as parental coaches very seriously. It started before our children were born. Everything had to be perfect. Everything had to be the best. Everything had to be exhaustively researched. Everything had to be in precise alignment so that little Justin or Kaitlin could get into the best nursery school and the best grade school and the best middle school and the best high school and the best college and the best, best, best. Of course, we wanted them to get good grades and succeed and feel good about themselves so we could feel good about ourselves. We often went the extra mile to make sure that happened. We took over and completed their science projects for them. We took extreme, extravagant, and sometimes perhaps close-to-unethical measures to make sure they were properly prepared for whatever came their way. Some of us even went all the way and took our kids out of school to educate them at home so we could better control their learning experiences and social interactions. Exerting control became the habit of our middle years. Relaxing that control requires mindfulness.

Don't Tell Me What to Do, Just Send Me Money: The Essential Parents' Guide to the College Years by Helen E. Johnson and Christine Schelhas-Miller (St. Martin's). Witty, practical tips about how to weather your kid's first year out of the nest.

Ambition has played a part in our parental behavior, absolutely, but so has fear. How many of us have ruled out some new experience for our kids because we were simply too afraid to let them try? How many of us realize how dramatically we were affected by the national campaign in the 1980s that placed pictures of missing children on milk cartons and ran during our formative parental years, causing us to exercise a nearly paranoid vigilance over our little ones? Never mind that no one ever really made it clear to us that most of those "missing" milk carton kids had been taken, not by strangers, but by a disgruntled parent in an acrimonious custody dispute. Fear had been planted, and once fear is planted it takes root and grows, wrapping its tendrils around our consciousness and our unconscious, informing our behavior and decisions. To this day, many of us still keep our kids in protective bubbles.

But keeping our kids in a bubble hasn't lessened our fears any, has it? The bubble is a fantasy. It's time to come to terms with our fears and let them go. Haven't we dragged our fears around with us, from playground to schoolroom to ball field, long enough? Do we have to drag them all the way to the college dorm and beyond?

Letting go of fear and letting go of absolute control over our children are two things we must do if we want them to be successful adults and if we want to have a successful second half.

It may be several years before your kids are ready to take their first steps outside the nest, steps that are as exhilarating as they are terrifying. Or maybe you're ready for them to fly, but they keep finding themselves back in the good old nest. Either way, there are specific ways you can prepare yourself for these challenges. And what you learn, practice, and demonstrate will help prepare you for the day they hop off the edge and fly into the world on their sturdy fledgling wings.

Now it's time to use our seven strategies to shed light on specific ways you can begin to let go of your teen or college-age child. As you set about devising your plan for letting go, keep your personal challenges in mind.

CREATE TIME

The time you spend now with your teens can be important preparation for letting go. As you start to plan the second half of your life, get into the habit of talking about it in front of your teens. It's not necessary to make them feel as if you are eager to be rid of them so you can start in on the rest of your life, just don't make a state secret of it. Make it clear that the second half of your life is something you are thinking about and very much looking forward to, that you have worked hard for it and deserve it, much as they are looking forward to their own high school or college graduation. Get them used to thinking about your future as an adventure that is very much on par with theirs. Talking about it in front of your teens, perhaps the toughest audience there is, will make your plans more real. Saying it aloud is nearly as important as writing it down. (And, remember, writing things down helps make them happen.)

Recognizing and sharing the similarities between your life and that of your teens is a mature form of what early-childhood educators term "parallel play"—playing alongside your young adult as you cultivate, separately, your age-appropriate plans. Here are a few suggestions for parallel play:

- You are looking for a new part of the country in which to live. They are looking for a new part of the country in which they might want to study.
- You are looking for ways to prepare for a time when you won't be devoting 60 percent of your waking time to working. They are looking for ways to prepare for a time when they won't be spending 60 percent of their time in high school.
- You are researching a midcareer change; they are researching colleges and careers.
- You are both in transition mode and full of ideas, questions, and concerns. Share them with each other.

REFLECT

Fear exerts a potent force in our daily lives. It can hobble you just as it can hobble your child. Spend some time, in quiet thought or meditation, reflecting on your fears for your child. Try to imagine your fears as flat stones. Some of the stones are white, and some are blood red. Make two piles. Let the white stones be fears you can diffuse, fears you know are just not plausible. Make the red stones the fears that you just can't push away.

Here's our list of piping-hot red stones: Do any of them set you off? I am afraid my child will:

- Do lots of drugs or drink and become an addict of some kind.
- Do badly in school/not finish high school/opt out of college.
- Hang out with "bad" kids or get involved in abusive relationships.
- Drive recklessly while under the influence.
- Get into trouble with the principal/police/somebody else's parents.
- Become anorexic/bulimic.
- Get kidnapped.
- Drop out of college and flush my investment down the toilet.
- Lose him- or herself on the Internet and meet strangers at fast-food restaurants.
- Become permanently hypnotized by violent video games.
- Get knocked up or knock someone up.

Have you come up with a list of red stones of your own, or were you sufficiently horrified by our list? In either case, now that you've gotten it out of your system, try recasting the negative thoughts to make them more manageable. Turn those red stones into white stones. We'll do this by approaching them positively. At the same time, start to assess how you can manage your emotions. Negative emotions can run around in a family a little like a stomach virus. Pretty soon everyone is picking up on your anxiety and everyone is anxious. Calm down. Breathe. That's better. Take a teen breather.

To get you started, we'll recast one of Buffy's red stones. Her daughter, Daisy, has lots of friends, some of whom might lead her astray. It is necessary for Buffy to take a deep breath now and then and remember that she trusts Daisy. Her daughter has good judgment and Buffy's occasional fear that something could go wrong has nothing to do with Daisy. It is Buffy's own shortcoming. Buffy cannot expect Daisy to make changes in her behavior if nothing is wrong. It is Buffy who must make changes in her behavior. Look within.

See? It's not magic. It's simply a way to act on and redirect your fears rather than letting them prey on you. Apply this transformative exercise to all of your potential panic attacks. It will give you an opportunity to express your fears openly and then change how *you* feel and act.

The Family Table

Here's an exercise that will provide you and your family with a forum in which to express your thoughts and fears. You can meet at any table—the kitchen table, the living room coffee table, the dining room table, even a picnic table out on the deck or patio. Or you can meet anywhere the members of your family are comfortable gathering. Declare this spot the place where family meetings will convene when necessary.

Call Family Tables with enough regularity that they become a natural part of the rhythm of family life. Call them to discuss the reassignment of household chores, the settlement of a family dispute, a crisis, any major changes in the economic picture (such as a new job, a lost job, a cut in salary, or a home improvement) that might necessitate rebudgeting, or a fear you have been struggling with. Try to let your family know in advance that a family meeting is in the offing and what the agenda will be. That way you and your kids will have time to think about it in advance. Schedule a time for the meeting, and let everyone know that attendance is mandatory.

Before the meeting, rehearse in your mind what might transpire. You might want to do a meditative exercise. Visualize yourself sitting at a family meeting. Put the topic out there and discuss exactly how you feel about the issue. You might even let this visualized discussion shape the agenda. Take care that the feelings you bring to the table are honest, loving, and totally without acrimony or hostility, but also charge yourself with expressing clearly and directly everything you want to say. When the meeting takes place, you might be surprised to find that it runs smoothly, as if your mate and children had themselves participated in your meditation rehearsal.

PRACTICE PATIENCE

Hey, you don't need us to tell you this: teens tax patience. Just as we are often overwhelmed by our jobs, our family responsibilities, the sense that our dreams may have gotten away from us, so is a teenager overwhelmed by the demands made on him or her by family, friends, school, and society. As adults, we have more and better skills for dealing with change, unhappiness, and setbacks. Teens are learning to find their way and are just beginning to develop their coping skills and mechanisms. Sometimes their behavior can push us to lose our patience if not our minds.

For instance, teens are not generally known for volunteering to do jobs around the house, and it's all too easy for us to give up the struggle of getting them to help and, instead, do those tasks ourselves, exhausted, angry, martyred. After all, no one likes a lazy lump, but nags are even less lovable. Also teens are not generally rays of sunshine. And so we pamper our teens in an effort to jolly them along. What we wouldn't do for a smile or a kind word! Don't get caught up in this cycle. Don't spend excessive funds, stand on your head, or wait on them hand and foot to get them to smile for you. They ain't in a stroller no more. By the same token, a teenage child demands and deserves at least as much patience as a toddler.

In order to practice patience successfully, you must set reasonable goals. What goals do you have for your children? When they were lying in their cribs peacefully sleeping, and you stood over them in hushed adoration, what grand and glorious goals were you imagining for them? What grand and glorious goals are you imagining now? Take those goals and, one by one, flick them out the window. They are *your* goals, not theirs. Like you, your children are entitled to set their own goals, to dream their own dreams. If you long in your heart for your child to go to Harvard and practice law, well then you need to look into going to Harvard yourself and studying law in the second half of your life. But don't force your child to live your dream; don't live your life through your child. Figure out ways to help your children realize their own goals and dreams.

It may be that your child is not goal oriented. Adolescence is a bit of a quagmire. It's hard to indulge your dreams when you're bogged down in the mire, just as it is hard for you to do so when you are bogged down in work. It's important to remind a teen in such a state that life will not always be that way, that life does not begin or end with high school. High school is not, as many teens might think, a seething pit of hellfire or a perpetual party. High school is a platform, a crucial way station, to be used to carefully prepare and formulate not just goals and dreams, but also work habits, that will set the tone and tenor of their lives.

To help perfect your patience, here are some positive everyday actions you can take with your teens.

- *Charge them with making their own decisions.* Without second-guessing or micromanaging their decisions, talk to your teens about their decisions while they are still making them. Let your teens suggest a curfew and then discuss whether it is appropriate or not.
- *Teach independence.* If, out of habit, they come to you to ask you what they should do, try to gently turn the question back to them, nudge them to find their own way. If you feel they are making an inappropriate decision, talk about how you feel about it rather than criticizing their decision. Let them take the lead about their plans after high school. If college is part of their dreams, let them come to you, and then by all means offer to help, but let them take that first step.
- *Applaud your kid.* When your child gets his social security card, driver's permit, driver's license, first job, class ring; when your child raises a grade of 80 to 82; when your child shows courtesy or consideration for a peer; when your child shares a thought or says something that you think is really wise or profound—celebrate it and sing his praises.

Kate Says You Are Only as Happy as Your Unhappiest Child — Not!

I sometimes think I have had more than my share of troubled children. I have agonized about them for hours with therapists and psychiatric social workers. I have asked myself what I have done wrong. What I could have done differently or better. In my darkest hours, I have actually entertained the thought that my husband and I are ill matched genetically, that our DNA combination makes for "defective" offspring. That sort of thinking has led me, on occasion, to want to dismantle my marriage, disband the family, and scatter us all to the four winds, on the theory that we bring out the worst in each other and that we might be better off apart.

But with the help of meditation, friends, and a good therapist, I have revised my thinking and now believe that it is only by standing strong together as a family that we will get through the rough times. Bipolar, manic-depressive, obsessive-compulsive disorder, attention-deficit disorder, attention-deficit and hyperactivity disorder are scary terms that can paralyze any person, let alone a mother. These are clinical terms for people with different behaviors and different types of brain chemistries. Some people are blessed with a balanced biochemical makeup and live happy lives naturally, and some people need help, in whatever form help might take, to find the right biochemical balance. But I do believe that some of these folks can, under constructive, loving, less panicked circumstances, not only live, but also live happily ever after. I also believe that their parents can live happily ever after.

Some of the techniques you have learned for practicing patience can be very helpful in loving a teen who may be struggling.

- *Practice deep breathing and don't panic.* Help your child do the same. If your child is prone to anxiety attacks, teach him how to breathe deeply and mindfully. See if you can help your now grown child to unclench his jaw, shoulders, and fists and rid his body of toxins and fears.
- *Beam megawatt smiles.* Celebrate even the most minor accomplishment, improvement, or milestone.

Think you've got it bad? Read these firsthand experiences of what it is to grapple, either directly or through your kids, with bipolar syndrome.

An Unquiet Mind: A Memoir of Moods and Madness by Kay Redfield Jamison (Knopf). A psychiatrist's account of her own descent into bipolar madness.

Acquainted with the Night: A Parent's Quest to Understand Depression and Bipolar Disorder in His Children by Paul Raeburn (Broadway Books). You think you've got it bad? This is one father's grueling account of coping with two children who are bipolar.

- *Join support groups.* Learn from other people who have been there how best to cope.
- *Acknowledge and admit that there is a problem.* Then, as a family, you can address it.
- *Meditate.* Meditate on the subject of your troubled child and see if you can find answers.
- *Provide your child with structure.* If she is lost and wallowing in anxiety and misery, get her onto some sort of schedule. Make clear your expectations and hold her to them.
- *Make little deals that you know are easy for your child to meet.* Don't set him up for failure. All things are possible, but manage your expectations.
- *Examine your child's diet and sleep habits.* See if these might be the source of her trouble.
- *Bombard your child with love.* Whatever toxic rays they might emit, resist giving off toxic rays in return. Love is the answer.
- *Ask yourself who the child is.* Is it possible that you are behaving more like a child than your own child? Or perhaps getting down to his level out of fear and frustration? Fear and frustration can actually make us behave childishly—pitching fits, weeping, pouting, throwing out unrealistic ultimatums. Meditate or take a Breather before you talk with your child.
- *Their fate is in their own hands.* When your children were little, you were inseparable. They rode on your body, their moods and experiences were your moods and experiences, their accomplishments were your accomplishments. Now your children are heading toward adulthood. Their lives are their own. You cannot let them—their ups and downs, happiness or unhappiness, victories or defeats—determine how you feel.

When Teen Blues Are More Than a Phase

Being sullen is typical teen behavior, but if you suspect that you have a seriously depressed teen on your hands, keep an eye out for these signs. There are so many different ways depression can manifest itself in an adolescent that it is important to be familiar with as many of the signs as you can and to pay attention to whether they are fleeting, recurring, or last for a prolonged period of weeks, rather than days.

- Dropping grades
- Loss of old friends; no new friends to take their place
- Doesn't laugh or smile, even around friends; inability to find pleasure in activities he used to love
- Sadness, excessive crying, feelings of hopelessness. Nothing seems worth the effort.
- Poor concentration, low energy, persistent boredom
- Mood swings, irritability, hypersensitivity to criticism, indecisiveness, low self-esteem
- Physical changes: weight loss or gain, poor skin, self-injury, frequent illness
- Drug or alcohol use
- Talk or threats of death or suicide

Be aware that plenty of typical teens are bound to show *some* of these signs. And while all of these signs should be taken seriously, if your teen shows even one of the last three listed, you need to take action — seek professional help immediately. Consider whether your teen has experienced any of the following recently:

- Has there been a divorce or some other problem within the family? Job loss? Illness?
- Does depression run in your family? Think about yourself, your partner, your parents. It is time to address this.
- Has your teen recently broken up with a girlfriend or boyfriend?
- Has your teen lost a job opportunity he was counting on, a role in the school play, a pet?
- Has your teen just become sexually active or experienced an unwanted pregnancy?
- Does your teen have bad eating habits? Too much sugar and junk foods can cause mood swings and depression.

- Is your teen being bullied at school because of his sexual orientation or for any other reason?
- Does your teen feel responsible for something bad that has happened to the family or to one of his friends? Are there legal ramifications?

Yes, many teens will experience some of these events and manage to find ways to get through them and keep their equilibrium, but other teens will not have the necessary coping skills and may lose their way. You can be their compass.

Earlier in the book, we talked about active listening. This is a crucial skill when parenting teens. Whether you think your teen is depressed or just mired down in normal adolescent angst, do the following:

- If the situation is urgent, get professional help immediately—whether that be medical, legal, or some form of counseling.
- Respond with love and support. (And remember, calling in the professionals doesn't mean you get to bow out.)
- Encourage your teen to talk to you, to trust that there will be no punishment for what she is confiding in you.
- Don't try to talk him out of his feelings.
- Let her talk. You listen.
- Spend time with him doing what *he* wants—going to a movie, listening to his music in the car. Stop what you are doing when he wants to talk or sits in the same room with you.

There are many ways you can help your teen. Here are some of them:

- Encourage your teen to be more physically active.
- Encourage your teen to volunteer or tutor a younger child.
- Encourage your teen to find his artistic voice; maybe it will be in writing, music, art, dance, photography.
- Talk to your doctor, therapist, friends, or clergyperson.
- Consider group therapy or family therapy.
- Research medication or nonpharmaceutical methods of address.

RESEARCH

Reading about the teen years, that delicate, exciting, and torturous time of life known as adolescence, will help you maintain your patience. And thanks to the power of literature, you will feel less alone. Your feelings and your teen's feeling are normal and natural. Reading about how others navigated this part of the journey will help you design your actions and reactions. Some books that come to mind are Meg Rosoff's *How I Live Now*, Sharon Creech's *Walk Two Moons*, and J. D. Salinger's *The Catcher in the Rye*. When your child shares her book list at the start of the semester, you might find some good titles to add to your own reading list. These books will succeed, possibly even better than how-to tomes, in shedding light on the teen years, taking you back to that time, and spurring your reflexes for sympathetic alignment.

FIND ROLE MODELS

It can be hard to parent a bright, reasonably well-adjusted child. But it takes a special kind of courage to parent a child in turmoil. By his own choice, Libby's son went away to college two years earlier than his peers. He was a bright boy, underchallenged and disenchanted with high school. Libby was concerned that he lacked the emotional maturity for college, but she didn't want to risk his dropping out of high school, so she consented to early admission.

Not long into the fall semester of his freshman year, Libby and her husband got a call from the school. Their son was in a nearby emergency room ward. He had, according to his roommate and the residence adviser, snapped. The psychiatric social worker called it a nervous breakdown. Possibly a psychotic break. Libby will never forget the ride she and her husband took to retrieve their son. She hyperventilated. She wept. She argued with herself. She argued with her husband. She blamed him. She blamed herself. She second-guessed every single decision she had ever made that concerned the rearing of her son. And, mostly, she was filled

www.focusas.com
This terrific Web site educates about adolescent depression and lists local resources.

www.borntoexplore.org
A lighter, enlightening look at ADD and ADHD; includes resources and references.

www.kidshealth.org
A comprehensive collection of health facts, advice, and information for parents, kids, and teens.

www.parentingteens.com
Helpful information for parents dealing with troubled teens.

www.teenlink.umn.edu
A variety of resources addressing issues such as eating disorders, sexuality, substance abuse, health, communication, and more.

www.sexetc.org
Sex etc. is a site written by teens for teens and is sponsored by the Network for Family Life Education at Rutgers University. It provides peer-to-peer counseling and important information on sex education, birth control, pregnancy issues, STDs, and more. Visit and you might find out what's on your teen's mind.

with dread. Libby is herself a psychologist, but she dreaded what she expected would be hours and weeks and months of dealing with the mental health establishment and of coping with her son's illness.

Libby's son stayed in the facility long enough to get diagnosed, stabilized, and on a regimen of medication, while Libby stayed in a nearby economy motel. Visiting hours were limited, so Libby kept to her room much of the day. But she didn't just sit around feeling sorry for herself. She got on the phone. She called her friends and wept. Then she pulled herself together and called her old college teachers, who were psychologists and psychiatrists. She discussed her son's situation, his symptoms, his diagnosis and medication. She reread the books she had read in college and found new ones. After a few days, her son was discharged.

It was a long, silent car ride home. The boy sitting beside her was not the sunny, chatty, intellectually engaged, outgoing boy she had sent out into the world. He was pale, thin, silent, withdrawn, utterly lacking in confidence, and terrified. Rather than panic or resign herself to the situation, Libby participated in the healing process. She found him a local psychiatrist to monitor the medication and facilitate therapy. She found him a therapy group. Her husband invited their son to work in his print shop. Bit by bit, he reentered the world. He took trips to visit friends. He signed up for just a few courses. She didn't push, prod, or interfere. She let him find his own way. She stopped herself from acting as if this illness were happening to her. And through it all, she never lost her sense of humor.

Then one day, her boy — the sunny, smart, confident, outgoing boy — returned. She didn't make a big deal of it. She didn't say, "Oh, thank God, you're back." She simply reengaged in their old habits of conversation and rejoiced to her husband, his therapist, her friends, at his safe return. While he's not back out on his own yet, they both look forward to the day he will be.

WRITE IT DOWN

In chapter 6, we talked about Childhoods (favorite childhood stories), their importance in our lives, and their power to sustain us. We have collected a lot of stuff—a lot of junk, a lot of fairly nice things, and a lot of heir-looms and memories. Share these memories, whether they are simply in your head or connected to a material object, like a picture, a piece of jewelry, a cake stand, or an article of clothing. Capture them. Tell them. Record them. Honor them. This is part of the important work of being an elder in a family. It is your duty to keep the family saga vital and alive. Find inventive ways to share these stories.

Unpuzzling Your Past: The Best-Selling Basic Guide to Genealogy by Emily Ann Croom (Betterway). A first-rate guide, enormously useful for adult and kid, computer maven and Luddite alike, to getting started tracing your family roots.

- Have your children interview you.
- Edit family photographs as a family.
- Edit family videos into a single seamless DVD. Let's face it, you can surely use the help of a YP (young person) here.
- Create e-mail trees—customized e-mail distribution lists including family members outside the home. If your teens see you reaching out to your family, they may very well do the same when they are older.
- Help your children design a special way to exhibit their memories.
- Write down five ideas, values you'd like to think your children have inherited from you. Share them with your kids.
- Take a few moments to write about your teen in your journal. You are likely experiencing some very complex emotions, and writing them down can help you sort things out and help you choose your words carefully so you won't wound a vulnerable or confused teen.

It can be useful to write notes to your teen. Buffy does this a lot. Sometimes it is just a sticky note left on a door to remind them to turn out the lights and lock the doors when they get home late. In doing so, a couple of mornings of being irritated because the lights were left on all night were handled with a minimum of aggravation. Buffy just assumes you have to tell a teenager everything more than once. She also leaves notes or sends e-mails about any upcoming projects her kids might want help on or any family activities she wants them to participate in. She also leaves them little love notes—on their bedroom doors, on the bathroom mirror.

Uncommon Sense for Parents with Teenagers by Michael Riera (Celestial Arts). A high school counselor makes sense of teen turbulence while managing to avoid making the parent feel guilty for not being a better parent.

GET TOGETHER

Get together with your friends and compare notes on your lives with teens. For instance, have they found a way of successfully dealing with curfews that might work for you?

Don't forget to get your laugh fix. Get together with your teen in an activity that enables you to let down your guard and drop your roles as parent and child. Try to notice how frequently you have to suppress the parent in you during your time together. Try to notice how frequently your child mommy-izes you. See if you can find a comfortable way to interact free of the trappings of your family roles. Discover how immensely liberating and enjoyable it can be. Start getting in the habit of interacting this way. It can be as simple as going to a coffeehouse together. It might be listening to a favorite CD.

Buffy Shares More Than a Kodak Moment

Last spring, my daughter said we were invited to her friend Lauren's house, with the other parents, to see all the girls and all their dates dressed for the prom. It was an unusual invitation. My husband and I do not know Lauren's parents very well, although I know the mother is quite close to many of the other moms. I had a fleeting moment of not wanting to go. I thought: I don't know these other parents well enough to share this night with them. Can't Phil just pick you up here, we'll take a couple of pictures, and off you'll go? But when Daisy patiently explained that her friends wanted to be together, get dressed together, come down the stairs together, and have a million pictures taken together before piling into the longest limo I had ever seen, I said, of course, we wouldn't miss it. It was a special night, and I'm glad we didn't miss it. Parents sharing the milestone of senior prom together, sharing recent horror stories of college rejections and joyful ones of college acceptances, was intimate and lovely. Suddenly we all realized the support we were giving each other as we shared a bit of sadness over the emptying nest. As the limo finally pulled out after Peter offered his credit card to settle a mix-up in the billing, we said our good-byes and drove home happy. There are many opportunities to be with your kids. Don't pass them up as I nearly did because of shyness or a need to keep the experience to yourself.

PUTTING IT ALL TOGETHER

Now it's time to design your program for letting go. Review the chapter, and remember:

1. *Create time* to practice parallel play with your older child.
2. *Reflect* on your fears for your teens and act to diffuse them.
3. *Practice patience* with your teens. Let them make their own decisions, and work to separate your goals from theirs.
4. *Research* the books that your teens are reading and read them to help you remember what it was like to live the daunting life of an adolescent. Doing so will help you practice sympathetic alignment.
5. *Find role models* of parents who have successfully let go or coped with difficult teens.
6. *Write down,* and share with your teens, childhood stories, albums, DVDs, e-mail trees, and shadow boxes. Write them notes to celebrate their accomplishments, to solve a problem that has arisen, or to help get them get organized without actually doing the organizing for them.
7. *Get together* with a friend to compare notes on teens and share a laugh or two. Get together with your teen in an activity that allows you both to drop your roles as parent and child.

You will be spending a lot of time together if you have high school juniors or seniors in your house who are in the process of choosing and applying to colleges. And it can be a difficult, highly charged time. (Unless you have a son like Kate's Luke, who has taken on this process with a calmness and capability that belies his age.)

www.collegeconfidential.com
College Confidential demystifies the college admissions process and helps parents and students make important decisions and understand what happens behind the scenes.

www.guideforparents.com
A guide for parents seeking advice and tips on how to prepare and send their children to college.

TO-DO LIST

Select at least three suggestions from the to-do list below, or put together three of your own, and prepare to let go.

- Practice some form of parallel play.
- Talk to your therapist about letting go.
- In your journal, write down ten sources of potential panic attacks, and diffuse at least three of them.
- Start a Family Table.
- Post a chore chart.
- Work out a system of bartering; for example, a month of chores for tickets to a rock concert.
- Take your teen to your workplace.
- Get your teen to open a bank account.
- Write a letter to your teen about some incident that upset you that you want him to understand from your perspective.
- Get your teen to plan a trip.
- Praise your teen.

- Practice deep breathing with your teen.
- Take a yoga class with your teen.
- Read some young adult books or books that your teen is reading.
- Share Childhoods.
- Edit family videos and scrapbooks with your teen.
- Help your teen to create a memory shadow box.
- Create a family e-mail tree.
- Work with your teen to bust clutter from her room.
- Suggest that your teen donate old toys, videos, and clothes to a center for homeless teens.
- Join a family support group.

KATE'S PLAN

I have so many challenges, it's hard to know where to start. For years, I have picked up after my three boys without requiring them to pick up after themselves, mostly because I'm fussy about housekeeping, plus I don't want to be a nag. My husband and I never developed a system of chore-based allowances, so it's sometimes difficult to hold the boys to either a weekly budget or a chore schedule. I don't always share the big emotional or crucial events in my life with my sons, so when I'm stressed out they don't understand why. My eldest son had poor preparation for going out into the world and, as a result, he's twenty-five, still finishing college, and I am still supporting him. I think that's enough for now, don't you?

My plan looks like this:

- Discuss my teens regularly in my therapy sessions.
- Establish a more formalized system for household chores.
- Practice parallel play with my two sons who are still at home.
- Establish a Family Table.
- Encourage the two sons still at home to open their own bank accounts.
- Put the twenty-five-year-old on a stricter budget.
- Make sure the sons still at home get part-time jobs before they graduate from high school.
- Make sure the twenty-five-year-old gets a part-time job to help support himself at college.

BUFFY'S PLAN

I don't know about you, but whenever I reflect on what kind of parent I have been, I want to start over from the very beginning because *now* I really know something. Then again, maybe I don't. My goal is to do everything better and have more patience, but for now I will settle for four things:

1. Better prepare my kids to live on a budget by designing a budget together that we both can live with. Only advance money in emergencies.
2. Encourage but do not take the lead in their decisions (even if I am paying).
3. Encourage them to integrate the habit of exercise into their lives now.
4. Reflect on my interaction, tone of voice, body language, and so on, when talking with my kids.

So my plan is:

- Allow my daughter and my son to take the lead in their college and graduate school applications. Control my need to make schedules and calendars and to nag about same.
- Have more candid financial discussions with both children.
- Invite both of my kids to take yoga with Peter and me on Sunday mornings. (Remind myself to scoff at the idea that they need to join a gym.)
- Take a few deep breaths before jumping into an important conversation; meditate to control my own fears; confide in them some of my own transitional fears, concerns, and worries.
- Use the Family Table.

Between the nest and the workplace, you've been busy for decades, haven't you? So busy, in fact, that you may have been neglecting one of the most important components of a happy and healthy life: friendship.

How Long Have You and I Known Each Other?

Reinforcing friendships and forging new ones

> Dear Kate: Do you remember when we first met? It was the first day of school, the very first day. We were all running around signing up for class. I thought you were this wild hippie from Long Island. Love, Buffy
>
> Dear Buffy: Which I was, and I thought you were a bitchin' surfer girl from California. (I guess Maryland was close.) Everyone else at Sarah Lawrence looked like they were dressed for a funeral. You were in lime green and pink. I think you were wearing a muumuu, in fact. Like you were on your way to a luau. It was love at first sight. Love, Kate

OLD FRIENDS

Are you a good friend? That seems like an easy enough question to answer. As we look ahead to the second half of our lives, friends will become as vitally important to us as they were when we were seniors in high school. Look at the older folks you know. Aren't those with friends more connected to the world, happier, and more content than those who have few or no friends at all? Maintaining friendships takes effort, consistency, and a willingness to give without necessarily getting anything in return. It is crucial for us to take the time to be a good friend.

In this chapter, we will explore how and why we make and keep friends. Love and friendship are the lifeblood of our existence, yet many of us let our friendships take a backseat to family, career, and other time-sapping responsibilities. Now is the time to renew old friendships and forge new

Over the years, Kate and Buffy have shared a love of the following people, places, and things:

Mysteries

The beach

Strong white tea and Peek Freans

Days and nights together (without the husbands or kids), but sometimes with bats loose in the house

Black clothing

Tiny earrings

Doris Lessing's *The Golden Notebook*

Tough-talking dame movies like *Mildred Pierce*

Tearjerkers like *I'll Cry Tomorrow*

Sgt. Pepper's Lonely Hearts Club Band

The Diaries of Anaïs Nin

Malcolm Lowry's *Under the Volcano*

Anything ever written by Henry James

Overlapping pregnancies

Learning Attic Greek (well, almost)

Lost babies

Anything and anyone to do with Marcel Proust

Monty Python and labor pains

Suzy T.

Friendship rings

Endless e-mails

Dinner parties with friends and family

Scary road trips in Mexico with Gogo

ones. Every day, new research reveals the healthful and sustaining power, both spiritually and physically, of friendship. In this chapter you will learn how to reconnect to friendship and to appreciate its power.

Being a friend is as natural as breathing. Yet, as we have learned, breathing well isn't always easy or automatic, is it? In fact, it can be difficult. Likewise, being a good friend is not always easy.

What does it mean to be a friend? Here are some attributes that might help you begin to develop your own definition of friendship:

- Someone you've been with at key times in your life
- Someone you can talk to about anything
- Someone you can turn to for help and comfort
- Someone you can be yourself with
- Someone you share memories and private jokes with
- Someone you trust

Now, think about your performance as a friend. How do you rate as a friend? Without being hard on yourself, you may discover that you have been a little lax. Perhaps you have faded in and out of your friend's life. Perhaps you forgot to call her on her birthday. Perhaps you forgot to celebrate a certain milestone.

Do you ever feel competitive with some of your friends? Maybe a little envious of another friend's lifestyle or career? Acknowledge those feelings as human, then push them aside. In their place put loyalty, understanding, and love — the bedrock feelings shared by true close friends.

We have talked about close friends. Now, let your gaze expand further to include other friends, those with whom you like to spend time and do things, but whom you may not count among your closest friends. Imagine you are skimming flat stones across a pond. The pond is life, the stone is you, the ripples are your relationships. The ripples are subsets of your full range of friends. The closest and smallest circle is made up of your intimates, your compadres, your closest friends. The next set of ripples includes people who are important but not quite as vital to you as your close friends, and so on. Let's call these people "ripple friends."

Although Ripple Friends may require less of your time and attention, they are still crucial to the well-rounded individual you want to be. These people do not know you as well as your closest friends, so you might have to be on your best behavior. Communication with them might require a little more effort. They do not necessarily share a history with you so there are no private jokes—at least not yet—and there is no excusing your behavior. It may not be possible for you to let it all hang out around them. They do not have full knowledge of your accomplishments or your defeats. In a way, this can be a good thing. They have befriended you for who you are right now, at this moment in time. Old friendships may be on automatic pilot. New friendships can be fresher, more spontaneous, more relevant to the life you are leading now. Ripple Friends might be neighbors, coworkers, parents of your children's friends, members of your extended family, buddies at the gym, fellow carpoolers and commuters, acquaintances and colleagues from community service or charity work or church, friends of your parents or siblings, and fellow hobbyists.

Close friends tend to have the same values we do; they usually have similar goals, interests, and lifestyles. Ripple Friends, however, may be completely different from us. They may have diametrically opposed political views, different backgrounds, values, interests, strengths, and talents. Ripple Friends might be younger or older than we are. Younger Ripple Friends can be exciting and may draw us into unusual and life-enhancing activities. Ripple Friends might promote risk taking, in that they often expand and flex our sense of self and require us to try new things and talk about new and different ideas. And keep this in mind: older Ripple Friends provide an excellent hedge against creeping ageism and can be excellent role models.

Peter's magical musical tapes: Buffy's Arias, British Invasion, Ella, Frank, the Vanster (aka Van Morrison), David Gray, Country Heart, Nancy Griffith, The Boss, Damien Rice, The Jayhawks, and on and on, supplying the soundtrack of our lives for over thirty years

Studying comparative revolutions with Ronald Florence at Sarah Lawrence

Julius and John

Sentimental gifts

A cactus called Leonard Cohen

Harold Weiner

Almost anything purple

Santha Rama Rau and "perfect" Curtis Harnack

Lake George in October; a pressed sugar maple leaf

Miss Bittberg

Buffy's "Bette Davis Eyes"; Kate's Ethel Merman as candy striper imitation

That fateful trip to D.C. freshman year

Pick a friend from your own tea party and, together, compose a list of the loves you share.

Buffy's Remembrance of Friendships Past

My daughter is in the final stretch of her senior year in high school. She and her friends are already planning what they will do to celebrate their graduation. I tell her that after my high school graduation, a bunch of my friends, my sister, and I rented a house at Rehoboth Beach, Delaware, for a week. She asks me how many girls. I pause. I'm not sure. "Six," I finally say. And then I wonder if the number six popped into my head because it's just one of the many details of a day that was indelibly stamped in my memory.

We were all sitting in the living room of this beach house, talking, when the phone rang, scaring us half to death — the way a bunch of girls alone together in a house can get all keyed up without the slightest provocation. Who knows we're here? We stared at each other, our eyes wide. It's somebody's parents. Something has happened! Which one of us would be struck by the hand of fate? As it turned out, all of us, in a way.

The person on the phone was another friend of ours, the one girl who hadn't been able to join us. She was calling to tell us that Robert F. Kennedy had been shot in Los Angeles. We were devastated. Now I remember the date he died: June 6. I tell my daughter I can't remember what girls were there. I can't remember their names. But I do remember the date of RFK's assassination. My daughter's eyes are wide when I tell her this.

"What do you mean you can't remember?" she says. I see instantly that she is upset and not about my specific memory loss or about RFK. What upsets her is the idea that I have forgotten the names of girls who were once my very close friends. She finds the idea that she might one day forget her girlfriends — girls with whom she is so close, girls she loves so very much — extremely upsetting. She simply cannot see how it is possible to be so close to a group of girls and then thirty-five years later not be able to remember them. This makes her very sad.

As it happened, the next day I was going through old boxes in our garage (still finishing the work from chapter 4, locker cleaning), when I happened on *The Cupola*, my senior high school yearbook. Life is funny, isn't it? Synchronicity, I think they call it. Like my daughter, I had also gone to a small, all-girls school. Mine was in Washington, D.C. There were fifty-six girls in my graduating class. I flipped through the pages and, in no time, tracked down the six girls who had rented the beach house with me that June week in 1968.

When my daughter got home that afternoon, my yearbook was waiting on the dining room table for her. Triumphantly, I reeled off the names of the girls: Robin, Judy, two Susans, Pam, and Sharon! Elated, my daughter threw her arms around me and hugged me. Then she flipped through the yearbook until she found my picture and pointed, laughing. "Did you really look like that?" she asked, charmed and vastly amused at my teenage self. "Was your hair that blond, or did you get it colored?" I told her it was Summer Blonde by Clairol. Somehow or other, her moment of crisis got lost in a discussion of mid-twentieth-century beauty aids. Still, I think she believes she will never forget her high school friends, and I like to think that she is right.

Using our seven strategies, let's continue to explore friendship in all its manifestations. We'll also provide you with specific ways to nurture friendships during the second half of your life.

CREATE TIME

We are all busy. That's a given. Let's agree that we are all equally busy. If that's true, why don't we give friendship the time it deserves? Why do we let friendships lapse? Do we no longer love our friends? Are we angry with them? Has a friend perhaps hurt our feelings? Are we no longer living in the same area? Does the distance between us seem simply too great to stay in touch as we once did? It takes time to be a good friend.

When Buffy hears her mother, Middie, talk about an old friend she hasn't heard from in a long time, Buffy says, "Call your friend. Just pick up the phone and call." But Buffy can see by the expression on her mother's face that doing this is out of the question. Sometimes too much time has elapsed and making an effort to reconnect feels like a risky enterprise. When you are older, taking chances is daunting. Middie explains her reluctance this way. "What if," she says hesitantly, "I call and find out she's, you know, dead? What if she's there, but she can't remember me? What if she doesn't feel well enough to talk to me?"

These well-marshaled what-if scenarios render Buffy practically speechless. She summons her empathy. She says, "It is hard, Mom. Maybe too hard." And Buffy pauses. Middie is a very positive, strong woman, and if it is too hard for her, it is possible it will be too hard for Buffy when she is in her mideighties, unless she works at it every day.

It may be too hard for someone you know, but don't let it be too hard for you. Don't deprive yourself of the joy of friendship because you're unwilling to take the first step. Be proactive. Send an e-mail, mail a card, exchange a recipe. Sharing simple expressions of friendship, whether with someone you see all the time or someone you have lost touch with, will enhance your life spiritually and physically.

REFLECT

Reflect on your circle of friends. Spend some quiet time or practice a meditation. Then try this exercise.

The Tea Party

Visualize that you are giving a special tea party for your best friends. There is a big round table, and you have spread it with your best tablecloth. The tea is steeping in the pot. You have set the table with lovely china and bought special scones and clotted cream. A pitcher of fresh daffodils sits in the center of the table.

Now, ask yourself how many places you will set. Will it matter who sits next to whom? For starters, invite only close friends.

At Buffy's tea party there are, including herself, eight women: her sister Susan (whom she calls by her childhood nickname, Gogo); her two sisters-in-law, Donna and Alison; her friend Kate; her friend and business partner, Kathy; her former next-door neighbor, Patti; and her friend from childhood, Molly. These are women she speaks to and sees as often as she can. When she turned fifty, she used some frequent flyer miles and had her party in New York City, instead of Los Angeles where she lives, because almost all of these women live on the East Coast. These are the women she invited to her birthday, and these are the women at her tea party. These are the women she thinks to celebrate with. When she is sad or having a crisis, these are the women she needs to speak with.

Think about the people you have invited to your tea party. As your eyes move around the table, visualize their faces and glimpse the nature of your relationship with each and every one of them. Reflect on each friendship, its history, its dynamic, and how it has helped you to know yourself better. Think about how each friend helps you remember exactly who you really are: your essential self. These friends are a reflection of you: they represent your past, your present, as well as your future.

Then stop to consider whether there are any empty places at your table. Are there any long-lost friends who ought to be there? Now make the affair even larger to include your Ripple Friends. You might want to add another table for your Ripple Friends, or perhaps they are standing at a buffet of tea sandwiches, milling around and conducting a lively conversation among themselves, waiting for you to get up and spend time with them. Who is seated at your table, and who is standing at the buffet? Who are your close friends, and who are your Ripple Friends? Draw up a guest list, and review the roster of your friendships.

Things that can test a
friendship:
A wedding
A promotion
An illness
A careless word
Money not returned
Being out of contact
A husband or mate of
  whom we don't
  approve
Having babies
Raging hormotions
A confidence betrayed
Professional jealousy
Simultaneous stress

The Empty Place at Kate's Tea Party

The empty place at my table belongs to Justine. Now completely lost to me, she was once my best friend in the whole world. When we were very young, we shared a love of fantasy. When we got older, we explored together the world of boys and sex. We traveled to Europe when we were eighteen. It was a fabulous, reckless, madcap adventure: Thelma and Louise decades before they came to the big screen, minus the fatal car ride. We believed, during the time we were together, that we would always be friends, that our children would grow up, as we had grown up: together.

But that's not the way it happened. The dramas and demands of life drove us apart. We remained in touch intermittently, but just after the birth of my third son, I caused a major rupture. It was a single, simple, brutal, thoughtless act on my part that did it. Though she lived in California, she had been keeping track of my pregnancy, sharing with me its ups and

Justine is no longer in the phone book, so Kate will have to expend a little extra effort when she is ready to try to locate her old friend. These Web sites might help. Some sites, like www.bestpeople search.com and www.ussearch.com, are ones that private detectives, bail bonds-men, and professional searchers use as resources. Most require a fee, but when the time comes, for Kate it will be worth it.

www.friendster.com
www.classmates.com
www.reunion.com

downs by letter and by phone, the way friends love to do. She generally took the initiative, as I recall. Then Noah was born. Compared to my other two, it was an incredibly easy birth. My water broke at 10:30 p.m. during *L.A. Law* and by David Letterman's monologue at 11:45 p.m. I was holding him in my arms. I'm terrible with the phone, and afterward I let my husband make all the announcement calls from the hospital. He had no list — it was strictly seat of the pants — and he didn't know to call Justine.

A week or so later, Justine called me to find out how I was coming along. When I told her that Noah had already arrived, there was a long silence at the other end of the line. A continent stood between us, and yet I could feel the hurt welling up on her end. I ached for her, and because of the damage I knew I had done. I wanted to repair it, to apologize for leaving her out of this very important event. But I didn't have the courage to do it. And the longer I waited, the harder it was for me to even contemplate it. It was the last time I ever spoke to her, and that was more than fifteen years ago.

Not a week (not a day!) goes by when I don't think of Justine. I'm committing to tracking her down, apologizing, and reclaiming our friendship. I know it won't be easy, logistically or emotionally. But it's something I feel I need to do. Until I do, I have an empty place at my tea table and in my heart.

PRACTICE PATIENCE

Being a friend takes patience. "No kidding," you say! Seriously, being a friend requires a world of patience. In all of our relationships, we tend to have expectations about how each person should act, what should happen, and how we should feel. More often than not, these expectations are not met and we feel let down, disappointed, or angry. Managing our expectations can make our friendships more rewarding and less taxing. It can also make us more loving and more flexible. Do not confuse managing expectations with not expecting much from anyone. Managing expectations means that we must let go of our need for control and resist running ahead of the moment. We miss a great deal of life when we do this and, as a result, experience a lot of disappointments.

If you spend a few moments tallying up what your friend has to deal with in her life, you may be more understanding when she forgets your shopping date, is late returning your sweater, never offers to drive, and can't seem to find her wallet in the restaurant. It is easy to lose patience, but do you want to lose your friend or, worse, the love you feel toward your friend? Imagine what her challenges are, and be forgiving and supportive. Reflect love.

Being supportive and understanding does not mean that you become a doormat. A doormat never says anything directly, preferring instead to internalize her feelings, most notably her anger. Do not mistake being a good friend for being a doormat. What is more, do not be friends with anyone who treats you like a doormat. Buffy remembers when her mother would say how Buffy's friend, Becky, was not nice to her, that she took advantage of her. Buffy would argue and defend Becky, saying, "You don't understand how nice Becky is to me. You don't even know her!" Well, maybe, just maybe, her mother was right about Becky. Becky was Buffy's friend when it served her interest. She would forget to invite Buffy to sleepovers, renege on study dates, and often tried to exclude Buffy from the cafeteria table where all of their friends were sitting. It was hard for Buffy to admit that her mother was right, and it was hard for Buffy to admit that Becky wasn't a good friend. Just a convenient friend.

It is up to you to evaluate each of your friendships and determine which relationships offer you reflected love. Giving up on a relationship that is one sided is not giving up, it is growing up. And isn't it about time?

His Oldest Friend: The Story of an Unlikely Bond by Sonny Kleinfield (Times Books). A powerful account of the friendship between a poor Latino teen volunteer at a nursing home and a ninety-year-old resident and how they change each other's life.

Dear Kate: Freshman year was such a trip. Remember your roommate? So skinny and yet she was always eating. She used to pile the cafeteria plates up by her bed! There were heaps of dirty dishes in there. It wasn't until you moved to your own room that I realized you were actually neat. Love, Buffy

Dear Buffy: Not compared to you. You were the only one on our whole hall who cleaned her room. I remember you used to wet mop the floor. And no one was allowed in until it dried. It was like having a little mother living next door. Whenever I felt freaked out or homesick I'd come sit on your bed and you'd listen. Just listen. With interest. I was like a helium balloon and you were like gravity. You still are. Love, Kate

Dear Kate: I had forgotten about the mop. Love, Buffy

RESEARCH

By *research,* we usually mean reading about a topic to expand our knowledge. In this instance, though, we mean reading between the lines. Let's call it "intuitive reading." There are no books, but there are signs and symbols, and words spoken and unspoken. In your mind, revisit your tea party meditation. Go around the table of your close friends and go through your ripple friends as well, and consider whether one of them might currently be in need. Chances are, at any one time, one of your friends is going through a rocky period. Even if she doesn't say anything, you can sense it. Friends sense these things. It is intuitive reading.

How many times have we heard about a friend's misfortune and excused ourselves by saying, "Oh, gee, I didn't know that." Or, "Oh, if I had only known." Or else we admit that we knew something was wrong, but say, "I knew, but I didn't know what to say." Neither response is excusable or the appropriate behavior of a true friend. But at one time or another, we have all said these things. The next time you are doing some intuitive reading, go one step farther and take action. Be there for your friend.

Buffy's Confession
One of my daughter's friends suffered with anorexia for more than two years. I am not all that close to the mother. I'd consider her a Ripple Friend. We see each other regularly at school functions and when one of our

daughters goes to the other's house to visit. I saw this woman's face grow more and more lined and her demeanor turn more and more nervous and distracted with each pound her little girl lost. And still I said nothing. I wanted to. But, quite frankly, I was afraid to say the wrong thing. Secrecy and stigma surround anorexia. Even when I heard the young girl was in the hospital, I hesitated.

Now, two years later, my daughter's friend is better. And looking at her healthy body, her naturally rosy cheeks, I can easily summon up exactly what I should have said to her mother. Of course, it's never too late to be kind and supportive, but somehow I feel as if I missed my chance. My one consolation is that I have decided that I will never be that kind of coward again. The next time I see one of my close friends or Ripple Friends struggling, I will say something comforting and offer help. I will just say it. I chose this example; I might just as easily have chosen others.

Imagine that you are about to take a giant step and call a friend of yours (close or Ripple) who is having a problem. You want to call, but feel uncomfortable, not sure what to say or how to act. Take a few deep breaths and do the following:

- Listen to her talk about the problem. Express sympathy. Let her do most of the talking.
- Resist the temptation to say, "You'll be fine. This is nothing."
- Resist the temptation to say, "I know just how you feel." Or "I know someone who experienced the exact same thing." You really don't. Don't hijack her feelings.
- Keep your advice to a minimum unless you are specifically asked for it.
- Offer different kinds of comfort, such as taking a walk together, going to a movie, running errands for her.
- Remember, it is never too late to step in to help.

Some friendships find their most eloquent expression in letters. Check out the correspondence of some of these all-time great pen pals:

The Adams–Jefferson Letters, Lester J. Cappon, ed. (University of North Carolina Press).

Edith Wharton and Henry James: Letters 1900–1915, Lyall Harris Powers, ed. (Scribner).

The Letters of Vita Sackville-West to Virginia Woolf, Louise Desalvo and Mitchell Leaska, eds. (William Morrow).

www.postsecret.com

An ongoing community art project in which people anonymously mail in their secrets on a homemade postcard. The secrets are the art.

FIND ROLE MODELS

When Dania found out her friend Candy had cancer of the colon, she went to her supervisor and asked for a leave of absence. Dania had a big job and a career that was important to her, but she had only one best friend. Her boss, sensing that this key employee was in distress, told her to take a week, a month, as long as she needed. Dania's husband and kids told her they would muddle through in her absence. Dania packed her bags and flew to be at her friend's side.

The first thing she did was sit down with Candy's husband and kids and explain to them that she was moving in. She was going to be doing the "mother" things because Candy needed to spend her time getting better. At first, Candy protested. Dania had her own life. Dania had an important job. Candy and her family would be fine. But she finally relented and let Dania be her friend.

Dania cooked and shopped and waited at the bus stop for the kids. She and Candy instituted weekly girls' nights out during which they went to the movies, had their nails done, or sat in a neighbor's hot tub and relaxed. Dania stayed for two months and left when Candy finished her first course of chemotherapy. Two years later, Candy was in remission and grateful to be alive. For Dania's fiftieth birthday, Candy treated them both to a long weekend at a spa. Friends lend a hand in times of need and are there to celebrate the important moments.

WRITE IT DOWN

In your journal or notebook, write down your thoughts about what friendship means to you. Jot down moments of triumph in the lives of both your close and Ripple Friends. This is a way of connecting with your friends and remembering specific moments to recollect and celebrate later. As we said, defining friendship is a complex, personal, and wonderful task.

Let's return to the Tea Party meditation. As Buffy looks around her table, she is flooded with specific feelings for each friend. These are women who, over time, have come to embody the very definition of friendship for her. Susan, her older sister, loves Buffy with an unconditional love that is breathtaking. It still seems remarkable to Buffy that, growing up, her sister always included her in all of her activities. There was never any question that her friends were Buffy's friends. Susan thinks Buffy can do anything, be anything. She is Buffy's protector, her avenging angel, and her biggest booster. From Susan, Buffy has learned to support a loved one unconditionally.

Molly is the best friend Buffy's sister shared with her when they were girls. Buffy met Molly when she was eight. Molly and Susan were twelve. Molly has a prodigious memory and can recall legions of the tiny moments of their shared lives. Smart, funny, and temperate, Molly is tolerance itself. From Molly, Buffy has learned not to judge but rather to appreciate.

As we know, Buffy met Kate on their very first day of college. She had the room next door to Buffy's in the honeycomb that was their freshman dorm. They took the same courses. They did their homework together. They became inseparable friends. Twenty years ago, the movie business lured Buffy to Los Angeles. But somehow she and Kate have managed to stay in touch, even though they've had a continent between them all that time. Kate was Buffy's first friend as a fledgling adult. Buffy could try on ideas in front of Kate as though they were dresses from a vast and ever-expanding closet. Kate's mind is fast, open, and always receptive. From Kate, Buffy learned to trust her own instincts, to try new things, to dream.

Patti was Buffy's next-door neighbor when Buffy and Peter bought their first house. Patti met Buffy as a married adult woman. Patti had two children when Buffy met her. She was a bit older than Buffy and seemed to know everything about having a family. Patti is fun and funny. At a time when Buffy was a driven executive brimming with confidence about everything except domestic matters, Patti gave Buffy faith in herself as a mother and a homemaker.

Buffy met Kathy at work. Their friendship grew slowly and deeply over time. Work in the movie business is unutterably stressful and treacherous with politics. They watch each other's back, but their friendship offers more than political protection. It is a friendship that is constantly taking the measure of life. They sit in the same office together, car pool

Try meditating about friendship. Getting in tune with your innermost thoughts and feelings about your friends is crucial and may cause you emotional upheaval. You might want to listen to *Five Classic Meditations* by Shinzen Young (Sounds True). In this beautiful audio recording, Young leads the listener through a quiet journey to finding loving kindness.

when going on appointments, and talk on the phone when not together. They celebrate, observe, and cry over the triumphs and defeats of everyday life. From Kathy, Buffy has learned loyalty, trust, the power of encouragement, and compassion.

Donna and Alison are Buffy's sisters-in-law. Donna is married to Peter's brother Bruce, and Alison is married to Buffy's brother Topper. These two women have expanded the boundaries of family and infused Buffy's life with a sense of acceptance, devotion, and security in times of need.

These are some of the thoughts and phrases Buffy uses to define friendship. Now it's your turn to come up with your personal definition. As you go around the circle of your own tea party, think about how each friend helps you define yourself, then write it down.

- Unconditional, nonjudgmental love
- Deeply shared memories
- Intellectual stimulation
- Space for self-expression
- Esteem building in our many roles
- Loyalty and trust
- Compassion
- Commitment
- Helpmate
- Laughter

Once you've written down your definition of friendship, read it every so often. You may find that it brings you cheer and a comforting sense that you are not alone. In times of trouble, the power of friendship can surround you like a virtual cocoon, shielding you from the rough stuff. In times of joy, friendship can be a balloon of love that lets your spirit soar. Keeping, renewing, and creating new friendships is crucial to a successful second half of your life.

> ### Buffy's Ripple Friends Who Write
>
> About four years ago I was invited to join a writers' group. The woman who asked me was a business colleague, not a close friend but a Ripple Friend. I was hesitant, but my wish to reconnect with my writing overpowered my usual shyness with strangers and my reluctance to join things. The first night I was introduced to four other women and asked to say a little something about myself. I hesitated, realizing I could describe myself any way I wanted. I could say movie executive, wife, mother of two, but in that brief moment of freedom, I said, "Writer." And by saying it out loud, I was empowered in a very specific and personal way: these women would see me, talk to me, and treat me as a writer, and I would do everything I could to be worthy of that new title. There is no doubt that these Ripple Friends guided me back to fiction writing.

www.newcomersclub.com

An interesting, geo-specific Web site where you can find people with mutual interests

GET TOGETHER

Invite your friends for a real tea party. Go around the table and tell each friend what he or she means to you. Have your friends do the same. Consciously celebrate friendship. Take the first step—an e-mail, a knock on the door, a postcard, a phone call—and let the reflection of love surround you. Try to find ways to make getting together with a friend a regular part of your weekly or monthly routine. Look up or call an old friend and reestablish contact. Put your friends' phone numbers on your speed dial. Create an e-mail tree, a customized e-mail distribution list of your friends, so it's easy to reach them all at once.

Buffy's sister, Susan, has many friends, close and Ripple, and Buffy is always surprised at how far her sister will go to be a good friend. Recently, one of Susan's friends moved from Mexico City to New York City. Lily was recovering from a back operation when she moved, but her husband's work and her children's school deadlines forced her to move before she had fully recuperated. Susan surprised her friend Lily by flying to New York just one day after Lily had arrived. Susan unpacked Lily's boxes, hung her pictures, laid down shelf paper, filled the bookshelves, sorted

Read about friendship — literary, fiction, historical. Look into the lives of some famous friends, and you may find in their letters and writings a new understanding and commitment to being a friend: Houdini and Sir Arthur Conan Doyle (Sherlock Holmes), Franklin D. Roosevelt and Winston Churchill, André Gide and Oscar Wilde.

Norton Book of Friendship by Eudora Welty (Norton). A beautiful book on friendship by one of America's finest writers.

Truth and Beauty by Ann Patchett (HarperCollins). Tells of the complex and trying friendship between the author and Lucy Grealy.

www.myspace.com Check out this site to get a glimpse of how YPs (young people) stay in touch, and bring your networking to new heights.

out the kitchen. Susan got Lily's new apartment organized in a day and a half and then flew home. When Buffy told her sister how much she admired her, Susan tossed off the compliment, saying that's what friends do for each other.

> Dear Buffy: Just the other day, I was remembering freshman year. Do you remember how hard we worked? And how hard we played? And the male students who used to come through the dorm, looking for action. Oh, how we toyed with them. Love, Kate
>
> Dear Kate: Tormented them is more like it. Some of them didn't even realize we were making fun of them, but most of them left our hall not knowing what had hit them. The fact was, we were just too quick for them. They couldn't keep up with us. Most of them couldn't believe we weren't falling all over them. That we actually preferred each other's company to theirs. It was fun, wasn't it? Love, Buffy
>
> Dear Buffy: And then there was Peter. Love, Kate

PUTTING IT ALL TOGETHER

Now it is time for you to create a plan to keep your friendships vital and growing.

1. *Create time* to be a good and attentive friend.
2. *Reflect* on who your friends are and what they mean to you by visualizing a tea party to which you have invited all your friends.
3. *Practice patience* with your friends and work to manage your expectations. Remember that they have complicated and busy lives, too. Be sympathetic but don't be a doormat. Reflect love.
4. *Research* by reading your friends intuitively and responding to their needs.
5. *Find role models* of people who practice the art of friendship with skill and commitment.

6. *Write down* your definition of friendship. Include thoughts, anecdotes, and memories.
7. *Get together* with your friends and have a real tea party.

TO-DO LIST

Select three items from this list, and try to do them soon.

- Meditate on the value and meaning of friendship. Make friendship important and central to your spiritual growth.
- Invite a friend to exercise with you.
- Program into your cell phone the phone numbers of all your friends.
- Invite a friend to join you in reading a difficult book.
- Go back to school with a friend to learn a new skill.
- Do the Sunday crossword puzzle with a friend.
- Write in your journal how you feel about your friends. Explore your positive and negative feelings.
- Start a running e-mail correspondence with a friend with whom you've lost touch.
- Plan a special night with a friend. Make it a spa night. Do each other's nails, hair, and makeup. Do yoga together. Give each other a foot massage.
- Get an exercise video, and work out together at somebody's house.
- Rent the saddest movies you can. Have a triple feature with complimentary popcorn and Kleenex.
- Do a Thelma and Louise without driving off the cliff. Plan a road trip that lasts a day or more so you will have to read a map, pump your own gas, and navigate life's little difficulties.
- Have a slumber party.
- Decide to help each other spruce up a room. Prepare designs for each other, then go shopping to do your one-room makeover.
- Play Monopoly, Scrabble, cards, Cranium, Jeopardy, charades.
- The power of laughter to motivate, heal, and comfort is boundless. Go to a comedy club or watch Monty Python reruns.
- Call someone up and say, "I have been thinking about you." At best, this might provide her with an opening. At worst, she'll be comforted to know that she is in your thoughts.
- Encourage a friend in obvious distress to unburden herself.

- Offer to watch a friend-in-need's kids for a night while she goes out to a movie and unwinds.
- Send a card or note to a close friend or to a Ripple Friend.
- Bake bread or cookies or buy flowers, and leave them outside her door with a note.
- Invite her to a movie, a coffee, or a meal.
- Call or e-mail often.
- Find out the e-mail addresses of all your friends and create an e-mail tree so you can share news with ease.
- Help a friend in need. Go over and offer to help. It may take a few offers for the person to accept your help, but don't give up. We are all reluctant to accept help.

KATE'S PLAN

Except for Buffy, I'm not good at keeping in close touch with my friends, none of whom lives nearby. I don't like using the phone, and I don't have everybody's e-mail address. I have trouble managing my expectations with friends. I sometimes expect too much of them and then am disappointed and even angry. I have recently acquired some Ripple Friends at the barn where I ride. My friend Justine is no longer listed in the phone book, and the e-mail address I got from a classmate doesn't work. My plan is this:

- I will e-mail or phone a friend once a week. I will not procrastinate about returning e-mails or phone calls.
- I will get the e-mail addresses of all my friends and Ripple Friends and make customized lists for my e-mail tree.
- I will manage my expectations when it comes to friendships.
- I will continue to cultivate my Ripple Friends at the barn. Some of them have started taking line-dancing classes. I will try to join them when I can. I will initiate shopping expeditions to tack stores and encourage them to join me at various clinics and equine expositions.
- I will track down Justine and reestablish contact.
- I will try to be less of a doormat. When something is bothering me, I will try to speak up.

BUFFY'S PLAN

Friends are very important to me, and while I do not have a great many close friends, I could do a better job of staying in touch with the few that make up my inner circle. I have recently expanded my Ripple Friends, which is rewarding, if a bit unnerving. I want to keep expanding my circle of friends and learn how to read intuitively and more attentively. My plan looks like this:

- I will be more consistent about e-mailing my friends. I will try to write e-mails of substance whenever I can, not just "thinking of you" missives. I will exchange Web sites or magazine articles with my friends.
- I will be more open and friendly in order to make Ripple Friends.
- I will use my kids as role models, for they are both extremely attentive and supportive friends. I see in them the energy and thoughtfulness necessary to be a good friend.

With this chapter, we conclude our exploration of your immediate circle — your mates or dates, your kids, your parents and siblings, and your friends, both close and Ripple. Ideally, you've begun to pull together plans for dealing with these different layers of your life. Now it's time to expand your gaze ever further to include your finances, your community, your job, and the world around us, and to gear up accordingly for the second half of your life.

a r t   T h r e e

My Greater World

You are the world!

You hold multiple citizenships, don't you? First and foremost, of course, you belong to yourself. You also belong to your loved ones. But you belong to a larger world, as well, don't you? You are, as the saying goes, a citizen of the world. Now it's time to expand your view to see how the transition to the second half of your life will affect your standing in the larger worlds of finance, work, play, and community, both local and global.

How Much Money Is Enough?

Taking control of your finances

Dear Buffy: I don't think I've ever told you this, but I've always admired the way you've refrained from spending every penny you've ever earned. As in so many things, you are my idol. What's your secret? Love, Kate

Dear Kate: My parents were Depression era babies. Maybe money paranoia was passed to me through my mother's milk. I'm a freak in Los Angeles, where practically everyone lives so far beyond their means it's absurd. So you know, it doesn't mean I don't worry about money. My kids call me the B.D. — the Budget Director. Loving nickname, isn't it? Love, Buffy

Dear Buffy: The federal government could learn from you. Money is a little like sex, isn't it? Kind of a dirty secret. Should we tell all? Love, Kate

THE COLOR OF MONEY

Americans are now saving less money than ever before. According to a recent survey, only 39 percent of baby boomers feel they have sufficient savings to retire comfortably. Only 39 percent are prepared! Faced with a daunting statistic like this, we have to ask ourselves why. Why are 61 percent of us baby boomers so ill prepared financially for the second half of our lives? There is probably no single answer. There are very likely many answers. Here are a few. See how many apply to you.

- Minimal salary increases. Corporations and small businesses are offering conservative raises or no raises at all. Bonuses and perks are being frozen or cut.
- Rampant advertising. The U.S. economy is trying hard to stay on its feet. Advertising is a tool. Everybody wants your buck, so it's understandably difficult to hold on to it.
- Mass-market emporiums make it hard to resist bargain prices for items you may not even need.
- The rising cost of health care.
- Savings wiped out or unforeseen expenses after September 11.
- Uneven and unpredictable stock market.
- Saving money feels punitive. When we work so hard, we feel we are owed treats. Saving money translates as deprivation.
- Money lavished on our homes.
- Money lavished on the bubble we keep our kids in.
- Money spent on private schools and colleges.
- Ignorance of how to budget.

That last item is probably the one most of us can claim. What's that roaring sound? It's the sound of our overdraft accounts on overdrive. Our credit cards are starting to groan beneath the weight of debt. We tell our families that we have to go on a budget, that we have to become mindful of expenditures, and they whine. We start to slash budget items, left and right. The family hunkers down beneath the lash.

But after a week or two, everyone starts to rebel. Who can live like this? It's downright punitive! One by one, the slashed budget items get reinstated, sometimes with a bonus thrown in to compensate for the hardship of those two weeks of austerity. It's a classic cycle. Everyone does it. We overspend. We try to correct. We set impossible goals. We deprive ourselves for a week or so, then life gets so bleak and tiresome that we toss the budget out the window and go on a spree.

No wonder we hate and love money so passionately. On the one hand, we may feel oppressed by it because we have to keep jobs, secure mortgages, pay bills, be accountable, and work hard or starve. On the other hand, we love the comfort money can bring—the health benefits it secures, the education it funds, as well as the pretty things, the nice vacations, the delicious meals, and the fashionable clothes. Money can also give us power. Not the power to boss people around, although it can certainly give us that, but, more important, the power of choice. Losing control over money can make us feel lost, without options, embarrassed, inadequate, and exhausted. And it certainly seems that no matter how much money we make, there is never quite enough of it to meet all our needs.

Bobos in Paradise by David Brooks (Simon & Schuster). A book about "bourgeois bohemians" who grew up in the sixties and enjoyed all that the decade stood for but now drive SUVs, visit Starbucks religiously, and are a bundle of inconsistencies. Aren't we all?

In this chapter, we will explore our feelings and attitudes about money and confront our ambivalence about it. Then we will share a few simple methods to control spending so you will be able to save a little more for your future.

Try to be completely honest when assessing your feelings about money. By doing so now, you will be able to design a plan to take better control of your finances so you can enjoy a more secure second half, one relatively free of money cares. Start by asking yourself these questions: How much money do I really need? How much is enough? You're not fishing for a nuts-and-bolts budgetary answer here. It's more of an emotional, lifestyle, mind-set kind of thing. Because the fact is, if you are like most of us, no matter how much money you amass, you will spend every last penny of it and probably some pennies that you don't have. Go back to chapter 1 and the four things you said made you really happy. Consider them as you think about how much money is enough.

Get ready! As you work through this chapter, you'll need pencils, lots of scratch paper, a ledger (if you feel so inclined, or at least a section of a notebook), a calculator (or if you're making like Abe Lincoln, a pencil stub and the back of an envelope will do), and a willingness to lay yourself wide open to an honest and thorough appraisal of your financial situation, budget, savings, spending habits, and financial future.

But first, let's see what our seven candle strategies can do to shed blessed light into the dark, cluttered corners of our finances.

For Richer, Not Poorer: The Money Book for Couples by Ruth L. Hayden (HCI). Offers real insight into resolving money issues and learning ways to budget together. Whether you have been married for one year or one hundred years, whether you are two wage earners or one, give this book a look.

CREATE TIME

Because spending money is about consuming, let's use an eating metaphor to better understand how we consume. Before a nutritionist puts an obese patient on a diet, she will usually first ask him to keep an eating log of everything that goes into his mouth from sunup until sundown for a week. She makes a point of asking him not to change what he eats. The goal is to define and isolate his eating patterns for a week so they can eventually be reshaped. The spending version of this exercise requires a month-long log. This is where an old-fashioned ledger can come in handy. For the prescribed period of time, chart your family's expenditures—not the projected ones, the *real* ones. Write down everything.

Commit the time to keep track of checks you write and any automatic deductions from your checking account that you authorize. This is certainly an important part of the process, but it is fairly easy. Much trickier is keeping track of spontaneous cash expenditures. We like to call these cash expenditures the "black box," because they are such a mystery. The more family members you have being spontaneous, the more challenging this information will be to capture. Everyone must participate, so enlist your entire family in this record-keeping enterprise.

Start by calling a Family Table and declaring this National Mind-the-Money Month. At the end of the month, collect your data, reconvene, and let everyone know how each did. Focus on your teens' spending at the meeting. This will be an invaluable opportunity to teach them the value of money and make them aware of what they spend and why they spend it. Then discuss how many hours they would have to work to earn that money after taxes.

You can do the next step of this exercise alone or with your partner. First, total up your monthly receivables: your paychecks, freelance income, dividends, birthday checks, other monetary gifts or tips, anything green that's flowed into your family's coffers during the month. Place this on the black-ink side of the ledger. Then, based on the data you collected, tote up the myriad red-ink items: your expenditures. Include all expenses for the month, plus one-twelfth of yearly expenses (such as car and insurance premiums, school taxes), plus one-twelfth of unforeseen expenses—the ones you can't possibly predict but know will happen, such as the washing machine breaking down or your son's computer needing a printer. Be vigilant about recording your cash expenditures, especially items from the Black Box.

To get you started, we've prepared a sample log of expenditures for a family of four (two adults and two teens, one of whom is in college) and an older parent who does not live with the family but requires some support. If these line items correspond to yours, jot them down in a notebook or ledger and fill in the appropriate amounts. If you have expenses not included here, by all means add them. Use this list as a guide. Buffy has alphabetized our list because, well, she just can't help herself (another manifestation of bin syndrome, no doubt). Let's dig into these bins now.

Sample Monthly Expenditure Log

- Books, newspaper and magazine subscriptions, or newsstand purchases
- Cable and TV, including video rentals, Netflix, Pay Per View, TiVo
- Car maintenance and gas, registration fees
- Charitable giving
- Clothing, from coats to socks
- Commuting, including taxis, parking, and your share of a car pool
- Credit card bills, loans other than mortgage (include current bills and any outstanding balance you may have on a credit card)
- Drugstore, a major Black Box contributor (itemize your purchases: shampoo, razors, vitamins, batteries, pens, candy bars, chewing gum, etc.)
- Dry cleaner
- Entertainment, including tickets to movies, ball games, concerts, CDs, DVDs
- Exercise, including gym or YMCA dues, fees for trainer or classes, equipment purchases
- Food and liquor, including groceries, dinners out, dinners in, and lunches

- Garbage removal
- Gifts, including cards, flowers, picking up a tab at a restaurant, one-twelfth of birthday and Christmas gifts
- Hobbies and travel
- House cleaners
- Household items (for example, a new lamp, towels, a new rug for the hallway, a new mailbox); because these purchases will last, budget one-twelfth of the projected cost of these items
- Insurance (house, car, disability, medical, long-term)
- Kids' allowance, including kids in college whose rent and expenses you cover and kids at home who need spending money
- Lawn care, snow removal, pool maintenance
- Medical and dental care, including prescriptions, birth control, office-visit deductibles, medical expenses not covered by insurance
- Miscellaneous (aka the Black Box; for example, haircuts, extra cash to kids, snacks, field trip fees); take time with this category and break it down as completely as you can
- Parent's in-home caregiver, contribution for living expenses
- Pet care (grooming, veterinarian, dog food, cat litter, medicine)
- Phone, including cell phones, land lines, phone cards, fax, DSL lines, Internet access fees
- Rent/mortgage and taxes
- School/office supplies
- Therapy and/or body work
- Tuition, including tutors, SAT preparation courses, etc.
- Unforeseen expenses (for example, new tires for car, new appliance, roof repair, computer repair, trip to colleges, replacing lost eyeglasses); budget one-twelfth the projected cost of such items
- Utilities (electricity, gas, water, heating oil)

Total monthly expenses: _____

Now subtract your total monthly expenses from your total monthly income. Are you meeting your financial commitments, putting something away in savings, and earmarking some for charity? Good for you! Or, as might be the case, are you as red as Bozo's nose? Not so good, but not the end of the world, right? The point of this exercise is not to punish you but to open your eyes and help you develop money mindfulness. Money is like eating, in that we spend more, just as we eat more, than we think.

If it turns out that, theoretically, you have money left over at the end of the month, even as little as a twenty-dollar bill, will you save it or let it disappear into the Black Box? Concentrate and try to be aware where the money goes and where the leaks are. Only by finding out where the leaks are will you be able to stanch the flow and learn to redirect and use your resources more effectively and efficiently.

REFLECT

Does the thought of money and personal finances make you tense or queasy? Does it send you into a panic? Sometimes it bathes Kate in a flop sweat. Just contemplating National Mind-the-Money Month resulted in a sensation of wet concrete between Kate's shoulders. In an effort to break it up, she undertook a meditation. In her meditation, her family finances manifested to her as a large, semisodden lump of impossibly tangled yarn. So she concentrated on untangling and separating each strand, patiently, while breathing deeply. As the knots loosened, she assigned a name and a color to each strand: mortgage was red; insurance was green. By the end of her meditation, her finances had become a colorful, bright rainbow extending from her and her husband (and their joint checkbook) to the various services and people the bills represented. When she was finished, she felt more relaxed and even proud of this creation, which had been transformed from a lumpy knot to something that was actually sort of beautiful.

We are not asking that you turn your finances into macramé. We are, however, asking you to strive for greater clarity, control, and organization, which is, when you think of it, a beautiful thing!

The Complete Tightwad Gazette by Amy Dacyczyn (Villard). We like her attitude and tone, plus much of the advice she offers on how to fine-tune your frugality was suggested by the readers of her newsletter.

www.forbes.com/finance
Access helpful finance tips and advice from Forbes.

www.ourfamilyplace.com/finances.html
Financial resources and information for families on a budget. And whose isn't?

www.smartmoney.com
Articles and news on investing, saving, and personal finance.

Suze Orman is to financial advice what Martha Stewart is to gracious living: a powerhouse who truly wants to help her readers, listeners, and viewers. Suze is a no-nonsense adviser who will not let you get away with lying about your money, your actions, or your relationship with that icky thing called debt. She writes books, has a TV show, a radio show, DVDs, and writes a column for Oprah's magazine O. She knows her stuff.

A Suze selection:

You've Earned It, Don't Lose It (Newmarket Press)

The Laws of Money, The Lessons of Life (Free Press)

The 9 Steps to Financial Freedom (Three Rivers Press)

Play this simple word-association game to get at your feelings about money. What words pop into your head when you hear the word *money?* Bills, debt, envy, embarrassment, secrets, luxury, comfort, freedom, dreams, anxiety, power, IRS, unemployment? Is your list, like our sample, a complex mixture of pleasant and bad associations? That's because we love money and we hate money. Concentrate on neutralizing your feelings about money. Money just *is.* And the more control we have over it, the less important it will become to us, the less emotional we will be about it, and the fewer decisions we will make *based on money.*

PRACTICE PATIENCE

How many of the expenditures you made during the course of a month fell into the category of shopping therapy? You know. Bribing yourself to go on, consoling yourself, feeding the greedy beast within, or saying, "Darn it all, I've got it hard. I work hard, and I deserve to play hard." Working hard for a living doesn't make much sense unless you will have something left over for the years when, ideally, you will have more time to use it in a less neurotic and frantic, more mindful and enjoyable fashion.

During the past month, what have you spent that qualifies as therapeutic shopping? Here are a few of Kate's:

- Manicure/pedicure: $45
- Tape dispenser and stapler in the shape of frog and fish: $145
- Pair of French shoes: $250

Kate's not trying to make herself feel bad for having spent this money mindlessly. That would be pointless. Instead, she realizes that nearly $500 might have gone into savings. If she applied this mindfulness to curbing therapeutic shopping throughout the year, she might put away an extra $6000 a year, or more.

What are some of your recent therapeutic purchases? Do they add up to a substantial sum the way Kate's do? Shopping is fun, right? Advertisers and retailers love for us to think that way, but shopping is *not* a recreational activity. Let's say it again for good measure: Shopping is *not* a recreational activity.

Shop for what's necessary; do not shop to amuse or console yourself. Start to think of saving as the ultimate therapeutic activity and indulge yourself! Watch your muscles start to relax, your jaw unclench, your mottled complexion clear. Why, it's better than going to a spa—and a whole lot cheaper.

Sometimes budgets are so strict, they are doomed to fail. Like a dieter who fasts and eventually has to binge, you and your family will feel so deprived on a strict budget that eventually you will go off it altogether and once again relinquish control of your purse strings. It's a question of balance. Checks and balances. And setting reasonable goals.

RESEARCH

Let's return to the ledger where you recorded your monthly expenses. Our goal now is to subject each and every line item to ruthless scrutiny. Yes, that's right. You're going to research potential savings by organizing, analyzing, and categorizing each budget item. First we'll divide your expenses into five baskets. By doing so you can really focus on what you are spending your money on and how much you are spending. The five baskets are:

1. Expenses to keep the house running and in order
2. Expenses required to live as a family and to keep each family member fed, clothed, healthy, and educated
3. Expenses that protect and safeguard you and your family
4. Expenses necessary to earn a living
5. Miscellaneous/spontaneous expenses (the notorious Black Box)

Next you will scrutinize each expense and place a letter next to it.

    F = fixed expense; for the most part these costs are out of your control. (When you have a yearly bill to pay, as with property tax, you will enter one-twelfth that amount to represent a month's allocated expenditures.)

Women Who Shop Too Much: Overcoming the Urge to Splurge by Caroline Wesson (St. Martin's). At the end of the book is a very sensible eleven-step program for "balanced shopping" that's useful for run-of-the-mill shopaholics and shopping addicts.

Unbelievably Good Deals and Great Adventures You Absolutely Can't Get Until You Are Over 50! by Joan Ratner Heilman (McGraw-Hill). Just what the title says and more.

Not Buying It by Judith Levine (Free Press). This book is about the author's year of not shopping for anything except the bare necessities.

R = reduce expense; these costs can be reduced because they are excessive or because there are ways to better contain them.

X = eliminate expense altogether; this is a hard letter to write down.

Remember, whatever amount you manage to save is great. Five dollars, ten dollars, even a single dollar in savings can add up, over multiple items and over the course of a full year, into an appreciable sum. Be sure to set reasonable goals. As you go through the items, continually ask yourself whether there are any services being outsourced that might be handled more economically at home. Call a Family Table and figure out which items can be reduced, eliminated, or absorbed. Be reasonable. Try to shave rather than gouge. And remember that fasting inevitably leads to bingeing.

Basket 1: Expenses to keep the house running and in order

- Electricity: R
  Post signs around the house to remind family members to turn off lights, especially in the basement or playroom at night and in bedrooms during the day.
- Garbage removal: F or X
  If it is permitted in your area and you have a truck and the stomach for it, you could haul your own trash to the dump.
- Gas/heating fuel: R
  Because you don't set the price, the best way to save money is to conserve. Lower that thermostat. Put on a sweater. Put quilts or extra blankets on beds.
- Lawn mowing/snow removal: R or X
  Here is a place to call on each family member to participate in sharing the responsibilities for lawn maintenance. Consider bartering help in the yard for your teen's car insurance payment.
- Property and school taxes: F
  But they could go up.
- Rent/mortgage: F
  Research whether refinancing your loan would be advantageous to you.

Basket 2: Expenses required to live as a family and to keep each family member fed, clothed, healthy, and educated

- Allowance for kids: R

  The single best way to control this is to decide what you expect your child to pay for from his allowance. For instance, does he pay for his snacks but not the lunch card? Does he pay for gas but no part of an increase in the insurance premium? Be specific and detailed. Also, try not to advance additional money between pay periods.

- Books, magazines, newspapers: R

  As we learned in chapter 4, it is important to read. There are ways to gain access to information and books inexpensively, but some expenditure is required. Use the public library. Use the Internet as a quick and inexpensive source of information and news.

- Cable TV: R

  Clearly you want to enjoy films and music. Just be aware of what you are spending your money on. "Read my lips. No more Pay Per View!"

- Car maintenance and gas: R

  Depending on where you live and work, you may be able to reduce this item by walking or biking to certain destinations. The price of gas is a serious issue when trying to maintain a budget. And, hey, wash your own car.

- Clothing: R

  We probably have almost all the clothes we need except perhaps to keep pace with the office environment. This category is mostly for your kids. Slow down on the buying frenzy.

- Credit card bills: R

  If you have a lot of credit card debt, immediately cut up all of your credit cards except one, and use it only in emergencies. Even if you have no debt, minimize the use of credit cards. If you have to buy it on credit, reconsider buying it at all. Replace your current card with one that charges a lower annual fee or no annual fee and better APR. If you are in serious debt, seek help from a financial counselor or find a course that will teach you how to better manage your money.

We read about a high school that posed this question to its math students: "Suppose you purchased goods totaling $5,000 on your credit card. At 18 percent annual interest and paying $135 per month, it would take you fifty-five months to pay the bill. Defend your decision to do this." We love that students have to wrestle with their decisions, weighing whether what they bought is worth almost five years of payments.

- Drugstore: R

  A tricky area. Because drugstores now carry so many different items, you may find yourself going in for two things and coming out with ten. Many of these items cost less than five or ten dollars, so we tend to buy them because they are cheap. When added together, they aren't so cheap. Try to make a list of what you need, and shop only from the list. Do not let yourself wander aimlessly up and down every aisle because, as sure as shootin', you'll find something you need or want in every one. Much of the Black Box spending originates in this category. The same is true for home-improvement or big-box stores. Go there for something you need, but make sure you leave with only that thing and nothing more.

- Entertainment: R

  Yes, you can go to the movies or see Bruce Springsteen at the Westbury Music Fair, but you need to look closely at this area so it doesn't become the piece of candy you feel you owe yourself.

- Exercise: R

  As we learned in chapter 2, exercise is not an elective, although clearly there are many ways to exercise without spending large sums of money. Walking is free!

- Food/liquor: R

  This is a large part of anyone's budget. Reduce it by making weekly menus, using coupons, cutting down on takeout, exercising portion control, shopping from a list and not from memory or impulse, buying less junk food, eating leftovers, and drinking less liquor. Consider calling a Family Table to draft a week's menu.

- Gifts: R

  You may want to rethink gift giving. Are there other, less expensive ways to celebrate birthdays or to mark an anniversary? Sentimental gifts are often less expensive or free. For a graduation gift, Buffy's sister-in-law, Alison, gave her daughter a bird's nest she found while out walking in the woods and her daughter loved it! Gifts for family members can be necessities, like a new printer for the computer, rather than luxuries. If possible, try to wait for a special occasion (Christmas, birthday, graduation) to give such gifts.

- Hobbies and travel: R

  Hobbies will be important during the second half of your life. Find the money to finance them. To reduce travel costs, take advantage of earned mileage, special discount promotions, and Internet travel sites.

- Household items: R

  Your home needs to be comfortable, but it doesn't need to be re-designed every year. Unless you are drinking from old jelly jars, aren't the glasses you have nice enough?

- Phone: R

  Each member of a family of four, as ludicrous as this seems, may have a cell phone and probably shares multiple land lines (fax and separate Internet hookup for business). Most teens and YPs (young people) no longer use land lines, preferring to use their cell phones for all calls. Can you close down one of your land lines? Study all the ads for mobile phone service and switch to carriers that will reduce your monthly fees. Do not yield to YP pressure to consider more sophisticated phones—and limit text messaging. Enough is enough. Monitor use of cell phones. Review phone bills with your teens. Sometimes seeing it in black and white can be eye opening. Consider using a prepaid phone card even when using your home phone if it will reduce long distance costs. Buffy's daughter developed what Buffy called SCD (serious cell-phone disorder) one summer when traveling in New York. To pay off her phone bill, Daisy worked for free in Buffy's office until she had logged enough hours to clear her phone debt.

- Therapy: R

  This is an area that can go up and down as relationships and issues are worked out or need more work. Make a greater effort to get insurance reimbursement, then deposit the insurance checks directly into your savings account.

- Tuition/school supplies: R

  While tuition may be a fixed cost, the cost of supplies and books can be reduced by buying and selling used books on the Internet, using library books, and reusing supplies from semester to semester. Also research scholarships and grants.

- Unforeseen expenses: F
  We also need to make allowances for the fact that no matter how carefully and specifically we budget, there will always be an unforeseen expense that knocks us for a loop: root-canal surgery, new transmission, new septic tank.

Basket 3: Expenses that protect and safeguard you and your family

- Medical and dental insurance: R
  Shop around for lower premiums.
- Home or renter's insurance: R
- Car insurance: R
  Take advantage of discounts offered by insurance companies for good driving and academic records.
- Long-term health insurance: F
  You may not have this form of insurance but you should consider it. Premiums when you are still working and in your fifties are less expensive and easier to handle than when you are in your sixties and seventies.
- Disability: F
  Most people think life insurance is the most important form of insurance for their families, especially if they are the principal wage earners. But recent studies have shown that people are more likely to become disabled and therefore unable to work than they are to die.
- Life insurance: F
  To choose the right policy, consider your age, your parents' ages, the number of dependents you have, and whether you have a child with a disability.
- Parent's caregiver: F
  This could go up if your father's health declines and your siblings cannot make their contributions.

Basket 4: Expenses necessary to earn a living

- Commuting: F
  This is a difficult expense to bring down unless you commit to walking, car pooling, or negotiate some days of telecommuting.
- Dry cleaning: R
  In between wearings, consider hanging your clothes outside your closet or briefly outdoors to freshen them so you can wear them a second and third time. Remember that dry cleaning ages your clothes, too.
- Lunch: R
  Consider bringing your lunch or researching less expensive places to eat. Vary your menu and your eating habits.
- Clothing: R
  You probably have enough clothes, so consider each new purchase carefully. Avoid buying the same items over and over. (For instance, at one time Kate owned nine black blouses.) Be mindful of the added expense of clothes that require dry cleaning. Shop only if you need something specific. Buffy says that looking through catalogs works wonders. She folds down the corners, tears things out, but rarely takes it any further. Just the fun and relaxation of looking through catalogs or the big thick issue of September *Vogue* satisfies her recreational and therapeutic urge to shop.

Basket 5: Miscellaneous/spontaneous expenses (the Black Box)

This is, in many ways, the most important category because it is the most difficult to control. It includes trivial items that are often not necessary and that we lose track of. This is the place for expenses that don't fit into any of your other categories: raffle tickets for your daughter's school bake sale, ChapStick, Tic Tacs, birdseed, sunglasses to replace the ones you broke or misplaced and won't take the time to find, extra milk, the twenty bucks you hand to your son so he won't be walking around with only a dollar in his wallet. Taken by themselves, they are not very expensive, but they add up quickly if we aren't careful. We give this category a big R.

Consider taking these actions with your own budget:

- First, you must decide to be more mindful about money. If you are part of a couple, agree to do so as a couple, and then as a family.
- Determine how much money per month it will be possible for you to save.
- Consider making automatic weekly or monthly deposits in savings and retirement accounts. However much or however little you can put aside, in addition to anything you have already managed to put aside, can make a big difference in the quality and comfort of your life in future years.
- It's not too late to start reducing and controlling your spending. It is never too late.
- If you are bonus eligible, consider saving it. Don't even count it. Just pretend it's not available to spend.
- Roll out your savings program gradually.
- Encourage each family member to pick an item to reduce or perhaps even eliminate. You might want to bring a bag lunch to work instead of eating out. Your husband will settle for tap rather than designer water. Your kids will declare a moratorium on the purchase of new jeans. (Aren't thirty pairs enough?)
- Make sure that the money you save doesn't disappear into the Black Box. Make sure it gets banked on a monthly basis.
- Once you've established consistency in your methods over a couple of months, introduce a new item to reduce or eliminate. Start with something really easy. For instance, Kate's friend Cathy treated herself to two Starbucks Mocha Grandes every day. Cathy figured she was spending $60 a week on caffeine. That's almost $250 a month, or $3000 a year. She switched to tea, which is probably better for her health anyway, and realized that amount in savings. And that's only a single budget item! Just imagine what's possible if you put your mind to it.
- All things are possible if you set *reasonable* goals.

FIND ROLE MODELS

Try being a financial role model for your children. This is an important one. Teens are major targets of consumer advertising. Millions of dollars are spent every year courting the tween and teen dollar, as if they had dollars of their very own to spend. Because their dollars are your dollars, it's important to be aware of this phenomenon. As much as the media, our society, and our economy would like to make us think otherwise, shopping is *not* a recreational activity. One more time and all together now: shopping is *not* a recreational activity.

Try to remember that shopping is what we do when we need something. When teens come to you and talk about really wanting or needing something badly, do the following:

- Have them examine this urge. Don't let them make reckless purchases. Don't let them be wasteful or irresponsible with their, and your, money.
- Try to examine with them the notion of how much stuff is enough.
- Try to get them to recognize the difference between spending money mindlessly at the mall and the real enjoyment they feel when they go out on their own with friends and have fun. The last time we checked, fun was still free. Stuff, however, is generally not free.

You have now fully entered the process of planning and designing the second half of your life, and chances are that you are already beginning to become more mindful about the ways you spend money. You are starting to eliminate unnecessary and thoughtless expenditures from your budget. This is a good thing, because if your kids see you being less reckless with your money, they just might start being more careful with their own.

As in all other areas of your life, strive to be the first and best role model for your kids. If your teens see that your enchantment with the galleria is waning and that you no longer consider the shopping experience a recreational activity, they may find it less attractive and amusing themselves. Your teens are now at an age when your daily example can make all the difference in their character and integrity. If you spend too much—

For your kids (or, more likely, for you to get ideas to share with them): *Don't Spend Your Raise (and 59 Other Money Rules You Can't Afford to Break)* by Dara Duguay (McGraw-Hill). One chapter title speaks to us loud and clear: Don't Cure Boredom by Going to the Mall.

www.themint.org
A good Web site for parents to help kids learn to budget, save for big purchases, and put some money aside for charity. Click on Tracking to find some good worksheets.

www.teenanalyst.com
Started in 1999 by three teens from Illinois, this Web site offers tips on how to invest and good info on all sorts of topics, ranging from internships to planning for college to how to pay for it.

www.nate.org
The National Association of Trade Exchanges uses the power of the Internet to help connect people who want to barter goods and services.

www.timedollar.org
Time Dollar USA trades services with others without exchanging money. Earn time dollars for contributing your time, then spend your time dollars to receive help in return.

www.timebucks.org
Time Bucks is a social network that uses time bucks to exchange skills. Earn time bucks by providing a service or item, then spend your time bucks to receive services or items.

just as if you drink too much or swear too much or show too much impatience—your children are more likely to develop these same habits. One of the most positive legacies you can give is to not set your child up for a lifetime of debt and money anxieties. Start being a role model today.

Buffy's Son, Jesse, and the Thrift Store

My kids surprise me sometimes. When Jesse was old enough to start buying his own clothes — that is, still using our money, but taking the initiative to do his own shopping — he frequented thrift shops, secondhand stores, and flea markets. Part of the impetus for shopping in this unusual, eclectic way was that Jesse is an artist, and mass-market mall clothes do not appeal to him. Also, many of his friends were holding down part-time jobs while going to school, and he clearly saw — without our having to say it a hundred times — that earning money was hard and that buying a new shirt at the mall could easily take half a paycheck.

WRITE IT DOWN

This exercise will help you to figure out what your finances will look like when you are sixty-seven years old or older.

Studies show that each year you will need approximately 80 percent of your current income to support yourself, and you'll need to do so for an average of twenty to twenty-five years. Remember that while some expenses such as tuition, commuting, groceries, and mortgage payments will go down, others, such as medical expenses, property taxes, and recreation, will remain constant or go up. To simplify matters, let's assume that you want to retire in ten years when you turn sixty-seven. Assume your current income is $100,000. You will need $80,000 per year, or $6,500 a month, to support yourself. Where is that money going to come from?

- *Social Security.* If you make $100,000 a year and are able to continue to do so until you turn sixty-seven, your monthly Social Security benefit will be $2,178, according to the Social Security Administration Web site. You should be receiving an annual Personal Earnings and Benefits Estimate Statement every year. If not, contact the Social Security Administration and ask for it, or go online and request it. This report will give you your future projected Social Security earnings. Visit www.ssa.gov for information.

- *Pension.* Let's say you have worked at two jobs. From one, you will receive a small pension, and from the other your 401k savings. Your pension is approximately $1,200 a month. The projected total of your 401k is $67,000. (In the United States, this is the average 401k savings at retirement.) Only about 45 percent of us have a pension plan. If you leave an employer, it's a good idea to move your pension assets into an IRA or to roll them over into your current employer's 401k plan. (Check with your financial adviser.) If you have a 401k, are you putting away the maximum amount allowed tax-free, which is currently $18,000 per year? If you can swing it, do it, especially if your employer offers a company match.
- *Work.* You currently make $100,000 per year, but when you turn sixty-seven you plan to start working part-time and not necessarily for the same company. Let's estimate your yearly part-time income at $25,000. If you are working full-time and plan to continue doing so, project what your annual increase in salary will be over the next ten to fifteen years.
- *House.* The real estate market has been red-hot but will most likely cool off. The average cost of a home in the United States is $93,000. Assume you own your house outright. (This is a big assumption since most Americans carry mortgages.) You might sell your house and make money, but if you do so you will have to buy or rent another place. Be conservative in your estimates. You can also consider a reverse mortgage, a plan that is good for some people, but recent studies show home-equity loans are better. Research this carefully.
- *Savings.* Drawing from four different surveys, let's assume your savings matches the U.S. average: $38,000.
- *Investments.* Experts say that once you have stopped working, you should withdraw only 4 percent of your net savings per year. Let's assume you were a good saver and a wise investor and that 4 percent

www.seniordiscounts.com
Find the gold in the golden years with more than 125,000 discounts listed in the largest senior discount database online. Search and save.

From the bookshelf of Harry's Uncle Bob. Do the words *Wall Street* give you hives? Would you no more put your money in the stock market than you would shoot craps? If you're ready to take your money out of the mattress and put it to work for you, here are some books that Uncle Bob recommended to Harry so he can better take care of the money Uncle Bob plans to leave to Harry and his sister one day. Having just begun to acquaint himself with the brave new world of investment, Harry finds it much more like a role playing game than a game of chance.

Dictionary of Business Terms by Jack P. Friedman (Barron's). More than 7,000 clear definitions of key terms used throughout the biz world.

Dictionary of Finance and Investment Terms by John Downes and Jordan Elliot Goodman (Barron's). Covers stocks and bonds, banking, corporate finance, tax laws, mutual funds.

Wall Street Words: An Essential A to Z Guide for Today's Investor by David L. Scott (Houghton-Mifflin)

Dictionary of Investment Terms by Catharyn Martz (Thompson)

The Savage Number by Terry Savage (Wiley). This nationally known finance expert helps you compute your "Savage Number," the amount of money you'll need to retire with to comfortably support your lifestyle. Savage also strongly recommends paying bills online, because it offers you better control of your finances and a more comprehensive record of your accounts, both receipts and payables.

www.troweprice.com/ric This online calculator offers a tutorial to show how uncertainty can affect your retirement planning, helping you to properly manage uncertainty instead of ignoring it.

www.fool.com/retirement .htm Expert articles and advice on retirement saving and how to preserve your nest egg and make it last.

amounts to $60,000 per year. It's a good idea to find an investment counselor and calculate a potential revenue stream based on dividends. Plan for your future with help from the National Association of Personal Financial Advisors, www.feeonly.org.

So how do you reach the $6,500 a month you will need to live on? Your Social Security benefit ($2,178) and pension ($1,200) will pay you a combined sum of $3,378. There is a shortfall of $3,122 per month. How will you bridge it? Probably from a combination of additional savings, investments, 401k, and equity in your home. Feeling the squeeze? Don't freak out. There's time to bridge the gap. You can increase your savings, work longer, or plan for part-time or freelance work. You can begin now to better manage your spending so that you'll have good habits well into the second half of your life. Consider the Dream Cake you envisioned in chapter 1, then figure how much it will cost to support that lifestyle on a monthly basis. (This will be your monthly budget in the second half of your life.) Then review that budget and see if you can locate any savings or ways to economize. This requires imagination and discipline, but you can do it.

Will you have an inheritance?

This is a tricky one. We don't want to sound ghoulish or predatory. Some parents, grandparents, and other relatives are more than happy to give you an idea of what you might expect. Kate's father-in-law calls up on a regular basis to report his net worth. While this makes his kids feel a tad awkward, for him it's a source of pride. Others are more private about money matters. Some can be cajoled into sharing if you tell them you're trying to plan your finances for your future. But with people living longer, few of us can expect to inherit much. You might want to ballpark this or not count it at all. Remember when we spoke about creating a medical family tree in your File of Important Things? Consider creating a family money tree. No, not the kind you shake, but one that assists every member of your family through a process of sharing financial information. For example, asking your parents to give you details about their finances is less about inheritance than it is about finding out whether they have enough to support themselves and whether you might have to begin setting something aside to help them out.

GET TOGETHER

Get together with family and friends and indulge in an activity that requires no major expense. See whether the enjoyment you derive from this activity is inversely proportional to the money you may have spent or not spent. Consider ways you and your friends or neighbors might share expenses by shopping together for bulk items or taking turns watching each other's pets to save boarding costs when one of you is away for a couple of days. There are many ways to stretch your dollars. Share what you find with your friends and listen to how they are managing.

PUTTING IT ALL TOGETHER

Now it's time to come up with your design for taking control of your finances. But first, let's recap what we've learned about your budget.

1. *Create time* to track your family's monthly expenditures.
2. *Reflect* on money and what it means to you. Do you control your money, or does it control you?
3. *Practice patience* and try to live your life without spending money to console, reward, or otherwise bribe yourself to go on.
4. *Research ways* you and your family can save money on a monthly basis. Carefully examine each monthly expense.
5. *Find a role model* in yourself for your teenage children and demonstrate, among other things, that shopping is *not* a recreational activity.
6. *Write down* and add up the money you can expect to receive and/or earn on a monthly basis beginning at age sixty-seven. Project your future expenses/budget.
7. *Get together* with friends and family and do something that doesn't require much money.

Coming to terms with your money, budgeting your money, and being mindful about how you spend it are the subjects of this chapter. It is not about how to invest or how to get rich. We loathe the word *retirement* because of its many negative connotations, but finding out whether you will have adequate resources after you stop working full-time at your current job is important. These books and sites can help you figure that out.

Retire on Less Than You Think by Fred Brock (Times Books/Henry Holt). Written by the *New York Times* columnist, this book is predicated on the refreshing notion that it's easier to cut back and simplify than to scramble to come up with a humongous nest egg for the future.

Retirement on a Shoestring by John Howells (Globe Pequot). Useful and imaginative tips for maximizing retirement benefits, tapping equity, and trimming budgets, while still having plenty of fun.

TO-DO LIST

Select strategies from the to-do list below, or come up with some actions of your own to take control of your finances and start saving. Don't let the length of our financial plans stymie you or freak you out. Once you get started, your plan will be fairly extensive. Managing money is in the details.

- Get a ledger or notebook.
- Declare National Mind-the-Money Month.
- Break into the Black Box.
- Reshape your budget.
- Get an accountant to help you review your expenses.
- Open a direct deposit savings account.
- Review your portfolio.
- Contact the Social Security Administration.
- Find out about your pension.
- Open a retirement account.
- Give up some small thing and realize the savings.
- Increase your monthly contribution to your 401k.
- Open bank accounts for your kids.
- Put your kids on an allowance.
- Put yourself on an allowance.
- Go to a flea market/swap meet/garage sale.
- Take your name off mailing lists.
- Consider one provider for TV, Internet, and cable service.
- Consider hiring a financial planner to look over your finances.
- Join a barter club.
- Join a food cooperative.

KATE'S PLAN

With a grown son not yet finished with college and two teens at home, I have three allowances that are not subject to any fiscal discipline. My family is careless about utilities. We scrape too much food off our plates and into the garbage every night. We order too much takeout. I tend to spend too much money when I am under stress. I have a compulsion about giving extravagant gifts all during the year, and it really gets out of hand at Christmas. The result is that we spend about 5 percent more than we're earning. My plan is to:

- Post signs about turning out all lights at night.
- Put all three boys on an allowance.

- Open savings accounts for the two boys still living at home.
- Reduce the weekly grocery expenditures by improved menu planning, eating leftovers, and limiting takeout to once a week.
- Institute do-it-yourself manicures and pedicures.
- Reduce the dry-cleaning bill by airing clothes outside of the closet and spot cleaning at home. Even better, when shopping for new clothes, select items that don't need dry-cleaning.
- Deposit tax refunds in an IRA or savings account instead of celebrating it as "found" money and splurging.
- Deposit into savings all insurance company refunds.
- Bank my bonus if I'm lucky enough to get one.
- Send cards or letters in lieu of extravagant birthday or holiday gifts.
- As Seinfeld taught us, regift! If you receive a gift that you can't use or don't like, give it as a gift to someone who can use it.
- Radically modify Christmas expenditures.
- Contact Social Security and get updated information on my projected Social Security income.
- Contact human resources departments of previous employers, and find out about any pension funds that may be forthcoming.
- Resist treating shopping as a recreational activity.
- Project a future post–age sixty-seven budget.
- Make up a savings plan for my final ten years of full-time work.
- Use the fireplace to save on winter heating bills.
- Turn down the furnace at night and use more blankets.
- Shovel the driveway instead of hiring someone to do it with a snowplow.

BUFFY'S PLAN

I don't think my children have ever turned out a light without my husband or me asking them to do it or my posting a sign to remind them. My daughter recently asked me if we could have another setup of TiVo in the playroom rather than sharing the one in our room. Sometimes I can't believe my ears! Recently, when my job status changed, I created a detailed budget and found three or four relatively painless ways to reduce our monthly nut, but they were all things that either my husband or I did or did without. So I want to be much more aggressive in holding my children responsible for their expenditures and making them really get in touch with what it means to save money to buy something, not to use the cell phone when they are a block from home, and to generally appreciate how hard it is to earn money, let alone save money. We have already instituted several savings initiatives, such as modest vacations and no personal exercise trainer. I take classes that are much less expensive and request that the kids carefully evaluate what they are asking for and how they will contribute something to finance it. My plan is to:

- Limit the number of times we have take-in food. (My business partner, Kathy, and I have decreased our lunch bills by buying premade salads. And for business lunches, we suggest inexpensive restaurants.)
- Post signs to remind us to turn out lights, turn down the heat, and conserve water.
- Be more imaginative, more personal, and more reasonable in my gift giving.
- Keep the clothes and shoes I have in better condition.
- No more lattes at the coffeehouse on the way to work.
- In-home pedicures/manicures.
- Track the Black Box!
- Start a post–age sixty-seven budget.
- Review insurance (one of our biggest expenses) and see if there are ways to reduce it. For instance, we recently decreased my life insurance policy and funneled the savings into a long-term care policy.
- Visit some of the sites listed here for saving tips.

Now that you have spent time focusing on money, your feelings about money, and your expenses, let's start to think about where you might want to spend the next thirty or forty years of your life.

Do I Want to Move Somewhere Else?

Finding a place to spend the rest of your life

Dear Kate: I keep telling you, California has nine — count 'em, nine! — growing seasons. A gardener like you? Aren't you even tempted to move here? You could ride your horse, like, practically every day. Love, Buffy

Dear Buffy: Unless there's an earthquake or a mud slide. And only if I win the lottery. Need I remind you, Mrs. Rockefeller, California is the most expensive state in the union? Love, Kate

Dear Kate: Then I guess we're just going to have to make that move to Iowa. Our Own Private Iowa. Love, Buffy

Dear Buffy: Don't laugh. I know a friend who relocated, kicking and screaming, to Iowa and wound up loving it. You never know what place you might fall in love with, given half a chance — and, of course, wherever you go, there you are. Love, Kate

---

A SENSE OF PLACE

Whether you're coming or going, you need to take into account something known as a sense of place. What is a sense of place? There are many theories and many different interpretations of what it really is. But most people agree that having a healthy, well-developed sense of place is as necessary to your health and well-being as the right soil is for a plant. There are three

To develop your sense of place, read some travel books. Also read books about where you are living now. It can be fun and illuminating to learn how other people describe what you see every day.

A Sense of Place: Great Travel Writers Talk about Their Craft, Lives, and Inspiration by Michael Shapiro (Travelers' Tales). A wonderful book of interviews with some of today's greatest travel writers.

Rand McNally World Map (Rand McNally). A bargain and a great way to learn about the world.

Listen to music that is specific to your region. If you live in New York, you might put on Gershwin or listen to the score of a Broadway musical. If you live in New Orleans, you might listen to jazz or zydeco. Music can remind you of the subtle reasons you love the place you love.

principal components to a sense of place: belonging, stewardship, and knowledge. Let's discuss them in a little more detail:

- *Belonging.* You feel a connection to a place, whether you've lived there all your life or you just moved in yesterday; you are passionate about it and would rather be there than anywhere else in the world. The climate, location, buildings, terrain, indigenous plants and animals, people, and cultural and recreational attractions all appeal to you on some fundamental, gut level. Some of you may have experienced this gut-level response when you took your son or daughter on a college visit. After making travel arrangements and taking time off from work, you and your daughter walked onto the campus, and in ten seconds she flipped her head around and said, "I could *never* go here." Having traveled one thousand miles and one leg on an airline you had never even heard of, you were hoping for at least ten minutes of consideration. But listen to that instinctive response and instant reaction. It can be negative or positive.

- *Stewardship.* You care what happens to and in a place. Whether it's a drought, a hurricane, a sewage treatment plant, or a galleria shopping center, you are willing to take a stand and fight to preserve what you love most about it. You are committed to participating in its care and upkeep, by casting a vote, picking up trash in the park, or going to town hall to protest a new ordinance that you feel might not be in its best interest.

- *Knowledge.* You are vitally interested in learning all you can about a place—past, present, and future—its history, its ecology, its politics.

In this chapter, we will show you some ways to figure out where you want to live in the second half of your life, and then help you design a plan to make it happen. If you're staying put, you'll need a plan for doing that, too. If you are planning to downsize, move but stay close to where you live now, or move far away, you still need a plan.

🕯🕯🕯

Now let's set up the candles and use our seven strategies to find out where—both geographically and emotionally—you want to live in your second half.

CREATE TIME

Whether you plan to stay in your house or want to move on, you need time to explore your options and carefully figure out how much money you have and want to spend.

Buffy loves Southern California. She knows the high cost of living there, in terms of both actual expense and natural disasters—earthquakes, fires, and mud slides. But she has come to accept the high cost. Every place has potential problems. It is the warmth and beauty of Southern California that captivates her. The scent in the air makes her feel at home; the purple bougainvillea that flows like a waterfall over the pool house takes her breath away. Being able to cut roses from her own garden for the Thanksgiving table is a marvel to her. Buffy and her husband plan to stay in their home in Southern California for the foreseeable future. They love the climate and the lifestyle, and while their house has appreciated in the red-hot LA market, research shows that they cannot really reap the full benefits of a sale unless they leave the market altogether. So they plan to stay.

Buffy believes in planning capital improvements carefully. She thinks it makes sense to do them while she and her husband are still earning income rather than waiting until they are on a tighter budget and have to finance improvements with savings. But it also makes sense not to do them all at once. So Buffy and Peter have taken on their home improvements systemically. A shower had to be completely replaced, but they decided to add a steam component when it was being fixed.

As they look around their house and yard, they realize there are other improvements they want to make. They will prioritize them, budget them, and start to research what they want done. Just as Buffy looks at catalogs and magazines rather than actually shopping, she also gets satisfac-

HGTV has many shows that offer wonderful ideas for the average homeowner. You don't have to be Rockefeller to fund improvements for your own home. Check out *Curb Appeal, Designed to Sell, Landscapers' Challenge,* and *Design on a Dime* for ideas and inspiration.

www.handyman.com Find an experienced, professional contractor in your area who will help you accomplish your remodeling goals or get repairs to your home done quickly.

www.doityourself.com Empowering you with the techniques, knowledge, and materials lists needed to do your own home improvement and repairs with how-to tutorials, instructions, and more.

tion watching HGTV (the Home and Garden television channel). Her urge to refit, refurbish, and retool is often satisfied by watching these shows, and she usually gets a good tip or a wonderful idea that she can file away until she is again in the market for home improvement.

Kate and Harry agree that they will not stay in their current house for much of their second half. For them, living the next five years in their current house will be an exercise in restraint. For two decades, they have invested rather lavishly in their house by making constant, often extravagant, improvements. Now is the time, they realize, to taper off and exercise some discipline. That doesn't mean that if the furnace goes on the fritz they won't replace it, but their first impulse will probably not be to replace it with something top of the line. If a window needs replacing, by all means they will replace it and attempt to match the older ones. But they won't replace all of the windows in that part of the house just so they match exactly, which is something they might have considered doing as recently as a year ago. In short, Kate and her husband will not spend any money on the house unless it is necessary to its upkeep and they are absolutely certain they will get the money back when they sell.

REFLECT

Remember the Dream Cake meditation you did in chapter 1, when you pictured yourself in fifteen years? Let's revisit it, only this time emphasize place rather than self. First, make sure you have a notebook and pen handy so that afterward you can document your meditation and mull it over for content. Whether sitting or lying, cross-legged or prone, whether listening to a tape or guiding yourself, begin by breathing deeply, directing the energy of that breath throughout your body. Count back slowly from 20 to 1, and let yourself fall deep, deep, deeper into a state of relaxation and readiness.

Keeping your eyes closed and continuing to breathe deeply, start to create a picture in your mind. The picture is of yourself fifteen years from now. Where do you see yourself? Imagine you are looking out a window. What is the view? Is the view the same as it is now? Or is it markedly different? Are you in the woods? At the beach? In the desert? Are you in a city? A small village? Open the window if you can. Are the people outside your window speaking with a regional accent? Or are they speaking another language? Lean out and take a deep breath. What does the air smell like? Pine or sage? Salt or city? Is it warm or is it bracing? Spend some time in this place and see if you can figure out where it might be, what you might do there, and how you feel about it.

When you have completed your visualization, open your eyes and write down your impressions, what you saw and felt during your meditation. What does your meditation tell you about your projected sense of place in the second half of your life?

Kate shares her meditation and her interpretation of it here. Use it to get started on a meditation of your own.

Kate's Dream Cake — Redux

I'm back in that cool, one-room house with the picture window and the horses outside in the paddock. I see even more out the window now. There are flower and vegetable gardens. And off to the right, there is another structure, slightly larger than this one. Glory be! My husband's here. This is my husband's house. It has a studio for him to paint and sculpt in and also a TV. There is no TV in my house, so I have to go to his house to watch TV. But that's OK because there is only a hot plate in his house so he has to come to my house for meals. When we have guests, he moves into my house and the guests stay at his place. I don't have to clean his place. Or do his laundry. He is responsible for that. (Hmm, I wonder how he'll feel about this? My guess is, he'll be fine with it.)

There is a third structure, more crude, an arbor perhaps or a garden house, partially open to the air. Under it is a hot tub and a hammock, a table and some chairs and chaises, an outdoor grill. In milder weather, guests might stay there too. Town is about half an hour away by foot. It is a small college town. There are a couple of good restaurants, a library, and an assortment of classes is available: yoga, Pilates, meditation, cooking, and art history. I might want to volunteer at the library or teach a class at the college.

Building a new home for your second half? Check out these books by eco-architect Sim Van der Ryn, and find out how green architecture can help save the world: *Ecological Design* (Island Press), *Design for Life* (Gibbs Smith).

From this meditation, I have learned:

- I want to simplify my life and surroundings.
- I don't want to be living on top of my mate for the second half. I want to lead a freer and more independent life.
- Friends and family visiting is important, but I don't need a big house in which to entertain them. A smaller house means less fuss, less cleaning, less expense, fewer things to worry about. It is simpler and less expensive to maintain.
- I need to be in the country, but I also need to have some access to culture. I need a good library, a theater, good restaurants, and the wherewithal for a continuing education should I so choose.
- I will need to look for a small house with maybe a garage or other outbuilding that can be converted into my husband's studio/house. The rest of it — the paddock, the gardens, and the garden house — we might have to build from the proceeds of selling our current house.
- We need a couple of acres, ideally abutting or at least near public lands where there will be bridle paths.
- Having a town within walking distance will encourage a more aerobic lifestyle.
- I will want to give something back to the community, whether by volunteering or teaching.

PRACTICE PATIENCE

When you choose a place, you can be as staid or as daring as you like. All things are possible. Just remember that what's important is that you thrive in your chosen place. If you have no problem — or even feel more comfortable — being part of the flock, you can always choose one of the areas that are fast replacing Florida and Southern California as retirement destinations. The Ozarks; the Valley of the Sun in Arizona; the Rockies near Denver; the Pacific Northwest; Myrtle Beach, South Carolina; Anchorage, Alaska; and the Dallas and Austin areas of Texas are just a few of the areas that are attracting large numbers of people who want to pare down their lifestyles and live on limited incomes.

Live your dream, by all means. But avoid pursuing unrealistic dreams. If you always dreamed of living at the seashore, you might want to consider that seashore real estate sells for a premium, draws crowds in summer, is often desolate in the winter, and tends to be vulnerable to natural disasters. Living on a lake or river somewhere inland might be an acceptable compromise. Stay away from posh resort areas; they cost posh, too. If you have no clear idea where you want to live and are the adventurous type, you might want to post a map of the world on the wall, blindfold yourself, and point a finger at a random spot. Unless it's the middle of the Indian Ocean, you might find it a grand enterprise to go and experience living wherever your finger landed. With the proper research and preparation, you can do it.

Whether you are staying where you are or moving, living in the American desert or on a desert island, it's important that the abode you'll live in for the second half of your life meet a set of reasonable criteria. Don't jump at the first house you see that you like. Practicing patience has never been more important.

Here are a few important questions you need to ask yourself about the house or apartment you are living in now, and about any home you are contemplating, before you make a single move:

- Is the house or apartment the right size? Do you really need four bedrooms and a cavernous recreation room? Do you need a four-acre lawn to mow or a quarter-of-a-mile driveway to shovel in January?
- Is the house or apartment accessible? Are the stairs to the basement laundry room potential hip busters? Is there a spiral staircase to the second floor? Is the house a single level or an easy split?
- Is the house within walking distance of a town, not only to encourage walking, but just in case driving becomes problematic at some time in the future?
- Is the house or apartment economical to run and maintain? Is it practical to heat and light? Are the school taxes manageable? Does

In the sixties, it was Maggie's Farm. In the new millennium, it's "intentional communities," a term for eco-villages, cohousing, residential land trusts, communes, student co-ops, urban housing co-ops, and other projects where people live and strive together with a common vision. Intentional communities are springing up all over North America, centered on everything from organic gardening to bicycling to green living to horses to religion.

Check out *Communities* magazine (a project of the Fellowship for Intentional Community), which since 1972 has been the primary resource for information, issues, and ideas about intentional communities in North America. Visit www.ic.org for more information.

Builders of the Dawn: Community Lifestyles in a Changing World by Corinne McLaughlin and Gordon Davidson (Book Publishing Co.). Offers advice on how to start your own intentional community.

www.bestplaces.net
More than 20 years ago, Bert Spelling developed a patented software program called "Places U.S.A.," which allowed people to enter their personal preferences and find out the best place for them to live. Access the software with online membership.

Ingredients for your Dream Cake. Check out these sites for ideas of places and houses that may appeal to you. Most exchange sites require you to become a member if you want to list your home, but you can spend hours checking out all kinds of homes and arrangements for free:
www.intervacusa.com
www.digsville.com
www.craigslist.org (no membership fee)

your house come with built-in budget busters, such as high property taxes, clapboard that needs to be scraped and repainted every four years, or an inefficient heating system?

- Is there a rent-producing property on the land? This would provide extra income and, when the time comes, house a caregiver for you and your mate.
- Is the climate to your liking?

RESEARCH

If you anticipate moving, start reading the local real estate section of the newspaper or check out properties online—and start this week. Notice how long the houses in your area stay on the market. See how much they sell for. Track this activity periodically over the next few months and years to understand the highs and lows of your market area. Become a veritable local real estate minimaven. There may come a time, in the next few years, when houses in your area reach an all-time high selling price and stay on the market for a mere two or three days. This would be the optimal time for you to sell your house.

Be flexible and ready to hang out that FOR SALE sign at a moment's notice. Shop for and line up a local real estate agent you like and trust. Or research and become knowledgeable enough to sell your own house. However you choose to conduct the transaction, be prepared to make your move when the market is at its apex. Make sure your papers are in order: mortgage, deed, major appliance manuals, and any other information that a prospective buyer might find useful. Go back to chapter 4 and review your strategies to organize all aspects of your life. Get a head start on organizing the contents of your attic, basement, garage, yard, and closets. Don't let clutter reassert itself.

Whether you plan to sell your home or not, getting organized can make life decisions easier. Keep in mind that the money you stand to make from the sale of your home can be a major boost to your savings, so you might as well try to get the most that you possibly can.

Greener pastures

When you zero in on a place or two, whatever you do, don't pick up and move there, sight unseen. Take a trip to visit the place.

- Take a long weekend or even a vacation there. Explore house-swapping opportunities. When you arrive, visit the chamber of commerce. Get all the information they have to offer.
- Shop in the supermarkets, browse the shops, sit in the parks, and stroll in the public places. Soak in the sense of place.
- Visit the library and read up on local history and color. Research geological factors, such as fault lines, rivers, wetlands, and flood plains. Find out if this place is vulnerable to natural disasters such as hurricanes.
- Have any large factories pulled up stakes and hightailed it out of town, leaving toxic sludge in their wake? As a potential citizen, you need to be aware of the potential for toxic waste dumps and other dirty little secrets about which the chamber of commerce may not be forthcoming.
- Call on local real estate agents and make friends. Get on their mailing lists.
- What are the restaurants like? Check them out. Kate's neighbor John is a successful restaurateur who uses restaurants as criteria for judging the caliber of a town. According to John's Law, people who care about food also care about other good things. A bad restaurant town may not be a town you want to live in, if you care about food. And, let's face it, who doesn't?
- Talk to people who live there. What kind of vibe do they give off? Confide in them that you're thinking of coming to live there. Ask them how they like living there and what they recommend about the place.
- If you are still interested, subscribe to the local newspaper. Reading a local paper over time will give you invaluable information about the community's cultural and educational offerings, crime rate, expansion plans, and level of citizen involvement.

If you are still working on clutter busting, you may find these resources helpful.

And if you need the cavalry — and let's face it, some of us just can't bear to part with one thing — visit www.napo.net, the nonprofit site of the National Association of Professional Organizers, to find ideas, speakers, trainers, authors, consultants.

www.organizedhome.com This site will help you determine your clutter personality and provides strategies for starting the decluttering process. Even if you aren't drowning in clutter, learn valuable organization tips and how to save energy by doing it.

Research all the possible options for the second half of your life.

www.villasofamerica.com
www.lennar.com
www.activeadultliving
.com
www.retirenet.com
www.seniorresource.com
www.retirementliving
.com
www.retirementhomes
.com
www.senioroutlook.com
www.moving.com
www.homestore.com

> • Remain in touch with the place through a real estate agent or resident you may have met, and keep track of the real estate. If something comes up, whether or not you are ready to relocate then, you might want to buy it while the price is right. If it's your perfect place, it will be worth your while to get a jump on it.

College Admissions

If, like Kate, you long for the serene joys of the country, with some of the snap and sizzle of culture, you might want to focus on small college towns. Get a notion of where in the United States you want to live, then get a list of the top twenty-five colleges in that region. See if you can narrow down the list to ten as you cast about for the right combination of countryside or small-town charm with the more sophisticated amenities of libraries, theaters, and cultural centers. If you're inclined toward a slightly more urban setting, get a list of the top twenty-five universities in the areas that attract you. Chances are that the scale of the town or city will correspond to the status and size of the university. Consider how extensive their public transportation system is and whether there is an airport nearby. What about medical facilities—a teaching hospital, perhaps?

Do online research about the handful of towns and cities you have on your list. Start a file for the ones that pull you back to them again and again. Be on the lookout for articles and books that feature these places, famous or distinguished people who were born there, lived there, taught there—anything that will give you some background and color about this place you might one day call home.

Just as it is a good idea to simplify in your second half, so is it good to look for a place where the taxes and the cost of living are less than the place you will leave behind. There's no sense in ratcheting up your challenges exactly when you want to wind down a bit. So you don't plan to move for another six to ten years? Perfect! It's never too early to start the process.

FIND ROLE MODELS

Eddie's wife, Marnie, had always been fascinated by her roots in the Alsace region of Germany, on the French border. After Eddie stopped working full-time in the telecommunications business, he and his wife arranged to swap their house in Connecticut for one in a town in Alsace during the summer months. Once they were over there, they were able to drive to the town where Marnie's ancestors lived. It was a small town, having a population of no more than one thousand, but they both fell wildly in love with it.

Every summer for four years, they house-swapped and visited this village. They took German classes at home, and each year gained a little more fluency. They fell in love with the wines, food, land, and people. They made friends with people who lived in the town, one of whom was the lord mayor! One year, a house that they had always admired went on the market. With very little hesitation, they put their Connecticut house up for sale and made an offer on this one. Their children were upset, even angry at first, but all ill will melted when they realized how much fun it would be to spend holidays in one of the most beautiful spots in Europe. Eddie and Marnie visit their children at least twice a year, and their children come to visit them at least four times a year. All told, they see their kids more frequently, and under more exotic and stimulating circumstances, than they ever did when they were living in Connecticut.

WRITE IT DOWN

If you start to fall in love with a place — even if you realize that the place you love is where you've been living all along — start a cap feathers and black eyes list, an itemized list of pros and cons. In Joseph Heller's *Catch-22,* this is the list Colonel Cathcart made up to judge whether Yossarian was worth keeping around. How many feathers did Yossarian put in Cathcart's cap versus how many black eyes did he give? After all, no officer, and no place, is perfect. What you are looking for is a place with many feathers and only a few black eyes.

The Art of Crossing Cultures by Craig Storti (Intercultural Press). A wonderful book about how to go about encountering a new culture, coping with "country shock," doing without American amenities, dealing with homesickness, and thriving on foreign soil. Contains passages by some great writers (Mark Twain, Graham Greene, E. M. Forster, Noël Coward).

Le Mariage, L'Affaire, Le Divorce by Diane Johnson (Plume). Johnson, herself a part-time expatriate, has written this handful of delicious novels about Americans abroad, living among the French, and coping with le culture shock.

www.ihen.com
The International Home Exchange Network ("Your Passport to the World") offers its online members multinational listings, as well as a wide selection of privately owned vacation homes available for rent to those not interested in swapping.

Escape to a Small Town: Create a New Life and Fulfill Your Dreams in a Place Where You Can Breathe by Lisa Rogak (William Hill Publishing). We think the title says it all.

www.pen-pals.net
Learn about other cultures and share common interests with new friends via the world's largest pen-pal site.

www.penpalworld.com
A powerful online pen-pal service for staying in touch with old friends or making new friendships.

www.beaconhillvillage.org
Beacon Hill Village is a "virtual retirement community" in the Beacon Hill neighborhood of Boston that partners with service providers to enable its members to remain in their homes and apartments as they grow older. The annual fee gives them access to cultural events as well as in-home help for repair work, bill paying, transportation, shopping, and errand running. Visiting nurses and home health aides are also available.

Here are some examples of Cap Feathers and Black Eyes:

Cap Feathers	Black Eyes
• Near your children or siblings	• Don't know anyone there
• Nice climate	• Too many hurricanes
• Don't need a car	• Public transportation leaves something to be desired

Start your list with quick thoughts like these, then dig deeper and make a more detailed list.

GET TOGETHER

If you currently live alone, explore the possibility of living with a friend who also lives alone. Make like the Golden Girls and research places together. Explore what living together would entail logistically, financially, and psychologically. What are the cap feathers and black eyes? If you are living as part of a couple, explore the possibility of living near or nearer to friends. Get together with your friends and compare ideas, options, and research. You don't need to be next-door neighbors (although that might be nice), but wouldn't it be great if you didn't have to get on a jet to drop in for a cup of coffee or a glass of wine?

You also might consider living not just near friends but actually *with* friends. Groups of people—couples and singles—are finding that living together in a large house, in houses near each other, or in the same apartment building offers a unique way of living. One group of ten friends carefully planned how they might live together as they grew older. Fortunately, one was an architect and designed a building that had apartments of varying sizes, communal spaces for dining and get-togethers, and a well-appointed apartment for a nurse the friends hired to be their wellness director. Many of their expenses were shared. They had company, and yet each was able to retain privacy and a degree of independence.

PUTTING IT ALL TOGETHER

Now it's time to design a plan for where you will live in the second half of your life. Before you get down to specifics, let's review what we've learned in this chapter.

1. *Create time* to think about, in light of sense of place, whether you will stay in your current home or move.
2. *Reflect.* Sharpen your sense of place, and find out where you see yourself living in fifteen years by revisiting your Dream Cake.
3. *Practice patience* by not jumping at the first house you fall in love with. Be reasonable and practical with your criteria.
4. *Research,* by various means, places you might want to live in the future. If you feel you might be in that place already, consider what changes you might need to make to stay there.
5. *Find role models* who have developed a strong sense of place and acted on it.
6. *Write down* a list of Cap Feathers and Black Eyes to consider the pros and cons of the place you zero in on.
7. *Get together* and research living with a friend or living near a friend in the second half of your life.

TO-DO LIST

Do at least three items from this list—or however many it takes to help you make a plan for where you are going to live in the second half of your life.

- Spend time thinking about your sense of place.
- Conduct a meditation on where you see yourself living in the future, and analyze your vision.
- Make a list of improvements your home needs in order for you to stay in it. Budget and schedule them.
- Make a list of improvements your home needs in order for you to sell it successfully sometime in the next five to ten years. Make a plan for carrying them out.
- Start researching retirement communities. You might be pleasantly surprised.
- Start researching college towns, large and small.

- Start reading local real estate listings and familiarizing yourself with the market-place; attend open houses in your neighborhood.
- Hook up with a local real estate agent or one in the place you are thinking of living.
- Find twenty-five places you'd like to live, and narrow down the list to ten.
- Research the ten places you'd like to live and start files on them.
- Make a list of cap feathers and black eyes about the five places you like best.
- Make a list of cap feathers and black eyes for where you live now
- Write down your future budget based on at least three different places you have researched.

KATE'S PLAN

My husband and I have fairly specific needs. We want to be near a small college town. We want to own horses, so we need land. We enjoy trail riding, so we would prefer to be near public lands that have trails. Based on our future projected budget, we are thinking of buying a place that includes a rental-producing property that will provide a steady stream of income and cover at least our taxes. So my plan is:

- Make a list of improvements our home needs in order to successfully sell it in three to eight years.
- Make a plan for carrying them out.
- Start to become familiar with the local real estate market. Research the real estate market near Buffy, so I can consider living closer to my best friend.
- Hook up with real estate agents in the places I am thinking of living.

BUFFY'S PLAN

Peter and I want to stay in our California one-level house for the foreseeable future. However, the Los Angeles metropolitan area is very expensive, so we may begin to research other areas so that we are able to make an informed decision about where to live, when and if we stop working in careers where being in LA is essential. College towns are almost magical to me with culture, education, and usually top-notch medical facilities, all in a potentially less stressful area. We live far away from Peter's brother, my sister, my brother, and my best friend, Kate, and I have no idea where our kids will ultimately settle, but I do think of this circle of love as an important consideration in a move. Peter would like us to travel and live in another country for an extended period of time. My plan is:

- Work on a detailed list of Cap Feathers and Black Eyes for my current home.
- Research and consider visiting college towns, but only ones with reasonably good airports that would make it easy for people to visit and for us to travel.
- Keep improving my current home and accelerate the simplification process — especially the attic! And the garage!
- Start to research how to trade houses, and consider using one of our vacations to exchange our house for someone else's in a place we might want to spend an extended period of time.

The next chapter addresses career and paid work. Even as we write this book, laws are being rewritten that may change the nature of Social Security but will certainly push back the legal retirement age. Retirement, as you may always have imagined it, may not be in the cards for you. Work will probably continue to play a part in your life well into your sixties and seventies. Even if you are liquid enough to be able to step down from a full-tilt career at age sixty-five, you might be interested in working part-time in the same field or exploring new part-time fields. Whatever your future job prospects, a little career counseling is now in order. Whatever you decide to do with the rest of your life, remember, it is the best of your life.

What Do I Want to Be When I Grow Up?

Recommitting to work and finding joy

> Dear Buffy: You know, it's funny. I used to say to myself: I can do this for five more years and then I'm outta here. Next thing I know, thirty years have passed, and I'm still here. I think of this last eight to ten years as my victory lap, and I'm going to enjoy every minute, or at least every other minute. Love, Kate
>
> Dear Kate: And here I am, back at the starting line. I never would have expected it. I thought I'd have that job forever. Love, Buffy
>
> Dear Buffy: In a way, I envy you. It's exciting. Just starting out, knowing what you know. It's not like you're starting out as a secretary. You're drawing on years of experience, and you have a huge network. You'll do great. Love, Kate
>
> Dear Kate: It's scary, though. I have to keep in mind that work is always a little scary. And sometimes a lot scary. But I keep telling myself to find the joy. Every day. Find the joy. Not just the paycheck. Love, Buffy

LIFE AFTER WORK — SOMEDAY

What kind of employee are you? Are you a hard worker? For many of us, our fifties and sixties may be the busiest and most demanding years of our lives. In fact, your career may be going full throttle. The financial demands

Work Is Hell by Matt Groening (Pantheon). The creator of *The Simpsons* will have you laughing about work with such "chapters" as Three Part Plan for Squelching New Ideas; A Tense Office Is a Productive Office; and How to Make the Veins in Your Forehead Throb Alarmingly.

placed on you and your mate may be at an all-time high. You are trying to save money to finance your dream.

At the same time, you may be paying one or more college tuitions, and you very well may be contributing to the care of one or both of your parents or your mate's parents. Right now, a voice inside you is probably beginning to whisper, or maybe even scream, "What about me? Can I please stop this bus and get off?"

While the answer is probably, "No, I can't stop now, although I sure wish I could," there are steps you can take to reduce the stress of the next few years and actually embrace the idea of working longer. You have been working inside and outside the home for thirty years or more. And you know it's important to take full advantage of these, your career-high years, and your seniority at work, not just to support your current lifestyle, but also to save as much money as you can. That way, when you do decide to leave the driving to someone else, you can hop off the bus with impunity and ease, or perhaps move to a seat farther back so you can enjoy the scenery a little more.

In this chapter, we will explore your work — your feelings, ambitions, goals — and the importance of mentally, emotionally, and spiritually preparing yourself to continue working well into the second half of your life. The current employment landscape is difficult to describe with any accuracy. On the one hand, unemployment is relatively low, while on the other, too few new jobs are created each month. Having a job is a good thing. Having a job you love is a great thing. You may swing back and forth between complaining about your job and knowing you are lucky to have one. This ambivalence is natural. As we grow older, however, it is crucial to use some life lessons to infuse our work with joy.

The importance of finding joy in your work is one of the most essential themes to take away from this chapter. If you allow yourself to think of your work as drudgery, boring, unfair, exhausting, mind numbing, and beneath you, then all is lost. Because almost all of us *must* work — whether it be in an office, factory, showroom, store, or restaurant — almost all of us must find ways to make work joyful. Of course, we all feel resentment and fatigue now and then, but at the core of your working heart, look for, nurture, and demand *joy*.

The Art of Happiness at Work by the Dalai Lama and Howard C. Cutler, MD (Riverhead). A question-and-answer session about the difficulties and rewards of working. The Dalai Lama reminds us that the highest purpose of work is helping others.

Let your family, mate, or close friend in on your life at the workplace. Describing your role at work can make accomplishments more real and setbacks easier to take. When you are finished with your day, talk about it. Work takes up too much of your time and occupies too central a part of your being not to share it with someone close to you. Talk it out, and by doing so help rid yourself of frustration and anger. Talk it out and savor the good moments; store up your heroic memories.

Many of us, over the years, have fallen silent about our work. We have unconsciously conformed to the image of workers who trudged home from the office or factory, loosened their ties or took off their uniforms, cracked open a beer or stirred a martini, and sat in front of the newspaper or television, silent. Was your father one of those? Or did he tell tales of his workplace exploits? Which are you? Stoic mute or fascinating yarn spinner? Buffy's father worked in the television news business when she was growing up. He worked long hours, traveled a great deal, and always came home with great stories about fascinating people—people in the world of politics and government. He was a wonderful role model, demonstrating how rewarding work can be, and how hard work can be its own reward. Buffy's father regularly communicated joy about his work.

It is in sharing our work—the good days and the bad—that we give ourselves and, perhaps more important, our children, nieces, nephews, and other YPs (young people) the tools they will need to participate fully and happily in a chosen career. By sharing our triumphs and our setbacks, we can be role models for our loved ones and colleagues. A positive view of work and a strong support system at home provide a good foundation for us when work gets tough, when we don't get the raise we have been expecting, or when we are transferred to another city or downsized or fired. Joy will carry us through even the longest days of hard work.

The seven candles, our trusty strategies, will help you cultivate positive feelings about your work and make you into your own workplace hero.

CREATE TIME

Create time to think about your work. Because work can so easily become habitual, we seldom stop to think about it. Here are some key words to help you capture your thoughts: *accomplishment, collaboration, money, structure.* Take time to dig deep into each word for its positive value in your work and, equally, to confront its potentially negative effect. Use these words as beacons to reveal your true feelings about work. Here are some tips for how to do this:

- *Accomplishment.* Looking back over many years is one way to tote up your personal success, but examining what you accomplish from Monday to Friday can be a more useful exercise. Come up with five things you accomplished at work last week.
- *Collaboration.* Do you thrive in an environment of contact, or do you work better alone and a little off to the side? Either is great, but it's important to know how you operate best. If you've been a reluctant collaborator in recent years or a lonely solo flyer, now might be a good time to consider a switch.
- *Money.* We work to earn money. Do we need to earn as much money as we are earning now? How much do we *have* to earn? How much is enough? Seriously, how much? If you were to lose your job tomorrow, how much of a pay cut could you take and still lead a rich and full life? How much you are paid for your work should be less of a benchmark of success than what you accomplish during your workday and how much fun and satisfaction you derive from it.
- *Structure.* Those of us who have worked inside and outside the home for many years have come to rely on work as a framework for our daily lives. We like the continuity and rhythm that work provides. We like the structure, even though we may sometimes rail against it. Does your job provide you with structure, or are you the architect of your own schedule? Spend some time thinking, then write about what your job is and what it might be like to have less structure or whether you actually might prefer more. Are you ready for a change?

Do What You Are: Discover the Perfect Career for You Through the Secrets of Personality Type by Paul D. Tieger and Barbara Barron-Tieger (Little, Brown). This book helps you figure out your "work personality." Seems odd that you might not already know your personality, work or otherwise, but if you aren't satisfied at work, give this book a try.

I Don't Know What I Want, But I Know It's Not This: A Step-by-Step Guide to Finding Gratifying Work by Julie Jansen (Penguin). "I'm turning forty this year and all of a sudden I'm questioning. . . ." Helps identify current problems you may be having at work and also helps you identify new work choices that might prove more meaningful and enriching.

REFLECT

Now that you are more in touch with your thoughts, or at least have begun to articulate them, try this exercise. It will help you get in touch with your feelings about work. Yes, that activity you've spent most of your life doing.

Sunday Blues

Silently contemplate how you feel on a typical Sunday night. Do you feel jazzed and excited, like a kid waiting for the first day of school? Or are you filled with dread and unease? Are you perhaps unable to sleep because you are preoccupied with all that you have to do at work? Are you day-dreaming about escaping the nine-to-five world, or fortified from your weekend and ready to meet the week's challenges? If you are anxious, try to explore why. Does it have to do with your performance? Is it someone at work? A problem that won't go away? Sometimes we can't bring ourselves to face certain problems we are having at work. Year in and year out, we practice avoidance techniques so successfully that we often develop little rain clouds that follow us around wherever we go. These rain clouds can obscure the sun not only for you, but also for your mate, kids, and cowork-ers. Reflect on exactly what it is you need to do in order to find peace on Sunday night and look forward to Monday.

PRACTICE PATIENCE

The mental and emotional work you are doing in this chapter is a game of inches. At this point in our careers, most of us will not be quitting our jobs to start new ones. Sure, some of us will, and that's great. But most of us will keep working at our current job, career, or trade for ten, fifteen, maybe even twenty more years, depending on how high the retirement age is hoisted over the next decade.

So where is the forward movement? How can we chart our progress? By practicing patience and, as always, by setting reasonable goals for our-selves. It is important to find satisfaction in accomplishing small things as well as big things. Sometimes, we lose ourselves if we derive our sense of self-worth only from really big accomplishments. Try to find as much satisfaction in answering e-mails and clearing your desk as you do in snagging a new client or making a huge presentation. God is in the details. Let each moment have its moment.

Consider how you define accomplishment and whether you are taking sufficient satisfaction in each task well done. For instance, are you getting better at balancing your time at the office? Are you better able to say no to your boss when you can't take on any more responsibilities? Are you proud of yourself for making two cold calls, even if the calls may not have resulted in new business?

Start to track your smaller accomplishments. Rather than setting huge goals for yourself, start to set many small, reasonable ones, and derive satisfaction as you meet them, one after another, day after day.

The Pathfinder: How to Choose or Change Your Career for a Lifetime of Satisfaction and Success by Nicholas Lore (Fireside). A counselor who understands how difficult it can be to find joy at work shares helful insights.

Diffuse the Sunday Blues: visit www.quietamerican.org and take a one-minute "sound" vacation. You can listen free or buy one. Buffy listened to a recording sent in by author Rick Moody. It was one minute of water splashing against a jetty on Fischer's Island, New York. Sweet.

Take a Sabbatical

Kate's company has recently instituted sabbaticals for employees who have worked for the company for ten years or longer. Unlike some companies that require employees to do something during their sabbaticals that increases their usefulness in the workplace, Kate's company lets the worker determine how she will spend her time on sabbatical. One woman went on an archaeological dig. Another took an intensive course in mountain climbing. Whatever employees choose to do, the company insists that they totally disengage from the affairs of the office while they are out.

While most of us aren't offered this option at work, we can create it for ourselves. Time away is good for our health and growth — physical, mental, and spiritual. Vacations are important, but vacations aren't quite the same: they are artificial, sort of an ideal way to live. A sabbatical is about stepping off the merry-go-round and taking time to think about your life. *Six Months Off: How to Plan, Negotiate, and Take the Break You Need without Burning Bridges or Going Broke* by Hope Dlugozima (Henry Holt) has a title that says it all. *Time Off for Good Behavior: How Hardworking*

Browse a newsstand. Get a coffee or, better still, a bottle of water, and treat yourself to a couple of magazines that might get you thinking differently about your job, your work, and your career. Check out these and any other magazines that catch your eye: *Fast Company* is an informative and vital voice for new businesses, especially those tied to the Internet. Smart articles give entrepreneurs and worker bees the particulars of leadership and organization, no matter the trade.

Mother Jones presents articles on national news topics, investigative reports, and commentary, as well as articles on the arts, health, the environment, and book reviews.

Entrepreneur features articles, interviews, and business profiles, as well as financing, marketing, advertising, and legislative news of note aimed at the small business owner and those planning to start a new business.

> *Women Can Take a Break and Change Their Lives* by Mary Lou Quinlan (Broadway) shares thirty-seven women's stories about how taking a sabbatical changed their lives. Pair this cheerleading book with a nuts-and-bolts plan of your own.

RESEARCH

One key way you can keep work vibrant and interesting is to read about and pay attention to what is happening in your workplace, within your industry, and in the business world at large. Being informed will keep you more engaged, and if you are more engaged you will be happier and more productive. You can use reading and research in a variety of ways. For instance, perhaps you should consider taking courses in your field of work to improve your competency. Often, employers will underwrite this. You can also use reading and research to expand your area of expertise, either to advance at your current job or to plan for a different career in the next phase of your life.

Active listening will help you hone your ability to read the corporate or bureaucratic tea leaves. The sad truth is that many of us will be fired, laid off, downsized, or asked to take early retirement in the next few years. It's called the silver bullet. We've been working a long time. We earn a good salary. Letting us go is the equivalent of letting two, maybe even three, younger or less skilled workers go. It's a budget cut often just too tempting to resist.

Think about the silver bullet. Think about it now. Do you hear it whistling toward you? Is the panic rising in you? Or are you thinking that the silver bullet is not meant for you? "Not me," you say. Are you paying rapt attention to the changes your company may be making in overhead, budget cuts, and new managerial styles? Active and attentive listening and reading will help you determine what is going on in your workplace, and it will let you know if you are vulnerable. It will help keep you informed without making you paranoid. Talk to your colleagues, talk to your supervisor about your job performance, keep an open line of communication between you and your boss. Sometimes, you can jump to the wrong conclusions and cause yourself more stress and anxiety by listening to office gossip.

So let's say you are vulnerable. How can you prepare? In some ways you can't. If something bad happens, it will hurt and may be truly unexpected, but you can absorb the blow more easily if you start to articulate your fear, confusion, anger, and perhaps even your sense of relief. The sooner you admit to your feelings and acknowledge the setback, the sooner you will be able to take the necessary steps to propel yourself forward.

Nice Girls Don't Get the Corner Office: 101 Unconscious Mistakes Women Make That Sabotage Their Careers by Lois P. Frankel (Warner Business Books). Talks about how women think, sound, look, and respond, in office situations. You may find yourself nodding your head now and again or even steadily.

Buffy and the Silver Bullet

One late spring night, walking back from our boss's office to our own, I turned to my business partner and friend, Kathy, and said, "They are going to be coming for us." I don't know why I used that particular phrase. It sounded like the good guys in a Western being tracked down by the bad guys. Even after I said, "We are going to be fired," Kathy laughed ruefully and said, "I don't think so." But our movie company had experienced a number of money-losing flops in a row. Someone would have to pay.

Two weeks later, we were fired. I was almost fifty years old and had never been fired from anything in my life. My firing was not private. It was public. I work in the movie business, a small community that thrives on learning and then repeating the gossip about anyone and everyone. So my firing was written about in the trade papers, *Variety* and the *Hollywood Reporter*, which you would expect. The trades covering any industry have a job to do. However, it was also written about in the *New York Times*, the *Los Angeles Times*, the *Wall Street Journal*, *Newsweek*, and on some Web sites, and probably other places I mercifully missed. It was in the paper my parents were reading at breakfast. For the most part, I fared pretty well in these accounts, but I still felt humiliated and angry. I did my job well, and I liked my job. It didn't seem fair. I was scared. And I was sad to be leaving my great staff.

I was luckier than most. I had a contract with my company that afforded me an opportunity to start a new job, albeit one that I would have

Try pounding the keys instead of the pavement. Visit these Web sites to look for work without aggravating your bunions.

www.seniorjobbank.org For people over fifty looking for full-time, part-time, temporary, or volunteer work.

www.salary.com Provides compensation data for different industries and thousands of job titles. Also provides salary advice.

www.jobsearch.org A public-funded resource for job seekers and businesses, this site posts résumés and job openings. Thousands of new jobs are listed daily.

to figure out from the ground up without the benefit of mentors or specific job training. I had to make a go of it in a truly entrepreneurial way in a highly competitive business as an independent producer.

Once the anger and the sadness lifted, I found myself face to face with what I thought about work: what I liked and disliked about it and how, in my new venture, I could set about fashioning the work to better suit this new iteration of myself. What did I like about work? I liked the structure, the collaboration, the sense of creating something specific in a short amount of time, and I truly enjoyed the fun we all had doing it. What I didn't like about it was the inordinate number of hours it required away from my family, the stress and anxiety of performing well and of taking on the well-being of my staff as if it were my own. Over the next months, I tried to keep these related but opposing views in mind as I went about the slow, meticulous work of rebuilding my confidence and building a new business.

FIND ROLE MODELS

Trisha is a gifted artist. She casts big beautiful bronze pieces. Sometimes she works on commission, as when she created a beautiful climbing rose arbor for a couple in the Hamptons, and sometimes her work is funded by grants, as it was when she created a memorial to commemorate a small village in Germany that had been decimated by World War II. Trisha's sculptures are so physically demanding to create that she has had two operations to repair her hands.

Trisha teaches art to college students as a way to augment her earnings and stay in touch with young people, academic circles, gallery owners, and curators—all necessary to keeping her on the exhibition circuit. Recently, Trisha decided that it was too hard at age fifty-four to keep cobbling her income together from the various commissions, teaching, sales of her works, and grants. So she studied and received her real estate license. At first, she was reluctant to tell people that she had passed the exam and would soon be an agent, but after telling a few friends, she received not only support, but also admiration for having the gumption to pursue another business while continuing to work as an artist. She took many of the skills and gifts she had used during her career as an artist—taste, organization, writing grants, persuading people to part with their money—and applied them to the field of real estate. She has been a great success and continues to keep her art alive and thriving.

WRITE IT DOWN

Writing down our thoughts, feelings, and plans of action makes each thought that much more real, each goal that much more attainable. If you have been fired or downsized, if you are about to reenter the workplace after an absence, or if you plan to change jobs, here are some strategies for taking control of your life:

- *Write down how you feel.* Write in your journal or, better yet, write on index cards so you can discard the negative cards as you work through the emotions. Write down your fears—everything from "I will never get another job" to "I am too old" to "I was a fraud and it all caught up with me." Write down everything you felt when your boss or human resources representative sat you down and told you that you were no longer part of the organization.
- *Now write down how you felt immediately following the dismissal and how those feelings morphed over time.* Pay close attention to your dreams, and try to record them faithfully, for they often reveal important clues to your deeper well of emotions. Next, undertake an exercise in catharsis. Write two letters, neither of which you will mail. (You don't want to burn any bridges by acting impulsively.) Write one to your employer, detailing how you felt after being fired and the effect it had on your family. Then write one to yourself—an e-mail, a journal entry, a postcard—describing how you felt when you were fired and how you want to feel in the near future. Writing these letters will help you let off steam and articulate your complex feelings.

  Here is the letter Buffy composed to her direct boss and to the head of the company but did not mail. (Remember this is just an exercise.) She wrote this letter in her head hundreds of times until finally she stopped writing it. She would have healed more quickly if she had written it down instead of stewing and stoking bad, recurring dreams. Usually she wrote one- or two-line missives such as:

> *I thought I could trust you. I did a good job, and I was a loyal employee. Why did you fire me? Why were all the women you fired (except one) of a certain age? You have embarrassed me in front of my family.*

Buffy wrote this in her journal three months after being fired:

> *I am not afraid. I feel freer than I have in years. I do not feel my pulse in my stomach. I will not allow myself to obsess over my age. Even though anyone over thirty in Hollywood is . . . stop!*

- *Now write about what you want.* Without overthinking, write about the kind of job you will be looking for. For example, you might write, "I want the same job at a different company" or "I want a job as a librarian" or "I want a job with less stress and shorter hours" or "I want to work outdoors." Write what you really want to do in this phase of your life to earn money.
- *Now write down your strengths and weaknesses.* If you go back over your journal or if you consult your dream log, the reflections you have made while reading this book, or your Personality Thumbprint, you might be able to see where you are strong and where you need shoring up. Ask yourself whether you like to collaborate with others. Do you like the structure imposed by an office environment? Do you encourage others easily or do you need to be encouraged? How would you manage in a one-person office?
- *Now write down your action plan.* Write a résumé. Go online or buy or check out of the library a book that tells you how. Ask a friend to help you write a résumé that reflects who you are and all of your job experience, paid or unpaid.

Write down your job criteria: salary (refer to your budget and determine what you really need to earn as opposed to what you want to earn or what you used to earn), location (are you willing to move?), title, responsibilities, benefits. Do you need to take a course or even go back to school to retrain yourself? Will age be a factor?

Write a list of people you can start to call or e-mail about potential leads. Begin to construct your network. A *network* is a group of people who may be able to introduce you to a job opportunity. Your network begins with your relatives, colleagues, and friends. It also includes people you know through church or the gym. To expand your network, join professional associations or reach out to your local chamber of commerce, alumni association, or a local service agency in your community. Track local events in your area through Yahoo. Visit online sites such as www.iVillage.com, www.jobsearch.com, or www.quintcareers.com and search under "networking." The Internet is a virtual network waiting for you to join.

Getting a new job or changing jobs can be a challenge, but there is a lot of information out there to get you started. You may want to hire a personal coach, a professional who will help you figure out what you want and how to get it. Perhaps you have an idea for a new business but aren't sure how to get started. Consider hiring a small business consultant who can help you organize your finances, establish a corporation, navigate the world of licenses, and prepare you for tax implications.

GET TOGETHER

Get together with a friend and consider starting a business. Let your dreams and your ideas range wildly. Start an exercise company. Become personal shoppers. Become event planners. Then narrow your sights and see if there's a practical scheme lurking in there somewhere. How would you go about implementing such a scheme? Would you open a storefront or start a Web site? Research what's entailed for each endeavor. The idea

Want a new career, a different job? Try these sites:

www.careerchange network.com
Been there, done that. Now what? Career Change Network is dedicated to helping you choose a new career path and change your life.

www.coachfederation.org
This site seeks to help people find the most suitable coach for their personal and business needs.

www.back2college.com
Find online, distance, and on-campus degree programs.

www.careersnet.com
Build the life you'll love with this powerful career change, job search, and outplacement portal, featuring career coaches and other helpful services.

Want to find another job? In your current field or in a related field? Try these sites:

www.linkedin.com
Unique networking site helps you discover connections to recommended job candidates, industry experts, business partners, and jobs by strengthening and extending your existing network of trusted contacts.

www.craigslist.com
Popular classified ads for jobs, sales, services, community, and events.

www.monster.com
Find that job that you are looking for faster and easier with Monster.com.

hotjobs.yahoo.com
Find the perfect job with Yahoo's popular job search site.

www.careerjournal.com
A career site from the *Wall Street Journal* for executives.

www.careerbuilder.com
Find jobs locally or nationally with the largest employment network.

here is to make money and have fun spending time with the friend or friends whom work has kept you from seeing regularly.

Partners?

Working as business partners can be a satisfying and exciting way to earn a living. Think of Rodgers and Hammerstein, Lennon and McCartney, Lewis and Clark, Kate and Buffy! Buffy and Kathy! Buffy and Kathy worked together in the same department for more than nine years, and their friendship and partnership developed naturally. When they decided to go into business together, it seemed a natural progression of their friendship. They knew each other well and how each worked, so creating a formal partnership was easy. They were lucky. (And Buffy thinks the fact that they were born one day apart has played a sort of mystical role in their harmonious relationship.)

Business partnerships can be difficult to maintain, but there are ways to make them work. You are all probably involved in a partnership of some sort right now, whether it be your marriage, your relationship with your exercise trainer, your relationship with your cohead of the PTA, your friend who helps organize the book club, a close colleague at work. All of these are partnerships, and all can shed light on what kind of partner you are and what kind of business partner you want.

In addition to drafting a legal document, consider writing a partnership promise document. Remember that a partnership is not about working autonomously, control or power, or seeing the world in black-and-white terms. Write down what you think a partnership is about, and imagine scenarios in which you want to know how you partner will act. Will she lose her temper easily? Does she raise her voice? Is she timid if someone tells her no?

Here are some ideas to get you started.

- *Money.* How will we handle money? Will we be generous and trusting with each other? Will we always split everything down the middle? What happens if one of us needs some money for our family, and the other partner wants to put money into the business to grow it?

- *Expectations and accomplishment.* Do we both define success in the same way? What if one of us is offered a higher paying job with another company? How much time should we dedicate to the new business before we call it quits?
- *Collaboration.* Do we both listen carefully to what the other person is saying? Do I have to get my way every time? Will I be confident when she represents our business and I am not there? Can we disagree in public?
- *Structure.* Will we both work equally hard? Will we divide up the work or work together on all projects? Will I feel guilty leaving early one night a week to meet a family obligation?

Go slowly, guard against naysayers, talk it over repeatedly, keep communication open, but remember, partnerships can be great.

Let's Go into Business Together by Azriela Jaffe (Career Press). Offers more than one hundred interviews about what works and what doesn't in partnerships.

www.personalmba.com Promises you can master business without spending a fortune on a master's degree. Fans of this site suggest getting the associated books on tape and combining exercise and learning.

PUTTING IT ALL TOGETHER

Now is the time for you to design a plan to recommit to work and finding the joy. Take special care to acknowledge any special issues or challenges you need to address.

1. *Create time* to think about work and your feelings about work. Find joy in your work.
2. *Reflect* on whether you suffer from Sunday Blues.
3. *Practice patience,* and set reasonable goals for yourself. Be sure to take satisfaction from each accomplishment, no matter how small.
4. *Research* your company and your career field; be attuned to the subtle changes in your company that could change your job status. Read the corporate tea leaves and pay them heed.
5. *Find role models* of people who have found and sustained joy in their work, or who have changed careers in midlife.
6. *Write down* your feelings, then your strengths and weaknesses, and finally your action steps. If you are in a transitional phase, describe your dream job and prepare a résumé or a biography of your work life.

7. *Get together* with a friend and brainstorm and research a business you might go into together. Explore partnerships.

TO-DO LIST

Whether you like your job, want a different job, or have been fired or downsized, these activities will get you thinking about how you feel about your work.

- Consult a life coach.
- Discuss work with a therapist.
- Work on your résumé.
- Draft a letter inquiring about employment.
- Assemble a list of people (with phone numbers and e-mail and snail-mail addresses) who might be helpful to you in a job search.
- Write a comforting letter to yourself.
- Research and consider taking the Myers-Briggs test to get a sense of your disposition and strengths.
- Talk to your boss about opportunities, or initiate a conversation about your performance.
- Chart your overtime. Determine how many overtime hours you were asked to work and how many you had no control over.
- Seek out and interview people who have undergone a job change to see how they have managed the issues surrounding downsizing and reentry.
- Share at least two workplace anecdotes with a family member.
- Communicate your joy about work to others.

- Talk to your mate about how much money you each need to contribute to the family.
- List some of your recent accomplishments, no matter how small.
- List the history of your accomplishments, from college to last week.
- Go online and register at job sites that offer or track job opportunities in your field.
- If you are thinking about changing careers, consider using a vacation to try out a new job. There are companies that arrange for you to run a business for a week, such as a bed-and-breakfast or a small food franchise. Visit www.vocationsvacations.com, for example. Tune in to your fantasy job — winemaker, dog trainer, makeup artist — and then spend a weekend or a few days performing that job to see if you want to make a change and pursue a new career. You may find that running a bed-and-breakfast is just too much work for you.
- Consider a midcareer sabbatical, and use the time to research other fields. Seek out foundations that provide fellowships and grants to pursue new jobs and special projects.

KATE'S PLAN

I think I always had a vision of retiring early. For the last thirty years, every year I have said to myself, "Ten more years." The years have passed. I am now fifty-five. And now, when I say "Ten more years," for the first time in my life, this statement reflects reality. And the funny thing is, instead of looking at the next ten years as drudgery, as the final mind-numbing stretch, I see it as a joy. In a very real way, I feel a little like I did senior year in high school after I got accepted to college. I was no longer working with a goal in mind (that of getting into college). I was working, learning, for its own sake. My plan is:

- Without being paranoid, read the corporate tea leaves and make sure my position is as secure as I can realistically expect it to be in today's corporate environment.
- Work to sustain joy and communicate it to coworkers, family, and friends.
- Consciously mentor the people who will replace me, rather than resent their breathing down my neck.
- Share as much knowledge as I can.
- Make decisions without fear.
- Set a dozen smaller goals every year, and at year's end do a personal reckoning.
- Sharpen my editorial skills so I can transition into freelance work.

BUFFY'S PLAN

Given that I am in a feast-or-famine line of work, I need to devote myself to meditating on how best to deal with the ups and downs. Because I am rather conservative in my approach to finances, I need to start expanding my horizons for additional revenue sources. I am teaching one course now and am enjoying it. I would like to continue to write both fiction and non-fiction and derive some income from it. Therefore, my plan:

- Write a résumé or biography of my work, and spend time creating different versions to target different lines of work for which I think I am eligible.
- Pursue silent contemplation and meditation to plumb my inner feelings about work.
- Compile a list of people who can serve as my network.
- Explore teaching at other colleges.
- Set reasonable goals for myself as a writer.

Now that we have covered work, one of the more substantial layers of our lives, it's time to turn to another, consisting of your activities after work, or, as we used to say on our college applications, those all-important, character-building, résumé-rounding extracurricular activities.

Is There More to Life Than Work?

Finding time for play

Dear Kate: You have riding, gardening, embroidery, and now you're talking about hooking rugs! How do you find the time? It's like the only kind of activity I think I should be doing is the kind that brings in money. Like, if I have free time, that means I can use it to work more. Love, Buffy

Dear Buffy: Maybe it's that Depression-era baby crying out for security. But I was a witness. I remember in college senior year when you very briefly took up a hobby. Love, Kate

Dear Kate: That's right. I embroidered that shawl for Gogo as a wedding present. It was a map that showed her path from Washington, D.C., to London to South Africa to marry Wesley. On white wool. I wonder if she still has it? Or whether she burned it after the divorce? I collect certain things — does that count as a hobby? Love, Buffy

Dear Buffy: Sure. You could also take up embroidery again. Or find something else. It's not about busy work or dilettantism. It's about balance. And fun! It's about getting one side of your life to feed the other and vice versa. Now you'll have to excuse me, I have gardens to weed before I weep, er, sleep. Love, Kate

EXTRACURRICULAR ACTIVITIES

When Kate was in high school, she loved extracurricular activities. She was a lead player in the Viking Masquers, her high school thespian troupe; an officer of the drama club; an alto in the varsity chorus and in the smaller vocal ensemble; and literary editor of the yearbook. As her mother drove her from one after-school activity to the next, Kate fretted. How was she ever going to handle it all? Get her homework done, keep up her grade-point average, get great SAT scores, and get into the college of her choice, all while avoiding a total nervous breakdown. Her mother would respond, in her cool, sphinxlike way, "The more you do, the more you can do."

While Kate admits that there were times when hearing those words made her want to lunge across the car and throttle her mother, in the intervening years she has come to accept their wisdom and has even, on occasion (she must confess), been known to intone them to her own children.

Why are extracurricular activities so important now? Over the next ten to fifteen years, your work-play ratio will probably shift gradually, with work occupying fewer hours and play more. If your idea of play is shopping or talking on your cell or spacing out in front of the tube or working more overtime, then you need to address that now. You need to invest, emotionally and perhaps even financially, in an interest or interests that will nourish your mind, spirit, and heart. When work dwindles down to a few hours a week, you will need to be ready, and eager, to fill your hours with stimulating new interests that eventually could not only occupy your days but also provide an alternative source of income in the second half of your life.

In this chapter, we will assess the work-play balance in your life, the ratio of hours you spend at work to those you spend in the pursuit of, as the late great Joseph Campbell termed it, your bliss. We will show you how to address time, sort out time, and help you match up your particular set of aptitudes to pursuits that might pique your interest, mellow you out, or get your juices flowing again. The result will be a well-balanced plan for how to spend the ever-expanding extracurricular portion of the second half of your life.

The energy, wisdom, and pure satisfaction that you cultivate when pursuing extracurricular activities can, in fact, boil up and bubble over into the energy you bring to your job. And, since those extracurricular activities will eventually come to replace your paid work activities, you will benefit by starting to invest time, money, and attention in them now. Why, it is even possible that today's extracurricular activity could become a full- or part-time job during the second half of your life.

ⵊⵊⵊ

Now let's use our seven strategies to explore the wonderful world of extracurricular activities.

CREATE TIME

Creating time for extracurricular activities is vitally important to a well-balanced future life. Let's see if you can calculate your current work-play ratio. Start with the total number of hours available each week ($24 \times 7 = 168$ hours). For the next seven days keep a record of how you spend your time:

- *Tally up the number of hours you sleep during the week and on the week-end.* Some of us crash over the weekend and binge sleep in order to make up for the sleep deficit we've run up over the week. Don't forget to include power naps, too.
- *Tally up the number of hours you spend working.* Factor in your time commuting. Be sure to include your regular work schedule, but also add in overtime and any take-home work. If you check office e-mails at midnight, write it down.
- *Count the number of hours you spend preparing and eating food and doing chores on weekdays and weekends.* Like sleep, those hours get deducted as maintenance. Be sure to include all household chores — laundry, straightening, doing errands, chauffeuring the kids. Many of us have kids who drive themselves, so, hey, add in some worry time.
- *Count the number of hours you spend watching television.* Be honest. It doesn't matter whether you watch the History Channel or back-to-back episodes of *Law & Order,* just monitor your time.

- *Count the number of hours per week you spend exercising.* Exercise is required, as you'll recall. It is not an extracurricular activity.

Now add all the hours and subtract the total from 168. This is the number of downtime hours you have each week. Take some time to analyze, break down, and account for your downtime. It may be that you already have interests you devote time to. It may be that, as a result of chapter 4, you have already taken up a mindstretcher and are pursuing an interest outside your sphere of expertise. How many hours per week do you currently spend pursuing your own interests? Or, like so many of us, do you spend much of your downtime decompressing: loafing, noodling, puttering, and dreaming? Some time spent loafing, noodling, puttering, and dreaming is actually necessary to your mental health. We just don't want to squander all of our precious downtime in this fashion. The goal here is to create time to pursue interests. Keep in mind the following:

- Going to the movies or to a play or a concert counts as a cultural, nurturing pursuit so you get extracurricular credit for those activities.
- Visiting with friends or going to a party reinforces your social circle, so give yourself credit there, too.
- Doing household chores and driving your kids to their extracurricular activities or to their friends' houses does *not* count toward your own extracurricular credit.
- Spending quality time with your family, such as working on a model or a quilt with your child, is a happy combination of extracurricular and family fun.
- Gardening, if you are pursuing it as a hobby or an interest, rather than as lawn maintenance, can earn you credit, too.

Kate's Downtime Worksheet
- Sleep: 44 hours
- Work (including 20 hours commuting): 62 hours
- Shopping for, preparing, and eating meals: 12 hours
- Household chores/family maintenance: 4 hours

> - Exercise: 6 hours
> - TV: 4 hours
>   Total: 138 hours
>   168 hours − 138 hours = 30 hours of downtime
>   Breakdown of downtime hours:
> - Meditation/noodling: 3 hours
> - Horseback riding: 6 hours
> - Potential extracurricular activities: 21 hours

REFLECT

Are you a closet something or other? Is there something that you have always wanted to do but haven't gotten around to doing yet? Take some time to reflect on this question. Your case of the wannabes may take the form of frustration, a recurring dream, a deep-seated yearning, or an unfulfilled wish. Or you may simply feel the need to revive a childhood or early-adult interest. To get you primed, let's consider a few random scenarios:

- You've always suspected that you have a very good voice and that with a little training it might become an excellent voice. But you were always too shy to take it outside the shower stall. Perhaps now is the time to join a choir, start voice lessons, or hook up with a local theater group to audition for a role in the next musical comedy.
- As a young girl you once sewed a beautiful skirt, but you haven't used those skills in the intervening years because girls who wore homemade clothes to school were teased. Now might be a great time to pick up a secondhand sewing machine.
- Perhaps sewing is too solitary a pursuit for this stage of your life. Maybe you'll want to join a quilting class or group. Buffy has been saving pieces of her children's clothing for years with the intention of making a quilt, so she will be able to enjoy the memories and not imagine them packed away in the attic.
- How well you remember fly casting with your father in the streams

near your vacation rental when you were a child. You remember standing in your waders with the cold water flowing all around you, listening, watching, waiting for the trout to come up to the surface to feed. Maybe you can combine honoring your father with relearning how to tie flies. (As it happens, there are more books about tying flies than just about any other pastime. Fly tiers, for some reason, just love to write about what they do!)

- Your job is unduly stressful, and you need a specific antidote to it, something that will calm, renew, and center you. A friend of ours had a stressful, thankless job as a social worker in rural Maine. To relieve depression and stress, he started taking pottery lessons from a local ceramic artist. The pottery fed an interest in Zen Buddhism, or perhaps it was the other way around. The Zen Buddhism and the pottery nourished and sustained him. One thing led to another, and eventually he installed a kiln in his basement, quit his job, and started to sell his pottery to friends and in local shops. He's not making a fortune, but the work is tangible and deeply satisfying.

If your back burner has been untended so long that you no longer know what might be sitting back there, meditate to see if you can get a look at it. Or you might ask yourself this question: "If I win the lottery tomorrow, what hobbies will I take up? What will I do for fun?" (*Hint:* Splurging your winnings does not count.)

PRACTICE PATIENCE

It is not easy to learn something new or reacquaint yourself with something you haven't done in years. It is easy to get impatient with yourself when you make a mess of a project or a fool of yourself in front of your fellow hobbyists or students. It may be that you are accessing parts of your brain that you aren't accustomed to using. And, as Martha Stewart says, "That's a good thing."

Buffy took up tennis six years ago with her daughter, Daisy. Jimmy, a young tennis pro, taught them together. Buffy wasn't very good, and Daisy wasn't very interested. Like most teen girls, Daisy considered running around a tennis court cruel and unusual punishment. But the lessons afforded them time together, something they both loved. Jimmy was patient with both of them, and it was his patience that guided them through the lessons. Buffy watched her daughter take easy, relaxed swings at the tennis ball that Jimmy unerringly hit almost exactly to the point of her outstretched racket. Buffy, on the other hand, was nervous, tried too hard, and was anything but relaxed.

One night Jimmy told her to relax. Buffy asked what he meant. She thought her right arm *was* relaxed. Jimmy said, "Your arm. You are holding it at an angle, almost like your arm's in an invisible cast." Buffy was embarrassed.

Daisy came over to her and whispered, "You can do it, and who cares if you can't?" It was such a sweet thing to say, and Buffy found herself repeating it, "Who cares if I can't?" In this way, Buffy learned patience. She didn't have to be perfect. (As if she could.) And she didn't have to worry about her progress. She just had to relax. And be patient.

RESEARCH

If you have an interest or hobby, do some research to learn more about it. If you don't have an interest, do research to find one. Think about what kinds of skills and aptitude your work requires you to use. Think about what fields of interest you are exposed to every day. You might want to pursue hobbies and interests that take advantage of those same skills and interests. Or you might want to pursue an interest that falls outside your realm of experience and expertise. You might want to search for complementary interests. For instance, Kate exercises her verbal and written skills in her job as a publisher. She is looking for something physical or nonverbal to do so she can exercise a different skill set.

The world is teeming with things to do, so it might be easier to consider them in categories. These categories are somewhat arbitrary, and many interests span more than one. Use them to start brainstorming ideas. Here goes:

www.meetup.com
This site organizes local
groups of people who
share common interests
and meet regularly.

www.43things.com
Make a list of forty-three
goals or interests, and
this site will connect you
to others who share the
same goals and
interests.

groups.yahoo.com
Join online groups to
find and communicate
with people who share
similar interests.

www.about.com/
hobbies
Discover online
resources, expert tips,
and articles on your
favorite hobbies.

www.scrapbook.com
Find scrapbooking
ideas, supplies,
resources, and online
communities to join.

- Reading and writing
- 'Rithmetic and science
- History
- Nature
- Music and dance
- Arts and crafts
- Exercise

Visit Internet sites and chat rooms, look in your local paper, or ask a neighbor or friend where you might find classes, groups, and places where you can pursue your interests near your home or workplace. Before you invest in equipment, try to observe a class or group in progress. Interview a teacher or a student. Do research to find out what will be involved or required of you before you invest any time or money. Your downtime is precious; spend it wisely.

FIND ROLE MODELS

Kira is a magazine editor who loves to ski. One winter vacation at Bromley, she broke her foot on her first day on the slopes and had to spend the rest of the week in the lodge by the fireplace with her foot propped up on a stool. The wife of one of her friends had brought a basket of knitting with her, and out of sheer boredom and desperation, Kira (who had always thought knitting was the province of pregnant women and grandmothers) asked this woman to teach her how to knit. Her first project was a scarf.

When she got home, she went out to a yarn store, bought needles and some skeins of yarn, and started knitting more scarves, before graduating to hats, sweaters, and vests. Before long, she was designing her own patterns and experimenting with varying sizes of needles and types of yarn. After a while, three things occurred to her: (1) everybody in her neighborhood suddenly seemed to have taken up knitting, (2) there wasn't a single yarn store within walking distance, and (3) someone smart enough to open a local yarn store was sure to make a killing.

A year and a half later, her magazine went under and Kira found herself out of a job. She used her severance money to rent and renovate a small storefront down the street from her home. A small business loan enabled her to purchase enough inventory for the first six months. She didn't even have to advertise. The neighborhood knitters found her and a place where they could go to knit, talk to other knitters, and share patterns and ideas. Kira is a role model of someone who opened herself up to a brand new interest that, as fate would have it, transformed itself into a new career for her.

WRITE IT DOWN

Write down at least ten interests or activities you would consider pursuing. As you do, keep the following items in mind:

- Be sure your extracurricular interests harness at least one skill or aptitude that you already have and one that needs some flexing or exploration.
- Consider playing to your minor strengths as well as to your major ones. Perhaps you have overdeveloped some and neglected others.
- If multiple pursuits appeal to you, strive for balance. Stamp collecting, embroidery, and model making are similar in that all three involve sitting on your keister indoors and doing close work. If you were to substitute bird-watching for model making, you'd improve the mix. If you were to substitute tango lessons for stamp collecting, you'd be just about set.
- Should you decide to take up more than one new interest, avoid embarking on them at the same time. Immerse yourself in one at a time. Give yourself a chance to get one ball into the air before you toss up the next. If that one ball satisfies you sufficiently, you may decide to set the second one aside for another day.
- For variety, try entertaining some interests that can only be pursued in one or two seasons. That way, you can substitute something completely different in the other seasons.

www.traildatabase.org
The world's largest database of walking and hiking trails.

www.rvia.org
RVs allow you to combine travel and leisure and are enormously popular. This site is the Recreation Vehicle Industry buyers' guide to choosing, using, and maintaining an RV.

www.rvra.org
Recreational Vehicle Rental Association is a resource for people who want to rent an RV.

www.newrver.com
The beginner's guide to RVing. Everything you need to know about RVs and the RV lifestyle.

www.elderhostel.org
The nation's first and the world's largest educational travel organization for adults fifty-five years old and older.

www.roadscholar.org
For those who want to travel "outside" the tour, and who view travel to other countries as an opportunity to learn (rather than shop), this site offers travel packages of an enriching, hands-on, holistic nature, from Baja to the Tundra, from the Sargasso to the Sahara.

www.seniornet.org
This is a friendly, no-frills online place you can go to ask questions and get information on subjects ranging from hobbies to health to continuing education to travel to deals for seniors.

www.boomercafe.com
An ongoing, ever-changing e-zine written by and for baby boomers. Under its regular feature Play, you'll find articles on travel, pastimes, road trips, sports, and sex.

- Think of your extracurricular schedule as being a palette of paints that can change with the seasons and fluctuate over the years to keep you fresh, interested, and interesting.
- Don't exclude any possibilities. From skydiving to deep-sea diving, there are no limits to what you can do.

GET TOGETHER

Get together and enlist the aid of a friend to help you get started on something. For instance, Kate wants to start a novel, but getting started is the hardest part. So Buffy offered to be a one-woman writing group for her. Each Friday, Kate e-mails Buffy what she has written that week, and Buffy gives her a brief critique and support to continue. By giving Kate a deadline and by letting her know that someone is waiting to read her work, Kate has the structure, encouragement, and sense of urgency that is so vital to a writer. Do you have a friend who can help you in a similar way? Can you help a friend?

Get together with a friend to research a new activity you can take up together. Make sure it's right for both of you. Don't drag each other into it. Help each other stick it out through the discouraging times. Go have a cup of coffee or a glass of wine afterward and share your feelings, impressions, and maybe a few laughs.

PUTTING IT ALL TOGETHER

Now it's time to design a plan for your extracurricular activities. As you set out on your task, keep in mind the following:

1. *Create time* for extracurricular activities. Figure out how much time you could devote to an extracurricular activity.
2. *Reflect* on your hidden, back-burner, closeted, or shelved wishes, dreams, and desires.
3. *Practice patience* with yourself when you are trying to learn something new.

4. *Research* to find areas of interest and people and places where those interests are vital and thriving.
5. *Find role models,* people with a healthy work-play ratio and a well-balanced roster of extracurricular activities.
6. *Write down* at least ten activities or pursuits that really interest you.
7. *Get together* with a friend to find a new extracurricular activity.

TO-DO LIST

Don't be intimidated by the length of this to-do list. It is organized in the categories we suggested in the research section. If by some miracle or act of oversight we have neglected to include something you are interested in, add it to your plan. Follow Joseph Campbell's advice — follow your bliss!

Reading and writing

- Do crossword puzzles.
- Compose crossword puzzles.
- Write stories or nonfiction.
- Write your memoirs.
- Write poetry.
- Write plays.
- Write song lyrics.
- Write jingles.
- Join or start a writers' group.
- Join or start a book club.
- Keep a journal.
- Write for a local newspaper or periodical.
- Write for a professional journal.
- Start a blog.

'Rithmetic and science

- Design computer programs.
- Design puzzles.
- Make models.
- Study celestial navigation.
- Buy a telescope.
- Buy a microscope.
- Study oceanography/marine biology.
- Study geography.
- Study botany.
- Build a rocket.
- Build a weather station.
- Green your home (that is, find ways of making it more environmentally friendly).
- Take up carpentry.
- Study architecture.

History

- Go on an archaeological dig.
- Research your family tree.
- Study art history.
- Research the area where you live.
- Travel.
- Volunteer at a museum or historical site.

Nature

- Orienteer (use a compass to plot your way on a walk or hike).
- Letterbox. (This combines the use of a compass with the solving of riddles. There are letterboxing trails to follow in almost every state. Follow the clues, track down the letterbox, then mark the letter with a personal stamp to show you've been there, and take away a souvenir. Check out letterboxing Web sites.
- Bird watch.
- Press wildflowers or leaves.
- Garden (flower, vegetable, or herb; outdoors, indoors cultivating a terrarium, or maintaining a container garden).
- Collect and identify shells.
- Take up fishing.
- Take up fly tying.
- Learn to sail or operate a motorboat.
- Breed dogs, cats, birds, or fish.
- Study astronomy.

Music and dance

- Reacquaint yourself with the instrument you played in high school or college.
- Learn how to play a new musical instrument.
- Learn to read sheet music.
- Play in a musical group.
- Sing in a chorus or choir.
- Compose music.
- Perform in a musical comedy.
- Subscribe to a concert series and bring the sheet music with you to read along.
- Listen to music analytically.
- Drum and chant.
- Ballroom dance, line dance, jitterbug, and square, folk, or contra dance.
- Ballet, tap, belly, or modern dance.

Arts and crafts

- Learn to quilt.
- Study dressmaking or design.
- Embroider, do trapunto, or cross-stitch.
- Knit and crochet.
- Hook rugs.
- Weave rugs or baskets.
- Sculpt.
- Paint.
- Throw pots.
- Make jewelry.
- Build a dollhouse.
- Create your own stationery, journal, or greeting cards.
- Make a puppet.
- Bind books.
- Make candles.
- Work leather.
- Work wood.
- Learn photography.

Exercise

- Dance (modern, ballet, tango, ballroom, swing).
- Study Yoga.
- Study martial arts (karate, Tai Chi).
- Take up spelunking, rock climbing, rappelling.
- Take up snorkeling or deep-sea diving.
- Learn to drive a race car.
- Learn horseback riding.
- Learn massage therapy.
- Buy or rent an RV and travel.

Miscellaneous

- Become a life coach, professional organizer, arbiter.
- Join Elderhostel.
- Use a midcareer sabbatical to find your bliss. Research foundations that give fellowships or grants to individuals.
- Join Road Scholar, a new program that combines traveling with education. You can sign up for a trip to England to study antiques or stay close to home and visit Pennsylvania to study criminal forensics.

KATE'S PLAN

I already ride and garden, but these interests are more practical in warm weather. I'd like to pursue other interests, particularly in the colder winter months when I ride less and don't garden at all. When I check my back burner, I see there are several unwritten and partially written novels back there. Ever since I was a little girl, I have wanted to write novels. I have published one novel, written during a brief, blessed break between two babies, and I collaborated on another novel with Buffy. But career and small children overtook me, and I haven't really gotten down to serious fiction writing in more than ten years.

Every week I commute for roughly twenty hours on the train. Usually I spend that time working on take-home projects from the office. But if I budgeted my office time better, I could dedicate at least five hours of that time (more, if I need it) to writing. I could also allot five hours from my twenty-one hours of downtime for writing.

More than twenty years ago, my sister-in-law hooked a rug for me. She dyed the wool herself from plants I picked in the area. She designed the rug to match a mirror from Bali, which has a frame of pink flowers. The rug is a beautiful pale yellow with a border of pink flowers. It still lies on my guest room floor. Over the years, dogs have done their business on it, children have gotten sick on it, muddy shoes or boots have trod across it, but it still looks as fresh and beautiful as the day I first laid it down. My plan is:

- Commit to learning how to hook rugs.
- Start writing a novel.

BUFFY'S PLAN

Like everyone else, grabbing hold of the elusive downtime and doing something useful and tangible with it is my biggest challenge. I have approximately twenty-eight hours of downtime. (Unable to keep my competitiveness in check, I see Kate has twenty-one hours of downtime. I have more. I sleep more than she does, commute less, and watch more TV. Am I a worse person?) So my plan looks like this:

- Continue to write regularly and finish the first draft of my new novel.
- Begin to cook and share the cooking responsibilities.
- Learn the names and vital information of the flowers and trees in my backyard. Begin to garden more.

Now you are ready to move up to the final layer of your life. Let's call it the icing on your Dream Cake. It's the element without which your life cannot really be complete. For most of this book, we have spoken about the many ways you can build yourself up and make yourself stronger, smarter, healthier, and more thoughtful. If you can't take at least a little of that yummy cake and share it, what good is it, really?

13 How Can I Give Back?

Paying it forward

> Dear Buffy: When you asked me about where and when I volunteer, I immediately felt like a total hypocrite. I don't really give back, and I'm tired of feeling guilty about it. Love, Kate
>
> Dear Kate: Cut yourself some slack, why don't you? You *are* giving back. You're running a one-woman nursing home for your mother. If you need to assuage your guilt, why not research where you might volunteer once you get (create) the time? Love, Buffy

PEACE, MAN!

Winston Churchill said "You make a living by what you get, but you make a life by what you give." Giving back, or volunteering, has deep roots in our history. Volunteers have regularly banded together to address an apparent need and to bring social issues to the public forum. Groups of volunteers forced the government and society to address such issues as the abolition of slavery, women's suffrage, and prison reform. Elise Slobodin of the UJA Federation's Caring Commission said volunteers are like pioneers and experimenters. We like the idea of being a pioneer and we like even better the idea of not allowing our choice of activity or level of participation to depend on financial remuneration. Some people volunteer purely out of charity and expect nothing back. Others volunteer because it makes them feel good to help someone. Still others feel that volunteering is a form of karmic exchange program: help someone today—tutor a young boy in math three days a week, for example—and someone you don't know may drive your mother to church on Sunday. Any way you choose to think or feel about volunteering is just fine. But think about it you must.

Why do you volunteer? Why do you *not* volunteer? Answer both questions since you need to examine both sides of this complex issue. The statements that follow might apply to you and get you thinking about your feelings about volunteering. I give back because:

- It is my responsibility as a citizen and a member of my community.
- I believe that one person can make a difference.
- I want to participate in a free exchange of ideas that is not based on money.
- Blessings should be shared.
- It gives me a warm, fuzzy feeling.
- I feel guilty as hell and am afraid God will strike me down if I don't.

I do not give back because:

- I am just too busy. I don't have the time.
- I don't want to have to deal with strangers.
- It's just more pressure added to an already overscheduled life.
- I have to make money when I invest my time.
- I am suspicious of how most charitable organizations use the funds that are donated.
- The world is so screwed up, how can one person possibly make a difference?

Did you find yourself nodding vigorously at some of these statements? These feelings and excuses are shared by many of us. Why is it that the baby boomer generation—we, who might have joined the Peace Corps or VISTA or any number of benevolent organizations—find ourselves, at this stage of our lives, simply too busy to give back now that we have the experience, spirit, and maturity to do so? When you were an idealistic youth, did you give time and energy to causes that you really believed in? Whether it was politics or the environment, stopping the war or defending

Fun facts from the Bureau of Labor Statistics: 65.4 million people volunteered at least once last year; that's almost 30 percent of the entire U.S. population. Women tend to volunteer more than men (one-third of all women vs. one-quarter of all men). People ages 35 to 44 are most likely to volunteer. Teens have a high rate of volunteerism. People volunteer an average of fifty hours per year. Most people volunteered for one or two organizations. The number one reason for not volunteering? Forty-five percent said they had no time.

Need a little push into the civic pool? Check out www.civicventures.org/ nextchapter. The Next Chapter initiative provides expertise and assistance to community groups across the country and works to help people in the second half of life set a course, connect with peers, and find pathways to significant service. Click on Directory to track down organizations in your state.

September 21st is the International Day of Peace. Visit www.peaceoneday.org to learn more about the day and how you might participate.

the rights of women, it seemed that we boomers *owned* the concept of the just cause. We were fighters. And we were thoroughly convinced that we were fighting on the side of the angels. In that spirit, we put causes ahead of just about everything else in our young lives: ahead of money and personal comfort and sometimes even ahead of family and friends. We were acutely aware of what was wrong with the world and we wanted to right it now.

Let us summon some of the vibrant feelings we had when we truly felt we could make a difference. We'll focus on five points to help center our thoughts and prepare us for action: patience, energy, all things are possible, commitment, and experience. PEACE. When you review the five components of PEACE, let them roll around in your mind for a few minutes, then formulate a sentence for each that describes your personal feelings. To get you started, here are some ideas:

- *Patience.* I will forgive my limitations and forgive others theirs; I will manage my expectations and frustrations.
- *Energy.* Age is not relevant; my exercise program (physical and mental) will provide the necessary energy and strength for me to perform.
- *All things are possible.* One person *can* make a difference. Kindness and action are my goals.
- *Commitment.* I value self-reliance, determination, structure, and standing up for beliefs.
- *Experience.* I have talents and knowledge, and it is my obligation to share them in a modest, humble way.

Giving back — participating, volunteering, making donations of time, energy, and skills — is the focus of this chapter. It is not always easy to select how or to whom to offer yourself, your skills, and your services. Volunteering can be a complicated process. But what's important is that you give of yourself in some way or other. The very act of giving back is the icing on the cake. It tops off your life and holds its many layers together. Consider volunteering a crucial element in the overall design of the second half of your life. Volunteering keeps you healthy, thriving, aware, and loving. Volunteering makes you whole.

Give peace a chance and, of course, use our seven strategies to explore the myriad opportunities available to you.

CREATE TIME

At this period in our lives, we are facing a great many changes, but as we have seen, they are changes we can manage, adapt to, even control. What we cannot afford to do is let time pass. We cannot afford to wait to dive into the civic pool. In the previous chapters we have contemplated some very heady ideas and taken our raw feelings, fleeting ideas, and pent-up energies and started to transform them into a growing, tangible plan of action for the second half of our lives. Without this last layer, though, our plans will be flawed, our dreams not fully realized. The fact is that we have resources within us to contribute, to get involved, to ensure that our lives from here on in are the best they can be.

How do we begin? Take time to look at your community and the people you come into contact with on a daily basis. What or who may be in need of a bit of help from you? Make a list of places you could volunteer, people you could assist, and issues you could help to resolve. Take time to poke around, and you will, in surprisingly short order, discover a need. Then, in equally short order, get up off your duff to address it!

REFLECT

Think about the role giving back has played in your life. Think back to your high school and college days. Try going back even further to your childhood, for often it is in childhood that the patterns are set for giving back in later life.

UNICEF Meditation

What are your first memories of giving back as a young child? When did you first feel the golden glow of having done something good, something

Here are some sites to get you going. You will be surprised how easy it is to find a place, a person, or a group of people who need you.

www.volunteermatch.org
www.joinsenior service.org
www.idealist.org
www.itmagazine.net
www.helpyourcommunity.org
www.charityfocus.org
www.worldvolunteerweb.org
www.volunteerabroad.com
www.volunteer international.org
www.volunteersolutions.org
www.seniorcorps.org
www.worldvolunteer web.org
The World Volunteer Web is hosted by the United Nations Volunteers (UNV) program. This site supports the volunteer community by serving as a global clearinghouse. It is the global focal point for International Volunteer Day (IVD), celebrated around the world every December 5th. Mark your calendars!

www.networkforgood.org
A comprehensive site
for volunteering that
helps answer the ques-
tion: how do I begin?
Buffy found several
places where she could
volunteer to help home-
less teens within ten
miles of her house.
Check out their tips for
donating. Tell your teens
about the Youth
Volunteer Network.

www.globalgiving.com
Learn about locally run
social and environmental
projects around the
world. Decide if you
want to help fund one
closest to your heart.

Peace and quiet, please!
Check out www.
acousticecology.org. The
Acoustic Ecology
Institute works to
increase personal and
social awareness of our
audial environment.
Click on Soundscapes
and browse their sound
libraries.

unselfish? Surely, we all remember trick-or-treating for UNICEF. Remember the Thanksgiving canned good drives and the Christmas toy drives? Think about your history of giving. Go back as far as you can remember, and then come forward in time. Try to remember a Childhood (a favorite childhood story) in which giving back plays a significant role. It might have been a kind act by you or your mother or father or sibling. If, somewhere along the line, you stopped giving, can you remember when it was? How old were you? What was going on in your life at the time? When and why did that golden glow, at least for a while, fade to an ember?

Buffy was just a little girl when her mother would tell her and her sister to go up to their room and each fill a shopping bag full of nice things that some other, less fortunate little girls might enjoy. As they ran up the stairs, she would call after them and remind them to be generous. "Don't just give away the things you don't like," she'd say.

Kate doesn't remember exactly when her golden glow was nearly extinguished, but she does remember flying back from Rome on a business trip seated next to a priest, a man of advanced age who was returning from an audience with the pope. During the flight, Kate and the priest talked about charitable acts. Kate blithely and somewhat self-righteously listed the organizations to which she and her husband made donations. "Do you write off your donations on your taxes?" asked the cleric. "Of course," Kate said. "Ah," he said, "but don't you know that true charitable giving occurs only when you get nothing back, not even a tax credit?"

Before you start to chart your course, consider convening the Family Table to discuss with your mate, kids, siblings—whoever makes up your family—how you might approach giving back as a family. Solicit their ideas and support for the commitment you are about to make.

PRACTICE PATIENCE

Volunteering requires a world of patience. You must be optimistic and engaged. You must be patient with your fellow volunteers, with those you are trying to help, and most important, you must be patient with yourself. Volunteering means finding yourself in new situations, sometimes strange and strained situations, where you may know no one and not know what to do or how to help. Don't let yourself be intimidated. Give yourself time to adjust and respond.

When Buffy volunteered at a teen drop-in house on Hollywood Boulevard, she found it easy to pitch in and figure out what needed to be done, such as serve the food, offer the teens phone numbers for job counseling, and empty the trash. What she found difficult was understanding the strict way the full-time counselors treated the homeless teens. Buffy had to exercise patience so as not to question their methods, especially in front of the teens, and to learn to accept direction, even if it was not the way she might do it had she been in charge.

RESEARCH

Ideally, by now, you are in the habit of doing research to prepare yourself for any new activity. Reading up on your community and researching organizations you might want to join or issues you might want to tackle are crucial to a successful volunteer experience. Many of us may be exploring entirely new territory. Some of us may already have worked diligently in the parent-school network, so expanding our horizons may be somewhat easier. For others, reading will offer comfort and help keep us informed.

When was the last time you read an article on the subject of senior rights or legislation? When was the last time you read an article on elder law? When was the last time you read a story about a senior suffering at the hands of an insurance company or a hospital or some other nameless, faceless, ageist bureaucracy? Now is the time to start clipping those articles and doing research to become more knowledgeable about what's happening in the legislative and business arenas that affects seniors. Do an Internet search on an issue. Contact lobbyists for senior rights. This knowledge will help you in years to come, but it will also help your family members and friends right now.

Here are some selections that might help you sort out your reasons for wanting to give back as well as provide you with an intellectual framework on which to hang your plan.

The U.S. Constitution. If you find this rough reading, read *Constitution Translated for Kids* by Cathy Travis (Synergy Books). The original Constitution appears on the right side of the page, and on the left is a "translation" for a fourth-grade reader. Reading the Constitution will inspire you. It will cover you in a wonderful armor of purpose. Clearly, the United States is not perfect, far from it, but as citizens, it is our duty to know and understand the basic tenets on which this country was founded.

Rachel Carson's *Silent Spring* (Mariner).

Tom Paine's *Common Sense* (Signet), particularly the beginning in which he discusses the difference between government and society.

A Quaker Book of Wisdom by Robert Laurence Smith (Quill).

FIND ROLE MODELS

Having role models is a crucial part of creating a plan for the second half of your life. People who are our age or younger make exceptional role models in the area of volunteering because they have found ways to integrate giving back in their daily lives. Imagine how much easier it will be for you to do the same when you have more time available and when you can more easily schedule your days and evenings.

When Jesse went off to college four years ago, Buffy's husband, Peter, quietly said he was going to mentor a young boy. He says he was partly motivated to pay back a sort of karmic debt. His son had managed to weather the complexities and challenges of adolescence and had (knock on wood) started his young adult life on solid footing. Peter has seen Jason once a week for three years. He has missed maybe ten visits out of 156 occasions. Jason lives in a group home for kids who do not have a parent, grandparent, or any adult who will step forward and say, "I will take care of this child, and he can live in my home." The single most important thing Peter gives Jason is consistency. He tells Jason he will be there on Thursday at 3:00 p.m., and he shows up. His actions tell Jason, "You can count on me."

Roberta was laid off from her job but was lucky to get a two-year golden parachute. Had she gone back to work, she would have lost her severance, so she decided to take a break from her career, collect her severance, and take some time off. She went to the gym, spent time with her daughters, and took greater care preparing the meals and keeping the house. About two months into this new routine, she felt that something was missing from her life, and it wasn't a full-time job. She felt really lucky, but it didn't seem right that she was just collecting that luck and not paying any interest on it. So she decided to donate some time each week volunteering at the women's prison not far from her home in Westchester County, New York.

Roberta had never volunteered before, much less in a prison. At first, she was a nervous wreck, driving past the prison gates into the parking lot, passing through the elaborate security checkpoints, and dealing with the guards, not to mention the inmates themselves. The women in this prison were tough and hardened by the lives they had lived, the crimes they had committed, and the time they were serving. They were about as different from Roberta as you could get while still occupying the same planet. Her job was to give job counseling to young women who were coming to the end of their sentences. She gave them advice on how to dress, how to groom themselves, and how to prepare their résumés. She even conducted mock job interviews. This experience took Roberta so far out of her realm of experience, out of her zone of comfort, that her life since has never been the same.

Roberta is back at work now, but she still volunteers on the weekends with her "lady cons" at the big house. Some of the women keep in touch with her from their new positions in the outside world. They send her baby pictures and let her know when they've received a raise or a promotion. They express, in little ways, their gratitude to her for the advice, tips, and support she gave them back when they were incarcerated. And she is grateful to them for opening her eyes to the greater world.

Positive Change Starts at Home

Kate and Buffy's families are trying to reduce their energy use to help combat climate change. Here are some simple practices you might want to adopt:

- Change a light. Use compact fluorescent lightbulbs.
- Drive less, and walk, bike, and carpool more.
- Recycle. Visit www.earth911.org for ideas and help.
- Check your tires. Properly inflated tires improve gas mileage.
- Use less hot water.
- Avoid products with a lot of packaging.
- Visit your local farmers market. Support self-reliance by checking out www.arms.usda.gov for a list of farmers markets near you. Also check out www.ilsr.org, which is sponsored by the Institute for Local Self-Reliance.

- Adjust your thermostat. Set it two degrees lower in winter and two degrees higher in summer. Check out the Green Power Network: www.eere.energy.gov/greenpower.
- Turn off electronic devices when you're not using them.
- Plant a tree. Your local state agricultural department will be able to tell you about seedlings and forestry. They love to give away seedlings to anyone willing to plant and care for them.
- Get educated about other ways to save our planet. Check out www.stopglobalwarming.org, and join the virtual march. What could be easier?
- Join a local environmental group. If you can't find one, start one.

WRITE IT DOWN

Remember that writing things down helps to make them happen. Now that you have spent some time getting in touch with your feelings and researching your volunteer options, write down your ideas. Write down what organizations appeal to you, what ideas or issues interest you, and what you are good at. If you are going to be a successful volunteer, take care to determine how your skill set and experience can best be put to use, and what personality traits or quirks might help or hinder you in a given opportunity. Ask yourself what you are good at: working independently or working in groups; working with small children or working with teenagers; cold calling to register voters or cooking a dish for an informal dinner with fellow citizens who have attended and spoken up at a meeting of the planning commission. Consider your work experience and what skills and talents you can bring to an organization or issue. Jot down your managerial skills as well as your tangible, specific skills, such as computer fluency, second language, ability to operate a van or truck, or accounting know-how.

GET TOGETHER

Get together with friends who live nearby. Look around the community and find something that needs doing. Is it trash pickup in a local park or along the road? Is it reading aloud to seniors at the nursing home? Volunteering can be a slightly less daunting task if you are part of an army. Even an army of two!

Buffy met Jennifer at work. She is a young woman who single-handedly runs Art of Elysium, a charitable organization that assigns an artist to work one-on-one with a sick child as a form of art therapy. Jennifer is dedicated to her work, and her determination to help others is contagious. Jennifer asked Buffy's daughter Daisy to help her organize a fashion show for young girls who had had multiple surgeries on their faces. These girls had spent a lifetime hoping no one would look at them, and now they were being prepared to walk confidently down a runway and silently yell, "Look at me!" It was Jennifer's idea to help these kids find their self-esteem and begin to heal. The afternoon of the show, many in the audience were so moved, they were ready to sign up to help Jennifer continue to spread the love.

PUTTING IT ALL TOGETHER

Now is the time to design your personal plan for volunteering.

1. *Create time* to look around your community and see what needs doing.
2. *Reflect* on your history of giving (or not giving).
3. *Practice patience* with those you are serving, those with whom you serve, and yourself.
4. *Research* books, articles, and selections to help you reaffirm your belief in the power of active citizenship. Start to read up on issues such as elder law, health care, and pending legislation.
5. *Find role models* who give back graciously and regularly, and try to emulate them.

6. *Write down* what you are good at, and match your skills to the organizations you have been reading and learning about.

7. *Get together* with some friends, and find something that needs doing. Then do it.

TO-DO LIST

Here are seven arenas for you to consider. Determine which one suits you best or research others.

- *Education and literacy.* There are so many opportunities in this area, from campus maintenance to literacy tutoring, lending clerical help in an office, fund raising, becoming an ombudsman for a school within a larger school district, coaching sports, assisting teachers, after-school tutoring. Become active in the alumni organization of your high school or college.

- *Health.* Hospitals, hospices, Red Cross, Planned Parenthood. Take Emergency Medical Services courses and become a team leader for your community in case of a natural disaster or terrorist attack.

- *Caregiving.* Meals on Wheels; shopping for homebound seniors; serving, cooking, or doing dishes in a soup kitchen.

- *The arts.* Museums, botanical gardens, children's arts organizations, choirs, music organizations, student galleries, after-school arts programs.

- *Environment.* Join organizations such as ECHO, Heal the Bay, Friends of the Sea, the Sierra Club, bird and wildlife protection groups, search and rescue volunteers, graffiti and community cleanup activities. Join local organizations devoted to the study of and lobbying for sustainable growth and renewable energy.

- *Politics/activism.* League of Women Voters, Get Out the Vote, voter registration drives, carrying petitions for candidates who support senior rights, working phone banks. Volunteer at a nursing home to gauge what issues are important to seniors.

- *Virtual volunteering, also known as cyberservice.* Similar to telecommuting, cyberservice allows volunteers to donate their time and skills to many nonprofit organizations by completing their tasks via the Internet. Virtual volunteering does not mean you work only via the Internet. It is usually a combination of on-site and online work.

If you are not ready to join an existing group, perhaps you'd rather start something yourself, such as:

- A walking club that is also a discussion club for community issues.
- A system of recording or videotaping seniors to start a public dialogue about what's important to them.
- A dialogue with a member of your city council.
- A news show on a public access channel.
- A civic-minded blog.

- An e-mail/phone tree for your neighbors in case of an emergency. Buffy's next-door neighbor created one for their neighborhood. It lives on paper as well as online. She also drew a map of the street so everyone could see where everyone lived. What started as an emergency list is now a place to share resources, ask for help, and get to know neighbors.

KATE'S PLAN

I used to serve on the board of CityKids, a young adult peer-to-peer counseling group. I raised funds and was active in setting the agenda for the group. This was during a time when my own son was having some adolescent adjustment problems. As he grew out of his problems, my involvement on the board waned, and of course I've felt guilty about that ever since.

In my work in children's publishing, I actively support literacy and routinely pack up books to send out to schools and libraries with nonexistent budgets. But between my job, my lengthy commute, and caring for my mother, I don't think it's possible for me to donate any time to volunteering at this point in my life. Now that my mother lives with me, I feel it is time for me to gain a more formal knowledge of elder law. So my plan is:

- Research elder law and share my knowledge as widely as possible with my friends, both close and Ripple.
- In the future, I plan to become actively involved in therapeutic riding, bringing autistic or emotionally challenged kids together with horses. So I'll read up on this subject now.

BUFFY'S PLAN

I was probably more engaged by our most recent national election than I have been since college. My participation was confined mostly to reading and discussing issues with my colleagues and friends. I would like to turn my interest into a more active participation in the political process. We have a serious problem with homeless teens and a problem with lack of affordable housing. I would like to help get these two issues into the public debate. One of the arenas I am most interested in and have supported in different ways is literacy. I will continue to participate and support the organizations I am currently involved with. My plan is to find new and lasting ways to participate and to offer my skills to:

- Increase public awareness of homeless teens.
- Participate in organizations that seek fair elections.
- Continue to work with Women in Film's Mentoring Program and fundraising efforts; the Academy of Motion Picture Arts and Sciences Grants and Scholars Programs; and Sarah Lawrence College Alumnae Association.

Afterword: Taking the Cake

Dear Kate: You know, some of my clearest and best memories are about my mom baking cakes. She is an amazing baker and made beautiful, unusual cakes. German chocolate cake. A cake shaped like a lamb for Easter. A birthday spice cupcake with a dollar baked inside. And remember my wedding cake? Love, Buffy

Dear Buffy: With the champagne frosting and the lattice on top. Harry and I still talk about it. I think it was the most delicious cake I ever ate. Those who can't bake, eat. Love, Kate

Dear Kate: Wish I could bake. I think the baking gene was passed down to Daisy. Love, Buffy

Dear Buffy: You bake in other ways. For her eighty-sixth birthday, I baked Sandy an angel food cake with a light chocolate icing and apricot filling. It was a tad lopsided. But I don't think she noticed how funky it was. She was really pleased. We sat down to eat it and she said, "Too bad Kate couldn't be here. She would have loved this cake." So I laughed. And helped myself to another slice. Love, Kate

SOMETHING TO SHOW

You know the old expression, "You can't have your cake and eat it too"? Well, we happen to disagree with it. We think you *can* have your cake. You can bake a cake for every day of your life, devour every crumb, and at the end of the day, still have something to show for it.

When you really think about it, that's what we all want out of life, isn't it? We want something—whether tangible or spiritual—to show for our days and our nights, our time, our efforts. Isn't that what happiness is about? Isn't that what forming bonds and having children and making homes and undertaking any form of art or achievement whatsoever are really all about? It's about having something to show, when all is said and done, for our actions and our labors. Having something to show is at the very heart of self-esteem and contentment and good health—mental, spiritual, and physical. It also happens to be the very spice of life.

Studies show that people who retire into a life of structure and creativity are happier than those who think they can spend the rest of their lives playing golf, or shopping, or just relaxing now that they are free of strictly regimented schedules and the demands of others. Buffy's father's life revolved around his work, and he loved it. He played a little golf, gardened on most weekends, and spent time with the family, but his work was the centerpiece of his life and when it was gone, his life lost its structure, focus, and spark. Day after day, he felt like he was no longer productive. He had nothing to show. He is struggling to find that structure, that focus, and that spark, the baking powder that will make his cake rise, but it's difficult. Perhaps, had he thought ahead of time about his work-play ratio, among other things, this transitional phase would have been transformative and uplifting rather than trying and depleting. If only he had been ready with a plan for the second half of his life. But you are more fortunate, aren't you? Because you *are* ready. You do have a plan. In fact, by now you should have a plan, a design, for each layer of your life—and icing to boot. And now you get to eat your cake and have it too. *Yum.*

WHAT ARE YOUR INGREDIENTS?

Think of your ingredients as everything we have spoken about in this book: Childhoods (favorite childhood memories), writing things down, logging your dreams, walking and reading and breathing and sanding down your Edge Behaviors. Think of actively listening, giving PEACE a chance, abiding by the second-half health maintenance checklist. Create your Personality Thumbprint, update your File of Important Things, call Family Tables, and break into the Black Box. Get together with your mate or your date or your pet, your kids, your folks, and your friends—both close and Ripple. Toss in tea parties and romantic weekends and sleigh rides. Use your mental squeegee and turn up your back burners to find work, extracurricular activities, and interests you might pursue. Think of always having a little bit left over to give away. Each day, picture yourself making the perfect homemade layer cake for your own personal delectation. How many cakes can you dream up? How many of your designs can you work into each delicious confection?

And what is a cake without candles? Seven of them, in fact: create time, reflect, practice patience, research, find role models, write it down, and get together. Light them whenever you need them, and they will show you the way.

THAT'S THE WAY THE CAKE CRUMBLES!

This isn't to say that, even with excellent ingredients, you won't still produce some doozies, some truly inedible fiascos. Yes, in spite of your best efforts, there are bound to be days when your cake will fall flat. It will collapse in your oven or a whole layer will slide off onto your newly waxed kitchen floor. But with a little patience and self-forgiveness, you'll wake up the next day and try again.

Always keep in mind what we said about setting reasonable goals. Don't be too ambitious with your recipes. There will be days when, miraculously, without even trying, nearly every level of your life will find expression in your cake; days when you will manage to work, pursue your bliss, visit a friend, hang out with your kid, see your therapist, walk, scrub pots at the soup kitchen, soak in a tub of lavender, read a big fat book, and floss after every meal. But most days, your cake will probably be a more modest concoction, a sheet cake even, and that will be just fine.

We want to wish you a rich and full life, and we hope that we have helped to shine some light—lively, dazzling, even luminous—on this, the occasion of your coming of age all over again. This cake is for you. This cake is yours. Prepare to celebrate! Dig in. And savor every last morsel.

Acknowledgments

We wish to thank Dave Woolrich, Mary Bianco, Kevin Campbell, Laurie Horowitz, Diane Ryan, Jan Gerardi, and James Gaynor for their invaluable expertise and counsel. For their patience, humor, support, and love, we thank Peter Robinson, Harry Ross, Kathy Jones, Edite Kroll, Keith Walker, Lalo Vasquez, Jane Rosenfield Kolb, Karen Kolster, Suzanne Sheppard, Sandra Ross, Laurie Ross, Jesse Shutt Robinson, Daisy Shutt Robinson, Bruce Robinson, Ada Robinson, Chris Jones, Gogo Wolfe, Aaron Ross, "El" Ross, and Noah Ross. Thanks also go to the gang at Springboard— Michelle Howry, Karen Murgolo, Jill Cohen, Matthew Ballast, and Marie Salter. Finally, to our gracious tea-party hostesses in cities and towns across the country, thanks for your hospitality!

Index

About the Authors

Kate and Buffy met on their first day of college. Kate came from Long Island and loved the Beatles. Buffy came from Maryland and loved the Temptations. Having found common ground in Van Morrison, they have been fast friends ever since. Kate works in New York, where she is a publisher of children's books. Buffy works in Los Angeles, where she is a producer of movies and TV. They e-mail constantly and try to get together whenever they can. Thirty years ago in college, they shared the exhilarating experience of coming of age. Today, in their fifties, they are helping each other come of age all over again, and are finding it every bit as heady the second time around. You can visit Kate and Buffy at comingofageagain.com.